Concepts of Reason and Intuition

With Special Reference to Sri Aurobindo,
K.C. Bhattacharyya and S. Radhakrishnan

Concepts of Reason and Intuition

With Special Reference to Sri Aurobindo, K.C. Bhattacharyya and S. Radhakrishnan

Ramesh Chandra Sinha

DK PRINTWORLD
Publishers of Indian Traditions

Cataloging in Publication Data — DK
[Courtesy: D.K. Agencies (P) Ltd. <docinfo@dkagencies.com>]

Sinha, Ramesh Chandra, 1944 -

Concepts of reason and intuition : with special reference to Sri Aurobindo, K.C. Bhattacharyya and S. Radhakrishnan / Ramesh Chandra Sinha.
p. cm.
Includes bibliographical references (p.) and index.
ISBN13: 9788124606537

1. Faith and reason – Hinduism. 2. Intuition.
3. Philosophy, Indic. 4. Ghose, Aurobindo, 1872-1950.
5. Bhattacharyya, Krishnachandra, 1875-1949.
6. Radhakrishnan, S. (Sarvepalli), 1888-1975. I. Title.

DDC 294.5 23

ISBN 13: 978-81-246-0653-7 ISBN 10: 81-246-0653-6
First published in India in 1981
Second Revised edition, 2013

Printed and published by:
D.K. Printworld (P) Ltd.
Regd. Office : *'Vedaśrī'*, F-395, Sudarshan Park
(Metro Station: Ramesh Nagar)
New Delhi - 110 015
Phones : (011) 2545 3975; 2546 6019; *Fax* : (011) 2546 5926
e-mail : indology@dkprintworld.com
Web : www.dkprintworld.com

Preface

THE present book proposes to make a critical and systematic study of the two most important problems of philosophy, specially of Indian philosophy — "reason" and "intuition". These problems not only engaged the minds of the foremost Indian thinkers of the past, but they have also been given a fairly important attention by the great Indian thinkers of this century. This book is an attempt to study the concepts of reason and intuition as they have been conceived and developed by the Indian philosophers of the twentieth century, specially the three philosophers — Sri Aurobindo, K.C. Bhattacharyya and Sarvepalli Radhakrishnan. Here, I make an attempt to do relevant comparisons of the views of Indian philosophers concerning reason and intuition with some of the eminent philosophers of the West, of the past as well as of the present.

Indian philosophers of this century have mainly expounded and developed the philosophy of the Vedānta in their own ways. Though they accept the metaphysical doctrines of the Vedānta, absolutistic as well as theistic, yet one finds a good deal of originality in their world views. There seems to be a distinct change in their views concerning man's life in the world, the secular and spiritual problems of life, his aspiration and his destiny. One finds a good deal of originality and freshness in their approach to these problems. It can be clearly perceived in the philosophies of Sri Aurobindo, Bhattacharyya, Radhakrishnan, Tagore, S.M.Iqbal and J. Krishnamurti. Even where there is no basic difference in the metaphysics of the Indian philosophers of this century with those of the classical periods, one can see a significant difference in the application of the metaphysical or spiritual truths to the problems of life — temporal as well as non-temporal. It is this fact that gives the above-mentioned thinkers a place of importance and makes their study necessary and fruitful in the present situation.

The change that one perceives in their attitude and approach towards man's life in the world, in their formulation of the dynamic ethical, religious and social values and the goal of human life and of history has been largely brought about by the tremendous advances in science and technology, and the emergence of new ideologies and the philosophies of life in the Western world. The great thinkers of this century saw it clearly that unless they interpreted and formulated the great truths of the Vedānta and the philosophy of life based on them in a language and the framework of ideas which could be appreciated and understood by the modern man, they would cease to inspire him and would simply adorn the pages of history. These thinkers seem to be convinced that man's philosophy and life cannot follow separate courses. His philosophy cannot cut itself off from the mainstream of his life. Philosophy, according to them, is not something which concerns simply man's intellectual life.

Philosophy involves the whole man, his entire personality and is deeply concerned with his individual as well as collective life. Its main purpose is to provide direction to man's life individually as well as collectively by revealing the real nature of his existence, of world-existence and of the ultimate reality. It is these ideas concerning the nature and purpose of philosophy and the necessity of interpreting the perennial philosophy of life as propounded by the Vedānta in the light of the dynamism of modern life and the aspirations of the modern man that govern the twentieth-century Indian thinkers in the formulation and creation of their philosophies of life and systems. They have made it amply clear that the deeper truths of life as revealed by the ancient seers of India and propounded with great clarity and vigour by an unending galaxy of the great philosophers of India can still provide succour to the distracted modern man and guide the course of his individual and collective life. The present book, while focusing its attention mainly on the conceptions of Reason and Intuition in the twentieth-century Indian thought, also proposes to throw some light on the basic contributions of the great Indian thinkers of this century in the formulation of dynamic ethical and religious values, in their effort to reconcile the secular and the spiritual spheres of human life and in providing definite goals for man's collective life and history.

The book comprises of six chapters. The first or the introductory chapter presents, in brief, the concepts of reason and intuition as they were conceived and propounded by the seers of the Upaniṣads, the Mahāyāna Buddhism, the Vedānta and some of the philosophers of the West. It also gives a brief account of the role and importance of the concepts of reason and intuition in the twentieth-century Indian thought. The next three chapters try to throw light on the important contributions made by Sri Aurobindo, Bhattacharyya and Radhakrishnan respectively, on the fundamental problems of reason and intuition. The second chapter, which deals with the conceptions of reason and intuition in Sri Aurobindo, draws particular attention to his conception of the higher reason or the logic of the infinite, the integral knowledge, the distinction between intuition and integral or supramental knowledge, the relation of reason with the evolutionary process and Sri Aurobindo's views on the goal of human life and of history.

The third chapter, which deals with Bhattacharyya, tries to throw particular light on his philosophical method, which is analytic and critical, his conception of the metaphysics and the place and role of reason in the metaphysical enquiry, the realization of subject as freedom through the method of analysis and the spiritual and intuitive experience and his conception of the Absolute. The fourth chapter, which is devoted to the discussion of the conceptions of reason and intuition as expounded by Radhakrishnan, tries to throw particular light on the wider and richer meaning given to these terms by him and their application in the different fields of science, art, ethics and religion, and on some fresh ideas introduced by Radhakrishnan regarding the goal of human life and history. The fifth chapter deals with the three other great thinkers of this century — Rabindranath Tagore, Sir Mohammad Iqbal and J. Krishnamurti — with special reference to the light they throw on reason and intuition. The sixth or the concluding chapter points out some of the most important contributions of these thinkers in the different fields of ethics, religion and metaphysics, and particularly with respect to our understanding of the problems of reason and intuition.

I am well aware of the fact that there are other eminent Indian thinkers of this century, namely Bal Gangadhar Tilak, Mahatma Gandhi, Bhagwan Das and some others who do not find a place in the present book. The reason for confining myself to the study of the three thinkers in detail and other three thinkers in brief was that I did not propose to make a study of the twentieth-century Indian philosophy as such. I wanted to confine my study to the thinkers who have made significant contributions to reason and intuition. The six thinkers, who have been treated in the course of this thesis, represent the main tendencies of the twentieth-century Indian thought, so far as reason and intuition are concerned. This is all the more true of the three thinkers — Sri Aurobindo, Bhattacharyya and Radhakrishnan.

I offer my deep and sincere gratitude to my revered teacher and supervisor, R.S. Misra, Malviya Professor of Comparative Religion, Department of Philosophy, Banaras

Hindu University, whose kind guidance, sustained interest, valuable suggestions, constant help and encouragement have enabled me to complete the present work. I have derived enormous help from his authoritative work entitled, *The Integral Advaitism of Sri Aurobindo,* and his article on "The Concept of Reason in the Systematic Theology of Paul Tillich". He also took immense pains to discuss and make me understand the abstruse and difficult metaphysical problems of Bhattacharyya's philosophy. I deeply acknowledge his invaluable help without which this work might not have been completed.

Ramesh Chandra Sinha

Contents

Experts' Opinions!

THIS is an excellent piece of research work on the "Conceptions of Reason and Intuition in the Twentieth Century Indian Thought". It offers a good comparison between Reason and Intuition from the standpoint of eminent contemporary Indian thinkers — Sri Aurobindo, K.C. Bhattacharyya and S. Radhakrishnan.

The author has rightly pointed out that Reason is unable to know the thing-in-itself and God, Intuition alone had the experience of them. But all intuitions are not alike. Sri Aurobindo and Radhakrishnan conceive that there are higher and lower forms of Intuition. The Supramental Consciousness in Sri Aurobindo's thought and the Mystic experience in Radhakrishnan's view are the supreme forms of spiritual consciousness. They are higher than lower forms of intuitions manifested in the works of genius, poets, artists and scientists.

The scholar has rightly shown that Intuition is not only a way of thought, but it is a way of life. The human society has to undergo sufficient spiritualization in order to be free from discords, strifes and selfishness. Only after the purgation of all evils and after sufficient spiritualization can one achieve the Supramental Consciousness. The human life can be guided by the truth of Spirit only when there is spiritualization and divinization of it in its topmost perfection.

The thesis shows Krishnamurti's view of Intuition as unconditioned experience falls far short of the integral Supramental Experience as conceived by Sri Aurobindo. The unconditioned knowledge is also a low form of spiritual experience for it remains disconnected from the human life and its spiritual condition. As to how the unconditioned Reason, which is mere silence or peace of mind, comes into relationship with God, has not been rationally explained by Krishnamurti. His philosophical position is, therefore, much lower than that of Sri Aurobindo and Radhakrishnan.

It is a fruitful piece of research work which throws light on the unexplored region of knowledge, i.e. on the higher and spiritual forms of consciousness.

Dated 6-2-1970 **Dr. R.S. Srivastava**

Head, Department of Philosophy,
Ranchi University, Ranchi (Bihar)

This thesis is a brilliant piece of research work. The candidate has made a critical and comparative study of the two most important concepts of philosophy — Reason and Intuition — as they have been envisaged by the eminent Indian thinkers of this century. He has also made striking and relevant comparisons of the views of Indian thinkers with those of some of the eminent thinkers of the West. In his detailed study of Sri Aurobindo, K.C. Bhattacharyya and S. Radhakrishnan, the candidate shows not only a profound grasp of the concepts of Reason and Intuition but also his admirable understanding of other important metaphysical and religious problems. His treatment of Sri Aurobindo's conception of Higher Reason and its comparisons with the views of Kant, Hegel, Bradley and Paul Tillich are extremely illuminating. His comparison of Sri Aurobindo's conception of history with the Judaic–Christian conception of history seems to be quite original and suggestive and places Sri Aurobindo's evolutionary philosophy in its proper perspective.

The author has also succeeded in giving a clear, systematic and critical exposition of the philosophy of K.C. Bhattacharyya who is acknowledged as the most difficult and enigmatic Indian metaphysician of the present century. We do not have good studies on K.C. Bhattacharyya as yet and he is still somewhat unapproachable. The researcher's treatment of some of the important problems of the philosophy of K.C. Bhattacharyya may be taken as an important and significant contribution which adds greatly to the value of the thesis. He also brings out clearly the distinctive features of Radhakrishnan's ideas of Reason and Intuition in the deeper and wider meaning that the latter gives to these important concepts and their implications for man's life as a whole. His comparison of Radhakrishnan's view of religious experience with that of Rudolf Otto is also important and fruitful. His studies on the philosophical and religious thought of Rabindranath Tagore, Mohammad Iqbal and J. Krishnamurti are also marked by clarity, freshness and depth.

Ramesh Chandra Sinha has maintained an objective approach in his treatment of the different thinkers, and his criticisms and judgements are, on the whole, fairly balanced. His literary presentation is also clear, lucid and commendable. The book is a scholarly work of an appreciably good academic standard and will make valuable contributions to the existing literature on modern Indian Thought.

Dated 9-2-1970

Dr. R.S. Misra
Department of Indian Philosophy and Religion
Banaras Hindu University

Shri Ramesh Chandra Sinha has loboured hard in studying the vast material and to use it for his research. He has given a good exposition of the concepts of Reason and Intuition as conceived and developed by the three thinkers — Sri Aurobindo, Prof. K.C. Bhattacharyya and Prof. S. Radhakrishanan — and has discussed them in detail. It is possible to differ from the candidate on some important points and some of his statements can be challenged, yet, on the whole, his exposition appears to me to be correct. His book embodies a fresh approach in interpreting some theories and shows his critical insight to a fair extent. The metaphysical presentation of the thesis is satisfactory; its literary presentation is good.

Dated 7-2-1970

Dr. C.D. Sharma
Prof. and Head, Department of Philosophy,
University of Jabalpur, Jabalpur (M.P.)

1

Introduction

INDIAN philosophical thought has entered a new era in the present century. The eminent Indian thinkers, specially the Hindu thinkers, have generally made serious and sustained attempts to re-interpret the great Indian philosophical tradition of the past and to give a new orientation to it. They have also tried to introduce certain new values concerning man's ethical, social and religious life, and his ultimate destiny. Thus they cannot simply be called the interpreters of the past heritage. Thinkers like Sri Aurobindo, K.C. Bhattacharyya, S. Radhakrishnan and others also show a profound impact of the great stream of Western thought in the development of their philosophical views and systems. On the one hand, their philosophical views are largely derived from the great stream of the Vedāntic thought, on the other hand, they are also shaped and moulded under the influence of the great idealistic tradition of the West.

Thinkers like Sri Aurobindo, Tagore and Radhakrishnan also show considerable influence of modern evolutionary philosophy in the development of their thought. Thus, the twentieth-century Indian philosophy presents a happy confluence of the two great philosophical traditions of the world — India and the West. Though the philosophical systems of Sri Aurobindo, Bhattacharyya, Radhakrishnan and other twentieth-century Indian thinkers are largely founded on the ancient Vedāntic thought, yet they show disinct originality and freshness in respect of methodology and approach to the problems of man's life, world-existence and Ultimate Reality. They show the same freshness and originality in their treatment of the concepts of Reason and Intuition.

Meaning of Reason and Intuition

Etymologically, the term "reason" is derived from Latin word *ratio*. It means relation. "In the most generalized sense of all, reason might be defined as the relational element in intelligence . . . ."[1] Senses can apprehend "A" and "B" separately. Reason alone can relate them. Philosophical thinking starts at the level of reflection. It is only after attaining a certain level of reflection that man finds himself in a position to ponder seriously over the problems of life and reality. The distinction between true knowledge and false knowledge is possible only at the level of reflective consciousness. It is only at this level that one can determine the nature of knowledge and distinguish the different sources of knowledge. Sense experience, reason and intuition are generally treated as different sources of knowledge. Radhakrishnan puts it:

> While all varieties of cognitive experience result in a knowledge of the real, it is produced in three ways, which are sense-experience, discursive reasoning and intuitive apprehension.[2]

Cārvāka holds that sense-experience is the prime source of knowledge. All non-perceptual or indirect sources of knowledge like inference and testimony are unreliable and misleading. Protagoras asserts that there is no truth except that given by the sensations and impressions of each man. Locke makes knowledge dependent on sense-perception. Though sense-experience is a valuable source of knowledge,

---

[1] James Hasting (ed.), *Encyclopaedia of Religion and Ethics*, p. 125.

[2] S. Radhakrishnan, *An Idealist View of Life*, p. 105.

yet it is limited in nature, for it furnishes only the external features or appearance of the object. When eye perceives a rose, only its colour and texture are known; its essence remains unknown. Senses in themselves are not reliable sources of knowledge. They do not give us the knowledge of reality. Heracleitus said that reality was a process of ceaseless becoming and Parmenides contended that it was bare identity or pure being. These statements are in direct contradiction to man's sense-experience. Each sense apprehends its own specific object. Ear cannot see and eye cannot hear. This indicates the utterly limited nature of sense-experience. Man becomes conscious of the limitations of sense-experience only at the reflective level. But reflective consciousness or reason does not mark the apex of man's consciousness. It cannot be taken as the highest source of man's knowledge. There comes a stage in the development of reason when it becomes conscious of its own limitations. It becomes acutely conscious of its self-contradictory nature. It realizes that it is conditioned by time and other categories and it can operate only in the realm of phenomena and cannot touch the Being or the unconditioned. It is at this stage that reason points out to a dimension of consciousness or experience which transcends it and which is generally called spiritual experience or intuition.

D.D. Runes defines intuition as:

> The direct and immediate apprehension by a knowing subject of itself, of its conscious states, of other minds, of an external world, of universal, of values or of rational truths.[3]

It gives an adequate knowledge of the essence of things. It enables us know reality. Intuition is the special faculty which transcends the conditions of existence. It is not conditioned by the categories of understanding. The plane of mind

---

[3] D.D. Runes, *Dictionary of Philosophy*, p. 149.

immediately above that of reason is known as intuition. Intuition is defined by Webster as the act or process of "coming to direct knowledge" or "certainty without reasoning or inferring". Intuition is "direct apprehension" or "immediate cognition". Reason cannot give immediate and final knowledge. This knowledge is not the result of any process of inference. It is not mediated through rational concepts. It is a "direct-intuiting" or perceiving of "the supersensible". Thus, we can understand intuition as a direct, immediate and certain way of knowledge which dispenses with the logical modes of reasoning and sense-experience.

Reason and Intuition in the Upaniṣads, Mahāyāna Buddhism and the Vedānta

The concepts of reason and intuition find a place of great importance in the Indian philosophical thought. The problems concerning reason and intuition engage the attention of even the seers of the Upaniṣads. The Upaniṣadic seers seem to have a very close understanding and appreciation of the nature of reason and intuition. They seem to be keenly conscious of the limitations of reason and of its finitude. Reason, according to them, cannot comprehend the Real or the Absolute. The Real, according to the *Taittirīya Upaniṣad,* is that "from which all speech with the mind turns away unable to reach it".[4] The *Kena Upaniṣad* also declares that the eye does not go there, nor speech, nor mind. We do not know, we do not understand how anyone can teach it. The knowledge or realization of Reality cannot be attained by reason. Reason gives us imperfect and partial pictures of reality. It deals with relations and cannot grasp the relationless Absolute. The Upaniṣads also make a distinction between the *parā* and *aparā vidyā* (the higher and the lower knowledge). The higher knowledge is intuitive,

---

[4] *Taittirīya Upaniṣad,* 11.4.

whereas the lower knowledge is rational. Reason can know only the world and not the Absolute or *Brahman*. Man can attain unity with *Brahman* only when he transcends the level of reason and attains spiritual experience or intuitive consciousness.

The concepts of reason and intuition also figure prominently in Buddhism. The Buddhist philosophers make a distinction between *buddhi* and *prajñā*. The Mādhyamika School of Buddhism propounds the conception of two truths — *saṁvṛtti satya* (empirical truth) and *paramārtha satya* (ultimate truth). The *saṁvṛtti satya* is the truth attained by reason or *buddhi*, whereas the *paramārtha satya* is attained by *prajñā* alone. *Buddhi* or reason gives man the knowledge of the phenomenal world, whereas *prajñā* enables him attain the knowledge of the Real. It gives man absolute freedom from the sufferings of life. Reason is not in a position to fathom the depth of the unconditioned. It can only serve as a pointer to the Ultimate Reality, but it cannot reach it. The moment it tries to reach the unconditioned, it finds itself involved in conflicts and contradictions. Murty observes:

> Reason involves itself in deep and interminable conflict when it tries to go beyond phenomena to seek their ultimate ground.[5]

Buddha was conscious of the conflict of reason and then he declined to probe into metaphysical problems. The Real is utterly devoid of all conceptual constructions. Murty further observes:

> . . . it is transcendent to thought and can be realized only in non-dual knowledge, *prajñā* (Intuition), which is the Absolute itself.[6]

---

[5] T.R.V. Murty, *The Central Philosophy of Buddhism*, p. 40.

[6] Ibid., p. 86.

The Advaita Vedānta also throws a flood of light on the concepts of reason and intuition. It makes a distinction between empirical knowledge and spiritual experience. This is made clear in the doctrines of two truths propounded by the Advaita Vedānta, namely *vyāvahārika satya* and *pārmārthika satya*. The *vyāvahārika satya* is the empirical knowledge, the knowledge of the world and is attained by reason. The *pārmārthika satya* is the knowledge of the Absolute or the unconditioned which is attained when man transcends the level of reason and attains intuitive or spiritual experience. The Advaita Vedānta does not make any attempt to reconcile reason and intuition. Reason gives man the knowledge of the world, whereas intuition enables him attain oneness with *Brahman*.

The Advaita Vedānta makes a dialectical criticism of realistic categories and shows their self-contradictory nature. It makes it clear that the Absolute or *Brahman* cannot be comprehended in terms of any rational concepts and categories. They give only the appearance of reality and not the reality as it is. Thus, the Advaita dialectic shows the self-contradictory nature of reason and points out to the higher dimension of consciousness called intuition which is free from all antinomies or contradictions, which are inherent in reason. The true nature of self and the Absolute can be revealed only by intuition. Śaṅkara regards *aparokṣānubhūti* as the highest source of knowledge. When intuition or *aparokṣānubhūti* occurs, the knowledge, the knower and the known, all become one. Intuition alone can fathom the depth of the Ultimate Reality. Radhakrishnan observes:

> Hindu thinkers as a class hold with great conviction that we possess a power more interior than intellect by which we become aware of the real in its intimate individuality, and not merely in its superficial or discernible aspects.[7]

---

[7] S. Radhakrishnan, *An Idealist View of Life*, p. 100.

Intuition transcends duality and gives vision of the Ultimate Reality. Reason serves as a pointer to the Being but it cannot enter into its heart. Reason is not opposed to intuition. It, on the other hand, paves the way for it. By being conscious of its self-contradictory nature, reason points out to a higher level of consciousness, called intuition or spiritual experience. The Ultimate Truth can be realized by the higher source of knowledge known as intuition, *jñāna* or *prajñā*. Reason prepares the ground for intuitive realization of the Ultimate Reality. Intuition is non-rational but not anti-rational. It is supra-rational and not infra-rational. Radhakrishnan contends, "Intuition is the crown of reason".[8]

Rāmānuja denies the non-relational character of knowledge. He conceives that all knowledge connotes relation. It involves a relation between the subject and the object. Rāmānuja does not raise any opposition between intuition and thought. Though the knowledge of the Absolute is attained through intuition, yet intuition is not opposed to thought.

> In Rāmānuja, the apparent discord between reason and intuition has been set aside and it has been possible for him to show that intuition and reason give us the same truth. The fundamental points of difference between Śaṅkara and Rāmānuja, arise out of the relation between reason and intuition. Rāmānuja does not find any conflict between the two, for in his case reason and intuition function in the same way: they are relational consciousness. Reason conceives, intuition perceives. Reason conceives relations, intuition perceives them. Both of them work in the same way. We may go far and say that intuition is a form of judgement, since intuition intuits.[9]

---

[8] S. Radhakrishnan, *The Reign of Religion in Contemporary Thought*, p. 440.

[9] A.B. Sastri, *Studies in Post-Śaṅkara Dialectics*, p. 13 (as quoted in *Integral Advaitism of Sri Aurobindo*, by R.S. Misra, p. 350).

But Rāmānuja and other theistic Vedāntins do hold that the knowledge of *Brahman* cannot be attained by reason. It is possible only by intuition or spiritual experience which brings the individual soul into direct union with the supreme *Brahman* or God.

Reason and Intuition in Western Thought

Reason generally occupies a supreme place in Western philosophy. Anaxagoras distinguishes the two modes of knowing as "by rational consideration" and "by experience". Democritus declares that true knowledge is possible not by the senses but by reason. For Plato, real knowledge is possible through rational concepts and not through sense-experience. Kant makes a distinction between reason (*vernunft*) and understanding (*verstand*).

> Understanding relates one thing to another within experience, but does not go forward to the ideal completion of experience in a total system. Such an ideal completion is wrought by the reason, which rises above the bounds of experience and affirms the three transcendental ideas of the soul as a permanent being (the psychological idea), of the world as a totality (the cosmological idea), and of God as the necessary being who is the cause of the whole (the theological idea).[10]

Hegel identifies reason with reality itself. Paul Tillich uses reason in two senses — "ecstatic reason" or "ontological reason" and "formal" or "technical reason". He observes, "Ecstatic reason is reason grasped by an ultimate concern. Reason is overpowered, invaded, shaken by the ultimate concern."[11] Ontological reason, according to him, is predominant

---

[10] Hasting James (ed.), *Encyclopaedia of Religion and Ethics*, vol. X, p. 597.

[11] Paul Tillich, *Systematic Theology*, vol. I, p. 53.

in the classical tradition from Parmenides to Hegel. The technical reason has become predominant since the breakdown of German classical idealism and in the wake of English empiricism. We shall have occasion later on to consider in some detail Tillich's conceptions of ontological reason and technical reason.

Reason has from the very beginning occupied a pre-eminent place in the Western philosophical tradition. It regards reason as a supreme source of knowledge. A great difference that one finds between the Indian philosophical tradition and the Western philosophical tradition is that though Indian philosophy gives a sufficiently important place to reason, yet it does not regard it as a supreme source of knowledge. According to it, reason can speculate about and contemplate the real, but it cannot attain unity with it. The direct awareness of the transcendent reality is possible only through intuition. But the Western thought generally regards reason as the supreme source of knowledge. The Real, according to it, can be comprehended in terms of rational concepts. Reason finds its culmination in the Hegelian philosophy which regards the real and the rational as identical.

Reason and Intuition: Their Role and Importance in the Twentieth-Century Indian Thought

The Indian thinkers of this century mostly derive the fundamental concepts of their systems, as has been pointed out above, from the great Vedāntic tradition of the past. They also accept the Vedāntic concept of metaphysics that it is the inquiry into the nature of "Being". The fundamental question of metaphysics, according to Sri Aurobindo, Bhattacharyya and Radhakrishnan is, what is "Being" itself. Metaphysics is concerned with "Being as Being". It is concerned with the objects only in so far as they help to know the nature of Being. Thought can negate objects of experience but it cannot negate being itself. The negation of things is possible only on the basis of being. The unreal can be negated, only on the basis of the real.

Metaphysics not only tries to know the nature of being but it also tries to reveal the structure of being. This structure of being is revealed in terms of concepts, principles or categories. The function of revealing or grasping structures of being through concepts and categories is performed by reason. Indian thinkers like Sri Aurobindo, Bhattacharyya, Radhakrishnan and others do not regard reason as the ultimate source of knowledge. Reason, according to these philosophers, is not in a position to have direct awareness of Being or the transcendent Reality. It can only serve as a pointer to the Being but it cannot seek unity with it. The attainment of unity with Being is possible only at the level of intuition or spiritual experience. Unlike the Western rationalists, the Indian thinkers of the past as well as the present, do not regard reason as the ultimate source of knowledge. Unlike Hegel, Sri Aurobindo, Bhattacharyya and Radhakrishnan do not identify the real with the rational. But they also do not confine all human knowledge to reason as Kant does. They agree with Kant in holding that reason is confined to the phenomena and cannot touch the depth of Being. But unlike him, they do not confine all knowledge to phenomena. They believe in intuition and other higher source of knowledge which transcend the phenomena and have direct experience of the Transcendent or the Absolute.

It is due to this emphasis on the intuitive knowledge or spiritual experience by the Indian philosophical tradition, the Indian philosophy is said to be intuitive, while the Western philosophy is rationalistic. Northrop distinguishes between Eastern and Western philosophies as generally formed of "concepts by intuition and concepts by postulation, respectively".[12] In other words, the Eastern thought, according

---

[12] F.S.C. Northrop, *The Logic of the Sciences and the Humanities*, p. 128.

to him, is intuitive and the Western thought is rationalistic. It does not mean that the trends of rationalism are absent from the Eastern thought and of intuitionism from the Western thought. It simply means that the dominant trend of the East is intuitive, whereas of the West is rationalistic. Radhakrishnan observes:

> While the dominant feature of Eastern thought is its insistence on creative intuition, the Western systems are generally characterized by a great adherence to critical intelligence.[13]

The distinction seems to be relative and not absolute. He also points out:

> It describes the chief tendencies and there are in fact many exceptions. It is only a question of the distribution of emphasis.[14]

Here it may be pointed out that though Indian philosophical tradition does not regard reason as the supreme source of knowledge, yet it does not in any way minimize its importance. Reason plays an important role in the different schools of Indian philosophy. It is true that the fundamental philosophical concepts are mostly derived from intuitive experience; but it is reason which constitutes the different philosophical structures in terms of concepts and categories. It is reason which gives a coherent, systematic and consistent interpretation of intuitive experience. Reason should not be taken only in the sense of "reasoning". That is one aspect or function of reason. Reason develops different dialectical methods to examine critically the tenability or the truth of the different concepts or categories. But reason also, as has been stated above, reveals the different structures of Being. It is

---

[13] S. Radhakrishnan, *An Idealist View of Life*, p. 129.

[14] S. Radhakrishnan, *Eastern Religion and Western Thought*, p. 115.

through these structures that one can approach the Being and fathom the depth of reality. Indian philosophers of this century agree with their illustrious predecessors of the Vedāntic tradition in their estimating reason and intuition as the source of knowledge. They believe that man who is conditioned by time cannot know the unconditioned simply by the help of reason. In order to attain unity with the unconditioned, man has to transcend reason and attain a higher level of intuitive or spiritual experience.

In one respect, the approach of the twentieth-century Indian thinkers seems to differ in a significant way from that of the ancient *ācāryas*. It is concerning their attitude towards authority or revelation. Thinkers like Sri Aurobindo, Radhakrishnan and others do believe in revelatory knowledge or Śruti. But they do not seem to attach the same importance to the scriptures as the ancient *ācāryas* did. This change in the attitude of modern Indian thinkers is best illustrated by the following statement of Sri Aurobindo:

> For the *sādhaka* of the integral Yoga it is necessary to remember that no written Śāstra, however great its authority or however large its spirit, can be more than a partial expression of the eternal knowledge. He will use, but never bind himself even by the greatest Scripture. Where the Scripture is profound, wide, catholic, it may exercise upon him an influence for the highest good and of incalculable importance. It may be associated in his experience with his awakening to crowning verities and his realization of the highest experiences. His Yoga may be governed for a long time by one Scripture or by several successively, if it is in line of the great Hindu tradition, by the *Gītā*, for example, the Upaniṣads, the Veda or it may be a good part of his development to include in its material a richly varied experience of the truths of many Scriptures and make the future opulent with all that is best in the past. But in the end he must take his station, or better still, if he can, always and

> from the beginning he must live in his own soul beyond the written Truth — *śabdabrahmātivartate* — beyond all that he has heard and all that he has yet to hear, *śrotavyasya śrutasya ca*. For he is not the *sādhaka* of a book or of many books; he is *sādhaka* of the Infinite.[15]

Modern Indian thinkers also show, as has been pointed out above, a considerable impact of Western thought, specially of its great idealistic tradition and also of the modern evolutionary thought on the development of their views. This will become clear from our treatment of these philosophers and thinkers in the course of the present work.

Now we proceed to discuss the concepts of reason and intuition or spiritual experience as they have been envisaged by Sri Aurobindo, the great philosopher and sage of the 20th century.

---

[15] Sri Aurobindo, *The Synthesis of Yoga*, pp. 61-62.

2

Sri Aurobindo
(1872 – 1950)

The Finite Reason: Its Structure and Function

SRI Aurobindo observes, "Reason is science, it is conscious art, it is invention".[1] It can observe and arrange truth of facts. It can speculate, discard and forecast "truth of potentiality". It probes into immediate appearance and "unveils the hidden truth behind it". It tends to divide, analyse and assemble the facts of life. Reason is discursive but limited in nature. Its function is to analyse, delimit and depiece. It is a principle of ordering the inner as well as the outer life. It is a faculty of the intelligent will. Sri Aurobindo observes:

> Reason using the intelligent will for the ordering of the inner and the outer life is undoubtedly the highest developed faculty of man . . . .[2]

There may emerge another spiritual faculty in future but in the present stage of man's development, reason is the sovereign tool or source of knowledge. To quote Sri Aurobindo, "It is the sovereign because the governing and self-governing faculty in the complexities of our human existence."[3] The *manomaya puruṣa* (the mental being) is distinguished from animal and

---

[1] Sri Aurobindo, *The Human Cycle*, p. 121.

[2] Ibid., p. 123.

[3] Loc. cit.

other creatures because he is endowed with the capacity of reason. Reason exists for the sake of knowledge. Reason has the capacity to take decisions and can direct and guide man's activities. It can also keep itself detached from mental activities and be a witness and spectator. This fact shows that reason is not only involved in man's life and activities, it also enjoys freedom from all involvement and activities. It can check itself from being carried away by the man's activities. Reason, according to Sri Aurobindo, can reflect, intelligently study, accept, refuse, modify, alter, improve, combine and recombine the workings and capacities of the forces in operation. It observes, seizes and arranges truth of facts. It is the ". . . helper, instructor, elevating friend and civilizer of mankind".[4] It plays an important role in shaping faith and yielding intuitive vision. Sri Aurobindo aptly puts it, "It is the servant and yet the master of all utilities".[5] It is the servant because it serves as an instrument of knowledge. It is the master, for it can put away all interests and asserts its freedom.

Reason becomes a mere servant of life when it furnishes means and justification for the interests, passions and prejudices of man. On the other hand, it assumes the role of a master when it attempts a higher action and separates itself from life. It controls interests, passions, prejudices, etc. Its very attempt at a disinterested and dispassionate knowledge makes it the master of life. It can seek truth for its own sake. It may explore the world of new possible utilities. It is the servant as well as the sovereign power.

Sri Aurobindo contends that "Human reason has a double action, mixed or dependent, pure or sovereign".[6] Mixed or dependent reason keeps in view the practical side of life. It

---

[4] Sri Aurobindo, *The Human Cycle*, p. 127.

[5] Loc. cit.

[6] Sri Aurobindo, *The Life Divine*, p. 73.

keeps a particular end in view. It limits our intellectual gain. It confines our view of things. It distorts the truth becasue it is pursued with a particular idea in view. It is limited to the working out of certain preferred ideas. It ignores all that is not useful. The selection, rejection, modification and justification are prompted by the utility of life itself. Mixed reason confines itself to the sphere of our sensible experience. Its sole concern is the study of phenomena. On the contrary, pure reason operates in arithmetic, geometry and science. Mixed reason is certainly finite in nature but there are other levels of finite reason also. Reason that operates in mathematics or science is also finite. Pure reason asserts its pure action. ". . . when accepting our sensible experiences as a starting-point but refusing to be limited by them . . ."[7] It goes behind, judges, works in its own right and strives to arrive at general and unalterable concepts. Mixed reason is "practical reason" of Whitehead and "understanding" of Kant, whereas "pure reason" is "theoretical reason" of the former and "pure reason" of the latter. It may be pointed out that mixed reason and pure reason come under finite reason. Pure reason, however pure it may be, works on the data supplied by sense-experience. The finite reason functions under the limitations of the interests of life. According to Sri Aurobindo, the thinking man tramples down all truths of life which conflict with his chosen opinions and interest. Therefore, finite reason does not function freely and dispassionately. Sri Aurobindo observes:

> True, even Science and Philosophy are never entirely dispassionate and disinterested. They fall into subjection to the tyranny of their own Ideas, their partial systems, their hasty generalizations and by the innate drive of man towards practice they seek to impose these upon life.[8]

---

[7] Loc cit.

[8] Sri Aurobindo, *The Human Cycle*, p. 135.

The finite reason functions under the deep impact of interest needs, instincts, passion, prejudices, traditional ideas and opinions of the ordinary mind. It is not self-sufficient. It proceeds by observation and experiment. In spite of the inherent limitation, there is persistent faith that reason will overcome its difficulties. The finite reason is analytic and discursive but the higher reason is comprehensive and all-embracing. The analytic reason bisects reality into the "that" aspect and the "what" aspect, whereas the higher reason takes unitary view of the whole of reality. The higher reason or the logic of the infinite is dynamic and overcomes the oppositions between subject and object, self and not-self, indeterminate and determinate, one and many, being and becoming.

Finite reason makes distinction between the knower, knowledge and the known. It can, at the most, hold facts as an understood truth so as to correct and modify. Before Copernicus, scientists like Ptolemy believed that sun moved round the earth. Later on, Copernicus brought revolution and propounded that earth moves round the sun. Finite reason is able to correct it but could not abolish the artificial but practical arrangement by which the senses apprehend that sun moves round the earth. Scientific knowledge cannot be said to be the result of higher reason. Finite reason works at the common level as well as in the scientific field. The higher reason visualizes the universe and its contents in a single indivisible act of knowledge. Reason, working under the conditions of finitude, cannot apprehend reality as a whole. It cannot understand the mystery of creation and fails to apprehend even the relationship between the seed and the tree. To quote Sri Aurobindo:

> A tree evolves out of the seed in which it is already contained, the seed out of the tree; a fixed law, an invariable process reigns in the permanence of the form of manifestation which we call a tree. The mind regards this phenomenon, this birth, life and reproduction of a tree, as a thing in itself and on

> that basis studies, classes and explains it. It explains the tree by the seed, the seed by the tree; it declares a law of nature. But it has explained nothing; it has only analysed and recorded the process of mystery.[9]

Finite reason has got separative tendency. It regards itself also as separate existence, the conscious subject, and other forms as separate objects of its mentality. But higher reason works otherwise. Sri Aurobindo says:

> The tree and its process would not be what they are, could not indeed exist, if it were a separate existence; forms are what they are by the force of the cosmic existence, they develop as they do as a result of their relation to it and all its other manifestations.[10]

It is clear that the higher reason works in a different manner. The tree and its process could not exist, if it is a separate existence. Sri Aurobindo points out, "The tree does not explain the seed, nor the seed the tree; cosmos explains both and God explains cosmos".[11] The higher reason is Divine, all-comprehensive, all-embracing and indivisible. It links every finite entity to the infinite and knows it and explains it in terms of the infinite. The higher reason is ontological in nature. It is neither reason operating on sense-experience nor working on abstract concepts. Finite reason is prone to dismiss all the diversities as unreal but higher reason reconciles all diversities and multiplicities. Misra observes:

> The opposition between the Infinite and the finite or One and many is raised by the finite and abstract reason and not by the higher reason or Logic of the Infinite.[12]

---

[9] Sri Aurobindo, *The Life Divine*, pp. 163-64.

[10] Ibid., p. 164.

[11] Loc. cit.

[12] R.S. Misra, *The Integral Advaitism of Sri Aurobindo*, pp. 96-97.

The Finite Reason: Sri Aurobindo and Kant

The finite reason is not in a position to have a clear and correct appreciation of man's situation. It ordinarily takes a narrow view of man. Reason, in its essential nature, tries to probe into the depths of being. It realizes the unity of things and existence. But reason under the conditions of existence is not able to realize the basic unity of thing. It cannot unite itself with the unconditioned. As Misra correctly observes:

> As logos, reason constitutes the structure of mind and the objective reality and it enjoys unity with the ground of being or the unconditioned. But in existence this transparency becomes opaque. Reason under the conditions of existence suffers from finitude and has to work under the limitations of categories. It suffers from inevitable distortions.[13]

The finite reason is unable to grasp the Absolute. It fails to apprehend the unity between the objective and the subjective orders of existence. If we assume that the subject and object are unrelated, it may be difficult to pass from the one to the other. If subject and object are independent, we require a *tertium quid* to link them and it will inevitably lead to infinite regress. Thus, the dualistic view of existence appears to be logically untenable. This realization impels the finite reason to seek the principle of unity. It becomes theoretically conscious of the being or the unconditioned, even if it cannot have a direct realization of it. It is this situation which brings into operation the higher reason. Sri Aurobindo holds that the contradiction that seems to exist between *Brahman* and the world appears to be irreconcilable only to the finite reason and not to the higher reason. The structure of the finite reason has been very clearly portrayed by Kant. All human knowledge, according to him, is conditioned by space, time

---

[13] R.S. Misra, *The Concept of Reason in the Systematic Theology of Paul Tillich*, p. 22.

and other categories. Kant says that we do not see things-in-themselves but as they appear to us through space, time and other categories. So, the knowledge provided by reason remains confined to the "phenomena" and does not extend to the "noumena". Our finite reason cannot make any judgement about "noumena or things-in-themselves". It cannot even say whether things-in-themselves exist or not. Sri Aurobindo agrees with Kant and Spencer in so far as they exhibit the finitude of reason and its inability to grasp the reality. Thus, we see things or objects not as they are in themselves but as they appear to us through space, time and other categories. Our finite reason working under the categories of space, time, causality and substance cannot make any judgement about things-in-themselves. Kant has exhibited in his *Critique of Transcendental Reason* that whenever reason tries to pass beyond phenomena and make any judgement with regard to what is supposed to be beyond it, it is involved in contradictions. The categories of the understanding can be applied, according to Kant, only in the region of space and time and not beyond that. Thus, Kant confines human knowledge to the region of phenomena. The categories of understanding by means of which one comes to have the knowledge of the world are empirically real but transcendentally ideal. Reason operates on the sense-data. It cannot say anything about what Kant calls the "ideas of pure reason", namely God, the universe and the soul.

Kant is right in pointing out that man's knowledge or reason gives us only the appearances of things and not their reality. But his view — all human knowledge is confined to phenomena — is not logically tenable. In this connection Sri Aurobindo's view of the unknowable differs from that of Kant, Spencer and other agnostics. Whereas Kant holds that reason cannot fathom the depth of the "Absolute" or "Noumena", and, hence, the latter must always remain unknown and unknowable. Sri Aurobindo maintains that though the Absolute or the unconditioned cannot be realized by reason, it can be apprehended by other sources of knowledge — intuition and supramental consciousness. According to Sri Aurobindo, Kant is right to the extent he shows the inability of reason to know the Absolute or things-in-themselves, but he does not seem to be correct in so far as he denies the capacity of knowledge as such to know the Absolute or the unconditioned. According to the Vedāntins as well as Sri Aurobindo, there are certain higher sources of knowledge available to man through which he can realize the Absolute. Man has the power to transcend the level of reason and attain a higher level of consciousness called intuition and supramental consciousness. The abstract and finite reason does not enable us attain any insight into the world of supersensible realities. Kant cries halt to all ontological speculations.

Reason gives equally strong arguments for and against such problem as God, world, soul and immortality. But it does not mean that the ideas about God, soul, freedom and immortality have no importance for human life. These ideas are necessary for man's moral and spiritual life. As a matter of fact, Kant has not denied the reality of the transcendent, he only denies the possibility of proving the reality of soul and God or the Absolute by means of reason. Kant points out in his *Critique of Practical Reason* that the Absolute cannot be known by reason, but it can be realized through another avenue of approach, namely moral will and faith. Though the Absolute is not an object of knowledge, yet it can be an object of moral will and faith. It is necessary to postulate God, freedom, etc. with a view to satisfying the demands of the moral law. The moral law, or what Kant calls the categorical imperative, claims to be absolute and universal. Man can act according to the categorical imperative which shows his freedom. Freedom is the necessary pre-requisite of the moral life. So long as man remains confined to the phenomenal or rational level, he is conditioned by finitude and governed by the causal laws, by determinism and necessity in all his acts. Therefore, Kant thinks that there must be another and higher realm, the noumenal realm where man enjoys the freedom which the moral life demands. Misra observes:

> Thus man as a natural and intellectual being belongs to the world of sense and suffers from bondage and as a moral being is a member of the intelligible world and enjoys full freedom.[14]

So, the guarantee of the world of freedom or the intelligible world is given not by knowledge or reason but by the intuitive realization of the claims of the moral law. The finite reason is thus subordinated by Kant to moral will or faith. Here, it is observed that what is denied by reason is accepted by faith. Kantian approach creates a gulf between phenomena and noumena. Consequently, we find a chasm between knowledge and faith in Kantian philosophy.

According to Sri Aurobindo, there is no unbridgeable gulf between reason and faith, the phenomenal and the noumenal world, the world of necessity and the world of freedom. This is owing to the fact that unlike Kant, he does not confine all human knowledge to phenomena. The intelligible world, God, soul, freedom and immortality are not only articles of faith and belief, but they can be realized essentially and integrally through the higher consciousness. For Kant, the Absolute remains for ever unknown and unknowable. To Sri Aurobindo, it remains unknowable as has been stated above, only to sense and reason and not to the higher sources of knowledge. Sri Aurobindo contends:

> When we speak of it as unknowable, we mean, really, that it

---

[14] R.S. Misra, *The Integral Advaitism of Sri Aurobindo*, p. 38.

> escapes the grasp of our thought and speech, instruments which proceed always by the sense of difference and express by the way of definition; but if not knowable by thought, it is attainable by a supreme effort of consciousness. There is even a kind of knowledge which is one with Identity and by which, in a sense, It can be known.[15]

Like Kant, Sri Aurobindo also shows the futility of our formal and abstract reason or the finite reason so far as the knowledge of the higher realities is concerned. He agrees with Kant in holding that the finite reason lands us into inevitable antinomies and contradictions. But unlike Kant, his criticism of the finite reason does not land him into agnosticism. Man's knowledge in his view is not only confined to the finite level but transcends the limitations of his rational consciousness and attains a higher consciousness, the spiritual and the supramental consciousness which can enable him realize the Absolute in its essential and integral aspect. The Absolute is unknown but it is not altogether unknowable according to Sri Aurobindo.

> Finite reason as has been shown above falls short to comprehend reality. It gives us partial and abstract view of it. The abstract view is that which does not express the nature of reality as a whole. It is only a higher reason or a higher logic which can give us integral view of life and reality. Finite reason is usually involved oppositions and contradictions. Sri Aurobindo tries to remove the shortcomings of the finite reason with the help of a higher reason, a higher logic which is known as the Logic of the Infinite.

As Misra observes:

> . . . the conception of the Logic of the Infinite is Sri Aurobindo's main contribution to philosophy. It has a great significance

[15] Sri Aurobindo, *The Life Divine*, p. 15.

> for contemporary philosophy and specially for Absolutism, both Indian and Western, ancient as well as modern. It constitutes the very foundation of Sri Aurobindo's Integral Advaitism. The whole of Sri Aurobindo's philosophy, his conception of the Absolute, his theory of involution or evolution, his principle of transformation, his conception of cosmic salvation, his view of the supermind and the gnostic being, etc. follows directly from the principle of the Logic of the Infinite.[16]

Thus, the Logic of the Infinite makes it clear that the reality of the world is not incompatible with the Absolute. It is only our formal logic or lower reason which creates a barrier between the Absolute and the world. The Logic of the Infinite does not find any contradiction between them.

The higher reason or the Logic of the Infinite of Sri Aurobindo, is the Divine reason. It is the reason inherent in the Divine Being. The divine acts in accordance with its own reason. This reason operates in nature as well as in human life and history. Its nature and working can be directly apprehended in the supramental consciousness. Ordinarily, it remains unknown to the finite reason of man. But a stage comes in man's life when he becomes acutely conscious of the limitations of the finite reason. It is this awareness which engenders in him the consciousness of the Infinite and Unconditioned. He begins to have at least theoretical appreciation of the working of the Infinite, of the operation of Divine reason in nature, in the living creation and the historical process.

Before we proceed to discuss the nature of the higher reason or the Logic of the Infinite, I think it fit to show the operation of reason in formal logic and in the logics of Kant

---

[16] R.S. Misra, *The Integral Advaitism of Sri Aurobindo* (Preface), pp. vii-viii.

and Hegel. It will help us in having a better and clearer understanding of the nature and operation of the Logic of the Infinite as propounded by Sri Aurobindo.

Role of Reason in Formal Logic and the Logic of Kant

Formal logic is supposed to act in accordance with the law of identity, the law of contradiction and the law of excluded middle. Its principal aim is self-consistency in our thought. It attempts to deduce certain conclusions from certain established principles. For example, the system of Spinoza is founded on formal logic. He places substance at the apex. The rest of his philosophy has been deduced from it. But a serious defect of Spinoza's system is that he could not reconcile his doctrine of Being or Substance with that of attributes and modes. The geometrical method, based on formal logic, could not resolve the contradiction that seems to exist between absolute and relative.

Leibnitz also contends that formal logic can provide us necessary truths. Necessary truths follow with logical certitude. But, necessary truths fall under the logical law of contradiction. Moreover, necessary truths are abstract. They belong to the domain of mathematics. The real world cannot be understood with the law of formal logic. Therefore, he contemplated another principle — the principle of sufficient reason. Social, moral, religious and other spheres of human life are placed under the domain of the principle of sufficient reason. Leibnitz calls the truth, governed by the principle of sufficient reason, the contingent truth. Formal logic deals with necessary truths, while the principle of sufficient reason deals with contingent truths. Leibnitz puts the principle of sufficient reason in order to get rid of the limitations of formal logic, in respect of understanding the empirical experience. But he could not extricate himself from the influence of the formal logic altogether. He distinguishes between necessary truths, governed by the principle of contradiction and the contingent truths regulated by the principle of the sufficient reason. This distinction is in itself sufficient to show that Leibnitz is not aware of a reason which can comprehend the necessary as well as contingent truths and is altogether free from the limitations of the logical reason as well as the principle of sufficient reason.

Kantian logic attempts to liberate itself from the limitations of formal logic. Kant exhibits in his *Critique* that judgement must not be only self-consistent but it should be synthetic and *a priori*. An *a priori* synthetic judgement is possible when the categories of reason operate through the manifold of sensations. Now the question is: how the manifold sense-impressions received through different sense organs and arranged by categories of understanding, attain ultimate unity? Here, Kant contemplates ego which gives unity to our sense-experience as well as to categories. This unity of ego is known as the "synthetic unity of apperception". The synthesis of apperception in intuition reconciles the opposition between empiricism and rationalism. Kant holds that for real knowledge, sense-experience and reason must unite. This unity is not possible at the level of logical or formal reason as it fails to comprehend empirical or contingent truths. So, Kant develops a new logic — transcendental logic in place of formal logic, in order to comprehend and explain experience. He does not remain satisfied with mere analysis of propositions. Transcendental logic is the logic of experience. Here, reason does not remain a mere spectator. It plays an active role. The object is known when it is related not only with other objects but also with the subject. The unity of experience is possible when it is referred to the unity of self-consciousness. This unity of self-consciousness has been aptly called the synthetic unity of apperception.

Now the question is: does Kant succeed in uniting the subject and the object, reason and sensibility? When we probe deep into Kantian logic, we find that it could not escape all traces of formalism. The object is not integrally connected with the subject. The object is presented to the subject by our sensibility. Sensibility has got only external relation with the understanding self-consciousness, being destitute of content is simply a logical condition of knowledge. It derives its content out of sensibility. As a result, there is no pure self-consciousness. It seems that Kant fails to bridge the gulf between the sensibility and reason. Reason does not get objective knowledge without sensibility. If reason tries to go beyond sensibility, it is landed in antinomies as exhibited by Kant in his transcendental dialectic. The Kantian reason remains at the mercy of sensibility in order to comprehend phenomena. If it is divorced from sensibility, it is reduced to bare abstract identity. Reason sundered from sensibility is mere consciousness devoid of all contents. Thought, in Kantian logic, is yet analytic and discursive. It is unable to resolve the contradiction between subject and object, reason and sensibility, phenomena and noumena.

Sri Aurobindo, Hegel and Bradley

According to Hegel, thought is the constitutive principle of all the subjective and objective orders of existence. Reason is all-comprehensive in nature and it overcomes all distinctions of the knower and the known. Hegel does not refuse the reality of matter. He simply says that matter is ultimately spirit in nature. Hegelian logic attempts to reconcile the opposition between spirit and matter, subject and object, thought and sensibility, one and many, etc. Kant affirms that object is object in relation to self or subject. The concept of object necessarily points to the subject. But, unfortunately, Kant did not succeed in bridging the gulf between the subject and the object. In

Kantian logic, reason is understood as analytic and abstract. In the Hegelian system, it is synthetic as well as dynamic. Reason being analytic and static in Kant, it could not reconcile the antinomies and as such remained confined to the arena of formal logic. But reason in Hegel, being synthetic and dynamic, does not act in accordance with the laws of formal logic. It seeks to resolve the opposition between thesis and anti-thesis into a higher synthesis. The formal reason conceives the relations between cause and effect, substance and attributes, and subject and object as external. But the synthetic reason of Hegel conceives these relations as internal and attempts to reconcile all opposition between them.

Bradley holds that thought and reality cannot be identical as contemplated by Hegel. He adheres that reality is more than thought. Sri Aurobindo agrees with Bradley in so far as reality is taken to be more than thought. Thought, according to Bradley, is relational and discursive. It is fraught with contradictions. But reality is a supra-rational whole which is above all contradictions and oppositions. Thought being rational fails to grasp the supra-rational Absolute. Thought, according to Bradley, is inefficient to know reality. In order to know reality, it has to commit suicide. Thus, Bradley criticizes Hegel's conception of identity between thought and reality. He observes:

> For thought is clearly, to some extent at least, ideal. Without an idea there is no thinking, and an idea implies the separation of content from existence.[17]

Thought, according to Bradley, is bound to work under this distinction of existence and character. If thought attempts to transcend this dualism, it commits suicide. Bradley observes:

> Let us assume that existence is no longer different from truth,

[17] F.H. Bradley, *Appearance and Reality*, p. 143.

> and let us see where this takes us. It takes us straight to thought's suicide. A system of content is going to swallow up our reality; but in our reality we have the fact of sensible experience, immediate presentation with its colouring of pleasure and pain. Now I presume there is no question of conjuring the fact away; but how it is to be exhibited as an element in a system of thought content, is a problem not soluble. Thought is relational and discursive, and, if it ceases to be this, it commits suicide: and yet, if it remains thus, how does it contain immediate presentation?[18]

In case thought rises above and harmonizes all relations, then thought is no more thought as discursive and relational in nature. Bradley makes distinction between the world of sense and the world of thought. He makes distinction between "existence" and "content", "this" and "that", "what" and "that" aspects of reality. These distinctions are reconciled in intuition. Some critics like Mure hold that Bradley misunderstands Hegel's conception of thought. But the thought of Hegel is different from the thought of Bradley. We know that thought as conceived by Bradley is relational and discursive. In that case, the world of sense-experience remains apart from the world of thought. It is true that analytic and discursive thought cannot explain sensuous experience. Our sense-experience, our feelings, desires, will, emotions, etc. cannot be explained in terms of analytic and discursive thought. But it has to be pointed out here that thought according to Hegel is not essentially analytic and discursive. In its higher stages, it embraces all the diverse functionings of mind like feelings and emotions and also the objective world.

The criticism of Bradley is against the abstract, analytic, relational and discursive thought. It is not equally applicable to synthetic thought of Hegel which seeks to reconcile all opposition in its all-embracing unity. Thought of Hegel does

---

[18] F.H. Bradley, *Appearance and Reality*, p. 150.

not simply constitute the cognitive aspect of the individual mind. It is universal in nature which embraces both the subjective and objective orders of existence. So, Bradley is not wholly justified in making a criticism of thought which he takes to be merely analytic and discursive, which it is not.

Now the question is: can thought be identified with reality? The answer is in the negative. The gradation of categories puts a limitation on reality. Hegel's dialectic becomes a rigid and closed system. In its fairness, Hegelian system is not free from the traces of formal logic. The main defect of the formal logic is that it tries to circumscribe reality within the limits of mental categories. Reality is not supposed to work strictly in accordance with the mental laws or categories. Thought as imagined by Hegel proceeds along a fixed line. It follows a unilinear development. This unilinear development cannot express the process of the eternal. This makes it clear that thought and reality cannot be identified.

Further, Hegelian Absolute does not explain the world-process. The facts of experience cannot be woven as threads in ready-made logical scheme. Thought accepts the data supplied by experience. It can be expected at best to do scientific arrangement of the given material.

Hegel claims to have reconciled all the contradictions. We find that his thought has not been successful in reconciling the Absolute and the world. Hegel's Absolute is the Absolute of thought. The Absolute must not depend on anything else for its existence. But Hegel's Absolute is not self-existent because there is a relation of mutual dependence between the Absolute and the world. The relation between thought and object remains more or less external in other categories. It becomes internal in the Absolute Idea. But Absolute Idea depends on these internal relations. Hegel's Absolute is not differenceless and relationless. According to Hegel, the Vedāntic Absolute, being differenceless and relationless, is a mere abstract identity.

Hegel is not correct to hold that we cannot conceive a relationless, differenceless and transcendent Absolute. It will mean that we cannot conceive the Absolute apart from the universe. It means a relation of mutual dependence between the Absolute and the world. This relation of mutual dependence between the Absolute and the world affects its absoluteness. Relations are necessary marks of finite objects and not in the case of the Absolute. To say that the Absolute is a differenceless, transcendent reality does not mean that it is an abstract identity. It means, as Sri Aurobindo has clearly shown, that it is not limited by the relations and differences. The differenceless, supra-relational transcendent Absolute is found in the philosophy of Śaṅkara. While Hegel denies the reality of an indeterminate differenceless and supra-relational Absolute, Śaṅkara denies the ultimate reality of the concrete universal. Sri Aurobindo steers clear of the extremes of Hegel and Śaṅkara. Sri Aurobindo thinks of Integral Absolutism which takes into account both the essential, differenceless and transcendent aspect as well as dynamic aspects. It considers both universal and individual aspects.

Hegel's conception of thought is quite different from the ordinary, analytic and abstract thought. Hegel regards it concrete, synthetic and dynamic. Thought as analytic and static cannot reconcile the oppositions or contradictions. But synthetic and dynamic thought cannot lead us to accept the laws of formal logic as absolute.

This above conception of thought has led Mure to contend that Hegel's thought is not merely thought but also intuition. Mure conceives in his book, *An Introduction to Hegel,* that Hegel's conception of thought is intuitive. He calls Hegel's thought intuitive for the reason that it bridges the chasm between sensibility and reason, subject and object, spirit and matter. This leads to hold that Hegel's thought has got an intuitive element in it. Misra observes:

> Much of what goes by the name of intuition has been incorporated by Hegel in his conception of thought.[19]

Hegel and his followers may not admit this position of Mure for the reason that by intuition they meant some infra-rational principle and not something which transcends reason. But unconsciously, Hegel has incorporated much of the real essence of intuition. Had it not been so, Hegel would not have been able to resolve contradictions.

Now I proceed to consider Sri Aurobindo's conception of the nature and significance of the Logic of the Infinite.

The Logic of the Infinite or the Higher Reason

Sri Aurobindo has also made a distinction between the finite reason and the higher reason or what he calls the Logic of the Infinite. The Supreme Reality is indeterminable by the finite reason. Sri Aurobindo observes:

> It is indefinable and inconceivable by finite and defining Mind; it is ineffable by a mind-created speech, it is describable neither by our negations, *neti neti*, for we cannot limit it by saying it is not this, it is not that, nor by our affirmations, for we cannot fix it by saying it is this, it is that, *iti iti*.[20]

Brahman is indeterminable to our finite reason or intellectual understanding. But it can be realized fully by our higher reason or supramental knowledge. This experience cannot be expressed through our ordinary language. In ordinary metaphysical thought, we are content with the service of intellect because this suits our method of logical and rational understanding. Sri Aurobindo says that in order to have a full comprehension of reality, reason must consent to pass out of the bounds of a finite logic and accustom itself to the Logic of the Infinite. If we extend finite logic to the infinite, the

---

[19] R.S. Misra, *The Integral Advaitism of Sri Aurobindo*, p. 73.

[20] Sri Aurobindo, *The Life Divine*, p. 383.

omnipresent reality will escape us and we shall grasp instead an abstract shadow of it.

The way of the infinite seems to be a sort of magic to our finite reason. This is because of the fact that we try to grasp the way and action of the infinite with our finite reason which functions within the limits of space, time and other categories. The infinite has its own way of being and action, whereas our consciousness is limited, our reason is finite. Sri Aurobindo observes:

> . . . it is irrational to suppose that a finite consciousness and reason can be a measure of the Infinite; this smallness cannot judge that immensity; this poverty bound to a limited use of its scanty means cannot conceive the opulent management of those riches; an ignorant half-knowledge cannot follow the motions of an All-knowledge.[21]

As a matter of fact, finite reason operates within the limits of the spatio-temporal world. It does not extend to reality beyond space and time. Life and mind are supra-physical finites. They have got different modes of operation than physical nature. Likewise, there is something more and vital in our mental existence. The finite has behind it the infinite which supports and directs the finite. But:

> Our finite knowledge, conceptions, standards may be valid within their limits, but they are incomplete and relative. A law founded upon an observation of what is divided in Space and Time cannot be confidently applied to the being and action of the Indivisible; not only it cannot be applied to the spaceless and timeless Infinite, but it cannot be applied even to a Time Infinite or a Space Infinite. A law and process binding for our superficial being need not be binding on what is occult within us.[22]

---

[21] Sri Aurobindo, *The Life Divine*, p. 389.

[22] Ibid., p. 390.

It is evident that the finite reason cannot be necessarily applicable to the infinite. Sri Aurobindo points out that reason is limited because it cannot deal efficiently either with supra-rational or infra-rational aspects of life. Entire truths of life do not come within the purview of the finite reason. An instinct deals with infra-rational aspects of life. Reason cannot deal successfully in the field of instinctive apprehension. It is much more difficult for reason to deal with the suprarational. The suprarational is the realm of the spirit. Reason is constrained to grapple with the ways of spirit. Its ways are inscrutable, complex and subtle to our finite reasons. But the actions of the infinite or the Supreme Being are not void of all reasons. As Sri Aurobindo observes: ". . . there is, on the contrary, a greater reason in all the operations of the Infinite, but it is not a mental or intellectual, it is a spiritual and supramental reason: there is a logic in it because there are relations and connections infallibly seen and executed." Further Sri Aurobindo observes rightly: "what is magic to our finite reason is the Logic of the Infinite."[23] The mystery of the creation and of cosmic process cannot be unravelled by man's finite reason. It can be, in some ways, appreciated only in terms of the higher reason or the Logic of the Infinite.

> It is a greater reason, a greater logic because it is more vast, subtle, complex in its operations; it comprehends all the data which our observation fails to seize, it deduces from them results which neither our deduction nor induction can anticipate because our conclusions and inferences have a meagre foundation and are fallible and brittle.[24]

Does it mean that the higher reason negates the lower reason? The Advaitins like Śaṅkara may hold that the knowledge of *Brahman* necessarily implies the negation of the world. But,

---

[23] Sri Aurobindo, *The Life Divine*, p. 391.

[24] Loc. cit.

according to Sri Aurobindo, the knowledge of *Brahman* does not necessitate our rejection of the world or denial of its reality. We have to judge each thing in all its three aspects — the individual, the universal and the transcendent. The truth of the transcendent is understood fully when it is realized in its individual, universal and transcendental aspects. To quote Sri Aurobindo:

> The Infinite is at once an essentiality, a boundless totality and a multitude; all these have to be known in order to know truly the Infinite. To see the parts alone and the totality not at all or only as a sum of the parts is a knowledge, but also at the same time an ignorance; to see the totality alone and ignore the parts is also a knowledge and at the same time an ignorance, for a part may be greater than the whole because it belongs to the transcendence; to see the essence alone because it takes us back straight towards the transcendence and negate the totality and the parts is a penultimate knowledge, but here too there is a capital ignorance. A whole knowledge must be there and the reason must become plastic enough to look at all sides, all aspects and seek through them for that in which they are one.[25]

We can fathom the depths of the Divine and understand the full significance of these fundamental truths not by our finite reason but by a higher and more plastic reason called the Logic of the Infinite. The Logic of the Infinite is the logic of reality and not of the finite reason or mind. The finite reason cannot probe into the depths of the fundamental truths. It cannot fathom the full significance of reality. On the contrary, the higher reason or the Logic of the Infinite does not obey the dictates of the dividing mind. It is founded on reality. Does it mean that the validity of the laws of identity and contradiction are denied altogether? Sri Aurobindo simply denies their

---

[25] Sri Aurobindo, *The Life Divine*, pp. 393-94.

absolute validity. Kant's antinomies show that reason is involved in contradiction and the categories of reason are limited in nature. They cannot apprehend the reality or thing-in-itself. The nature of the Absolute cannot be understood in terms of the laws of identity and contradiction. The Absolute is unknown and unknowable to our finite reason. Like Hegel, Sri Aurobindo also does not consider them as ultimately and unconditionally true. The laws of identity and contradiction are conditioned by the law of relation. If, in some sense, it becomes necessary to study a thing by isolating it from other things, in some other sense, it is also necessary to study it in relation to other things. Kant determined the limits of knowledge. Hegel sets the limits of the laws of identity and contradiction. Sri Aurobindo upholds that the material, vital or mental laws cannot be valid unconditionally because they are unable to reveal the real and integral nature of reality. All earthly laws are abstract. Hegel conceives that an abstract law cannot comprehend the concrete whole or the Reality. The Absolute manifests itself in accordance with its own law. It works under the divine law and not in accordance with natural, the mental, vital and material laws.

Sri Aurobindo admits that our finite reason cannot apprehend the relationship between the indeterminate and determinate, one and many, etc. The mystery of reality eludes the grasp of mental laws. "The self-existent," observes Sri Aurobindo, "is the Infinite and its way of being and of action must be the way of the Infinite, but our consciousness is limited, our reason built upon things finite . . .".[26] The finite reason cannot be the measure of the Infinite. The finite reason is limited in its use and operates successfully in its own realm of phenomena, but it cannot effectively judge the immensity of the Infinite.

---

[26] Sri Aurobido, *The Life Divine*, pp. 388-89.

There are various orders of reality, and the conceptions, measures and standards suitable to one order need not be applicable to another order. The laws applicable to physical being are not equally competent to explain human body. The laws of life cannot explain fully the operations of mind. The laws of mind cannot explain what is beyond mind. Our reason is not proficient to deal with the subconscious level, as well as superconscious level, for an instinct is required to apprehend the subconscious and an intuition is needed to explore the superconscious level. Reason is in mid-way between subconsciousness and superconsciousness. It serves both. Its limitation is exposed when extended to the realm of spirit. In the subtlety and complexity of its movement, the reason is lost.

Sri Aurobindo does not consider reason as the supreme and the most reliable means of knowledge. But he does not discard and minimize the importance of reason in its own sphere. Reason finds itself on sure grounds in the domain of logic and mathematics. It also operates in a more or less effective way in the finite world. It is not quite safe to accept an undeveloped instinct and indistinct intuition in its place. Our reason should be large and plastic enough to accept the truth and significance of the supreme reality and its working or process. Sri Aurobindo is not at all against the use of reason as such to understand the nature of reality but he simply asserts the limited nature of abstract and formal reason. Finite reason bisects the integral reality into fragments. It cannot have comprehension of reality as a whole. But it serves an important and useful purpose.

By showing the limitations of the finite world or the conditioned reality, it points to the infinite or to the unconditioned. It serves as a pointer to the Absolute. But reason can perform this function only if it is freed from its limitations, its abstractness, and has attained a higher state.

The abstract or the finite reason remains involved in contradictions as has been shown with great clarity and force by Nāgārjuna, Śaṅkara and Kant. By the application of higher reason or the Logic of the Infinite, one can solve the contradictions inherent in the logical or the finite reasons. One can solve the contradictions inherent in the categories of reason, for example between indeterminate and determinate, one and many, being and becoming and so on. To quote Misra:

> The human reason can have a conceptual knowledge of Reality and its process, if it gets rid of the bondage of its own rigid, abstract and inflexible laws and takes recourse to a higher reason, a higher logic, the Logic of the Infinite.[27]

In literal sense, negation implies non-existence. But to Sri Aurobindo, negation is itself affirmation. The negative assertions are positive in its essence. The indeterminability of the Absolute is not in a true-sense negative but positive. According to Spinoza, every determination is negation. But Sri Aurobindo says that every negation is determination. If determination is limitation, the negation is also limitation. The Absolute is beyond the limitations of affirmations, determinations and negations. The Absolute should be understood in integral sense. If it is freedom to be away from cosmic play, it is also freedom to indulge in the infinite cosmic play without being affected by it. It is not negative freedom but positive one. Thus, *nirguṇa* and *saguṇa* aspects are complementary and not contradictory, as they appear to our finite reason. Therefore, the higher reason is not perplexed by such contradictions as one and many, being and becoming, finite and infinite.

To our finite reason, the one and many seem to be opposite. To Sri Aurobindo, the contradiction is due to the double error. First, it considers this oneness on mathematical basis. By

[27] R.S. Misra, *The Integral Advaitism of Sri Aurobindo*, p. 87.

oneness of the Absolute, we should not take it as a mathematical unit. This point can be best illustrated in Sri Aurobindo's words:

> It is thinking in the terms of the mathematical finite unit which is sole in limitation, the one which is less than two and can become two only by division and fragmentation or by addition and multiplication; but this is an infinite oneness, it is the essential and infinite oneness which can contain the hundred and the thousand and the million and billion and trillion whatever astronomic or more than astronomic figures you heap and multiply, they cannot overpass or exceed that oneness; for, in the language of the Upaniṣad, it moves not, yet is always for in front when you would pursue and seize it.[28]

It can be many without losing its oneness. Infinite oneness entails infinite multiplicity. But one is not plural. It cannot be described as the sum of many. This is the second error that the finite reason commits in conceiving relationship between one and many. The one can be the infinite many because it can be limited neither by multiplicity nor by plurality nor by finite conceptual oneness. The mental reason makes an opposition between the infinite and the finite. It associates finiteness with plurality and infinity with oneness. In the Logic of the Infinite, there is no such opposition. The eternity of the many in the one is perfectly possible.

In ancient times, some of the Greek philosophers viewed reality as being and some perceived as becoming. The silent and static Infinite Being without dynamics and becoming, cannot be regarded as Ultimate Reality. Infinite as infinite without infinite power is inconceivable. A powerless Absolute, an impotent Spirit, can be anything but not the Ultimate Reality. But the question is: what is the basis of becoming? The being

---

[28] Sri Aurobindo, *The Life Divine*, p. 398.

is the basis of becoming. The silence serves as the basis of the movement. The opposition between silence and dynamics is apparent and not real. The contradiction is merely conceptual. The dynamic aspect of *Brahman* does not infringe the static aspect. Force inherent in the Pure Existent may be at rest or may be in motion. Becoming is the state of movement and being is the state of rest of the Absolute.

The Logic of the Infinite makes it clear that there is no contradiction between the infinite and the finite. The finite is nothing but the self-determination of the infinite under the conditions of space and time. Sri Aurobindo observes:

> The finite is a frontal aspect and a self-determination of the Infinite; no finite can exist in itself and by itself, it exists by the Infinite and because it is of one essence with the Infinite.[29]

Infinite does not mean only self-extension in space and time but something that is spaceless and timeless. The supramental logic does not raise barrier between the finite and the infinite. Reality can be known by integral knowledge and not by limited consciousness whether it is sensuous, mental or intuitional. We have to view the unity in all diversities. It has been indicated in the famous verse of Upaniṣad:

> This is the complete and That is the complete; substract the complete from the complete, the complete is the remainder.[30]

Now it is clear that "one" does not cease to be "one" by manifesting the manifold objects of the world out of it or in it. To the higher reason or logic of the infinite, immutability of *Brahman* does not make it incapable of change and differentiation. The opposition between the infinite and the finite or one and many is raised by the finite and abstract reason and not by the higher reason or Logic of the Infinite.

[29] Sri Aurobindo, *The Life Divine*, p. 401.

[30] Ibid., p. 402.

As Sri Aurobindo holds that our surface reason is prone to conclude that the diversity may be unreal, an appearance only, but if we look a little deeper,we shall see that the real diversity brings out the real unity. It seems that Sri Aurobindo has given satisfactory solution to the baffling problem of existence or reality. In view of the higher reason to the indeterminate and determinate, one and many, finite and Infinite are not contradictory but complementary to each other. Our reason is constrained to characterize as one and many, and so on. But the Absolute, as has been shown above, is beyond the grasp of our finite reason. The higher reason or the Logic of the Infinite can alone, according to Sri Aurobindo, point out to the Divine or the Absolute and can ultimately attain it.

Sri Aurobindo and Paul Tillich

Paul Tillich was one of the greatest Christian theologians of this century. In his famous work, *The Systematic Theology*,[31] he has made a brilliant analysis of reason, of its nature and function. His conceptions of technical reason and ontological reason bear a close resemblance with Sri Aurobindo's conception of the finite reason and the higher reason or the Logic of the Infinite. So, I find it helpful to make a brief study of the views of these two great thinkers concerning the structure and function of reason.

Tillich has made a distinction between ontological reason and technical reason. He has defined ontological reason "as the structure of the mind which enables it grasp and shape reality".[32] The grasping and shaping functions of ontological reason are not confined to the field of cognitive experience. They are extended to the other field of human activities. The ontological reason operates on the entire field of human life. In this respect, it is akin to the higher reason of Sri Aurobindo,

[31] This work is in three volumes.

[32] Paul Tillich, *The Systematic Theology*, vol. I, p. 75.

which is characterized by him as the Logic of the Infinite. Ontological reason or the higher reason is concerned with the complete structure of mind. It is the activity of the whole mind. It does not remain content with its cognitive aspect. "It is," according to Tillich, "effective in the cognitive, aesthetic, practical and technical functions of the human mind".[33] Ontological or higher reason is *logos*. It embraces man's entire existence.

The function of the ontological or higher reason is to grasp and shape reality. The ontological reason or *logos* constitutes the rational structure of mind. It is called subjective reason. It also constitutes the rational structure of reality which is called objective reason. The subjective reason is always actualized in the inmost core of the self which is related to its environment and its world in terms of reception and reaction. In receiving reasonably, the mind grasps its world. In reacting reasonably, the mind shapes its world. "Grasping", in this context, has the connotation of penetrating into the depth of a thing. "Shaping" in this context has the connotation of transforming a given material into a living structure. The two acts — grasping and shaping — are interdependent. One transforms reality according to the way one grasps it and one grasps reality according to the way one transforms it. This function of grasping and shaping of reality takes place at different levels of human consciousness. The ontological reason essentially aims at attaining unity with the reality by penetrating into its depth. It is not satisfied with grasping the appearance of things or reality. The real nature of things lies, not in their surface, but in their depth. Tillich observes:

> The surface must be penetrated, the appearance undercut the "depth" must be reached, namely the ausia, the "essence" of things, that which gives them the power of being.

[33] Paul Tillich, *The Systematic Theology*, vol. I, p. 72.

This is their truth, the "really real" in difference from the seemingly real. It would not be called "true", however, if it were not true for someone, namely for the mind which in the power of the rational word, the *logos*, grasps the level of reality in which the really real "dwells".[34] This grasping of the deepest level of reality effects an inward change in man's total being and transforms reality itself. Man is no more under the spell of appearances of things. The grasping and the shaping functions of ontological reason are not only illustrated in the field of cognitive experience but in other fields of human activity as well. Tillich observes:

> Reason in the philosopher grasps the reason in nature. Reason in the artist grasps the meaning of things. Reason in the legislator shapes society according to the structures of social balance. Reason in the leaders of a community shapes communal life according to the structure of organic interdependence.[35]

Thus, the entire field of human life and the creative activities of man and nature reveal in a deeper sense the structure and operation of ontological reason.

The technical reason in Tillich is understood as the capacity for "reasoning". It constitutes the cognitive aspect of human mind. It does not embrace the aesthetic, practical, emotional and other aspects of it. In the cognitive realm, the technical or finite reason is concerned with "those cognitive acts which deal with the discovery of means for ends". Reason in the sense of *logos* is primarily concerned with determining the ends. Reason in the finite or technical sense determines the means and accepts the ends from "somewhere else". If finite or technical reason tries to grasp the essential nature of things, their meaning and value in an independent way, it reduces

---

[34] Paul Tillich, *The Systematic Theology*, vol. I, p. 101.

[35] Ibid., pp. 77f.

them to something less than their true reality. But, by reducing them to an inferior status, it deprives itself of the true knowledge of things. For example, one may know many aspects of human nature by studying the physiology, the anatomy and the psychology of man. One can utilize this knowledge to attain specific ends. This knowledge alone does not help one in coming to a deeper appreciation of human personality.

Technical or finite reason, according to Tillich, is "controlling knowledge". This knowledge is determined in a predominant way by the element of detachment. Technical or finite reason or controlling knowledge is governed primarily by the element of detachment. It unites the subject with the object with a view to enable the subject to control the object. The controlling knowledge always tends to objectify man. It takes man also as an object. Man is taken as a means to serve some end which does not constitute an essential part of himself. Technical reason has attained tremendous success in the field of science and technology. It provides a method of investigation or research which is objective, precise and logical. It claims to control every level of reality. It is not satisfied with its application in science and technology but it also claims to determine the ethical and spiritual values of individual life and of community. The method which it adopts in the study of the objects of nature is also applied in the determination of the values and meaning of life. Tillich observes:

> Life, spirit, personality, community, meanings, values, even one's ultimate concern should be treated in terms of detachment, analysis, calculation, technical use. The power behind this claim is the preciseness, verifiability, the public approachability of controlling knowledge, and, above all, the tremendous success of its application to certain levels of reality.[36]

---

[36] Paul Tillich, *The Systematic Theology*, vol. I, p. 99.

The application of the strictly scientific method in the study of man is already creating a serious situation for man's moral and spiritual life.

> In psychology and sociology, in medicine and philosophy, man has been dissolved into elements out of which he is composed and which determine him.[37]

But this way of studying man reduces him to the level of an object. He becomes an object among other objects and is altogether deprived of his subjectivity. Man, as a person, is lost in this enterprise. As Tillich observes:

> Man actually has become what controlling knowledge considers him to be, a thing among things, a cog in the dominating machine of production and consumption, a dehumanized object of tyranny or a normalized object of public communications. Cognitive dehumanization has produced actual dehumanization.[38]

The finitude of reason is represented by the four main categories — time, space, causality and substance. Time, according to Tillich as well as Sri Aurobindo, is the main category of finitude. Misra observes:

> To be finite means to be temporal. Reason cannot break through limits of temporality and reach the eternal or the unconditioned.[39]

Time can be viewed from the point of view of its negative and positive elements. The negative element points to the transitoriness and the perishable nature of all things within the order of time.

---

[37] Loc. cit.

[38] Loc. cit.

[39] R.S. Misra, *The Concept of Reason in the Systematic Theology of Paul Tillich*, pp. 22-23.

> They point to the movement of time from a past that is no more toward a future that is not yet through the present which is nothing more than the moving boundary line between past and future. To be means to be present. But if the present is illusory, being is conquered by non-being.[40]

The positive element in time is indicated by the "creative character of the temporal process, to its directness and irreversibility to the new produced within it". Tillich holds that the present cannot be called illusory, for past and future and the movement from the one to the other can be measured only on the basis of the experienced present. At the same time, the destructive element in time also cannot be denied. Time swallows everything that it creates, the new becomes old and vanishes. Evolution and the emergence of things are followed by their disintegration and disappearance. This is the picture of time when it is looked "from the outside", namely in relation to the world. The positive and negetive element of time must be considered "from the inside", namely in relation to the self. The changing character of time creates in man a sense of anxiety with regard to his own existence. Tillich puts it:

> This anxiety is potentially present in every moment. It permeates the whole of man's being; it shapes soul and body and determines spiritual life; it belongs to the created character of being quite apart from the estrangement and sin.[41]

Tillich holds that time engenders another feeling also in man which is opposed to anxiety. It is called courage. Negatively considered, it creates anxiety, positively considered, it creates courage.

---

[40] Paul Tillich, *The Systematic Theology*, vol. I, p. 193.

[41] Ibid., pp. 193f.

It is clear from the above discussion that the concept of time involves a union of being and non-being, and also a union of anxiety and courage. Time has got its positive and negative aspects. It has a creative as well as destructive element. It has an element of affirmation and an element of negation with regard to world as well as self. Space, causality and substance are similarly involved in the finitude. They are ambiguous in character. It means that reason is conditioned by time and other categories.

In spite of its finitude, reason is aware of its infinite depth. If man were totally unaware of the depth of reason or the depth of reality, then he would not have any realization of his finitude also. This is the inevitable result of the separation of finite reason or technical reason or controlling knowledge from higher reason or ontological reason or receiving knowledge. The essential nature of man and the meaning of life can be known and discovered only when reason is able to fathom the depth of man's existence and attain unity with the ground of being. Thus, finite reason or technical reason gives way to ontological or higher reason which is based on the awareness of unity. Finite reason or technical reason has to work in subordination to higher reason or ontological reason in order to have an understanding of the meaning and nature of human existence. The ontological, ethical and aesthetic realms of reality cannot be adequately comprehended and understood by finite or technical reason, if it separates itself from ontological reason or receiving knowledge. In order to avoid the limitations of finite reason or technical reason, it is required to be linked with higher or ontological reason. Reasoning, in this situation, is used to explain the contents of higher or ontological reason and to serve its ends. Technical or finite reason does not possess the capacity to penetrate the depth of things, to know their meaning. The essential nature of things, their meaning and value are to determine higher reason or ontological reason.

The higher reason or the Logic of the Infinite of Sri Aurobindo bears a close resemblance to Tillich's conception of ontological reason. Like the ontological reason of Tillich, Sri Aurobindo's higher reason embraces the whole of man's mind as well as nature. It is operating in an unconscious way in the material world, and with a very limited consciousness in the vegetable kingdom and the animal world. Even in human consciousness, the operation of higher reason is limited to a great extent. It does not manifest itself in its original form at the mental or rational level. But man is possessed of the capacity to take recourse to higher reason in understanding the nature of human life, the finite world and the infinite.

A deeper understanding of the nature of higher reason enables man overcome all the so-called antinomies and contradictions, as has been shown above and attain unity with the whole of reality. It is able to have an all-embracing knowledge of the whole of reality, including the individual, the universal and the transcendent. In this respect, it resembles the ontological reason of Tillich which enjoins unity with reality or of the depth of existence. But, this experience of the unity or the realization of the depth of existence remains more or less theoretical at the rational or intellectual level. Both Tillich and Sri Aurobindo admit that even higher reason or ontological reason cannot have a direct knowledge or immediate experience of the whole of reality or the depth of existence under the conditions of existence or finitude. It is due to this reason that Tillich and Sri Aurobindo believe in the fulfilment of ontological reason or higher reason in some higher consciousness which is absolutely free from all finite conditions. Tillich calls it revolution and Sri Aurobindo gives it the name of supramental knowledge. Tillich believes that the ontological reason can work in an unfettered way only in revelation, only in a person, who is completely transparent to the depth of his being. In the same way, Sri Aurobindo believes that the higher reason or the Logic of the Infinite can operate in an unconditional way only in a being whose nature is completely transformed by the descent of the supermind. This requires a long process of evolution. Sri Aurobindo has given a detailed description of the process of evolution. Evolution, according to him, has so far proceeded up to mental stage. Now, it has to proceed further from the stage of mind to the stage of supermind and it should culminate in the entire transformation of the nature by descent of the supramental force.

Reason and Evolution

Sri Aurobindo presents a dynamic and comprehensive view of evolution. It includes the individual as well as cosmic evolution. He is a firm believer in the evolution of man and the world to the higher stages of spiritual existence. But the evolutionary process, according to him, cannot be explained in terms of any principle that is known to man in the present stage of his existence. In this respect, his view differs from the Hegelian and other modern theories of evolution. The Darwin–Spencerian theory of evolution is naturalistic and mechanistic. It lacks spiritual purpose. Hegelian conception of evolution is dynamic. Its scheme is dialectical. It is the logical process of the development of reason. To Sri Aurobindo, Hegelian view of evolution is not satisfactory as it is too much conditioned by reason. Reason is a stage in the development of the life of the spirit. It redeems one from the arbitrary control of sensations and perceptions. But it is imperfect because it suffers from the "bondage of stereotyped ways of looking at things".[42] It is required to be transcended.

Sri Aurobindo takes evolution as the inverse of the process of creation. He shares Hegel's view that all evolution is evolution of the spirit. But Hegel identifies spirit with reason.

---

[42] S.K. Maitra, *The Meeting of the East and the West in Aurobindo's Philosophy*, p. 35.

To Sri Aurobindo, the scheme of evolution, based on logic or reason, cannot be the last word in evolution. The spirit must transcend reason. *Creative Evolution* of Bergson, established the futility of logic or reason. Logic is helpless to reach the highest ladders of evolution. Bergson has emphasized most strongly the futility of the mechanical theory of evolution. *Creative Evolution,* a great work of Bergson posed a challenge to the mechanical theory of evolution. He not only wanted to demolish mechanical evolution but he tried to destroy all kinds of teleological evolution. Bergson abandons teleology but does not substitute like Sri Aurobindo a higher for a lower teleology. The rejection of all teleology is tenable. Maitra observes:

> It has taken away from his creative evolution all its creativity and has reduced it to that same dreaded mechanical evolution from which its express purpose was to give us deliverance.[43]

The question arises: what is spontaneous movement if it is not movement towards anything, what is creative evolution if it does not know what it is to create, what is self-generative action if it is not guided by any purpose? Maitra raises a question:

> In what way is such movement and such action different from the purely mechanical movement and action controlled by physical forces?[44]

Bergson ignores the fact that freedom is not a negative but a positive idea. To be free does not mean to be free from all control, but it means to be guided and controlled solely by oneself. A free act does not mean an act which is absolutely undetermined. It is an act which is the expression of man's

---

[43] S.K. Maitra, *The Meeting of the East and the West in Aurobindo's Philosophy*, pp. 96-97.

[44] Ibid., p. 97.

character. It is an action in which man's full personality is manifested. Similar is the case with cosmic plane. Creative or spiritual evolution is one in which every movement bears on its face the stamp of its spiritual origin. In this process, every step reveals its spiritual source. If it cannot do that, then it may be anything, but it cannot be creative evolution.

Here, we find a fundamental difference between Bergson's theory of evolution and that of Sri Aurobindo. Maitra significantly puts it:

> Spiritual evolution does not mean for Sri Aurobindo merely self-generative movement, but it means an evolution in which every step in the process is directed by the spirit. The spirit is also not a mere silent witness of evolution, as it is in the Sāṁkhya philosophy, but it actively guides and directs every little movement of it.[45]

Bergson substitutes creative evolution in place of Darwin's mechanistic and naturalistic evolution. But his creative evolution frustrates the very purpose of evolution because it does not lead to any goal. In fact, a sourceless and aimless movement of Bergson can in no sense be called creative.

> A flow that is not a flow towards anything, a movement that is not directed by any end, is unrelieved mechanism. In fact, what Bergson has given us is a temporal mechanism, in place of the spatial mechanism of the nineteenth-century biologists.[46]

Sri Aurobindo contends that the blind movement may not be a good substitute for mechanistic evolution.

"Emergent evolution" of S. Alexander comes close to Sri Aurobindo's conception of evolution. Like Alexander, Sri

---

[45] Loc. cit.

[46] S.K. Maitra, *The Meeting of the East and the West in Aurobindo's Philosophy*, p. 38.

Aurobindo also talks of the emergence of higher and higher forms of consciousness. The consciousness higher than the present evolute is "deity", according to Alexander. When evolution is at the stage of matter, deity represents the stage of life and, in this way, the next stage of evolution represents deity for the lower stage. Sri Aurobindo's view of emergence is different from Alexander's in certain respects. In Alexander's scheme of emergent evolution, there is no change of the old principles on the emergence of a new one. The old principles remain as they were before; only a new one joins them. For Sri Aurobindo, however, evolution does not mean merely an addition of some new principles to those which are already existent, but it means that the old principles, by reason of the emergence of the new ones, change their character.

Life, for instance, as it was before the emergence of mind, is very different from life as we know it today, dominated as it is by mind. So again, he believes that when the principle of supermind will emerge, all the principles which are existent today such as matter, life, mind and soul will undergo a radical change. Even the physical universe will be very different from what it is at present, for it will cease to offer any resistance to the spirit, but on the contrary, will work in perfect co-operation with it. Alexander in his book *Space, Time and Deity* — has given us a theory of evolution which resembles in certain respects to Sri Aurobindo's theory of evolution. Both conceive of emergent evolution. Alexander, like Aurobindo, talks of the emergence of higher and higher forms of consciousness. Both express hope of the emergence of a higher consciousness than has so far emerged. The general name, which he gives to a consciousness higher than what has emerged at a particular stage of evolution, is deity.

Let us now proceed to consider how S. Radhakrishnan criticizes Alexander's views of evolution. Radhakrishnan observes:

> Alexander's brilliant attempt to frame a general metaphysical scheme in consonance with modern scientific developments suffers from certain fundamental disabilities.[47]

It is seen that an "anti-metaphysical bias"[48] is predominant in his whole enterprise. The position of space–time in his metaphysics seems to be ambiguous. Radhakrishnan observes:

> It is an abstraction, an assumption made to account for concrete existence, and is not itself concrete existence. Yet it is called the stuff out of which existents are made.[49]

Since from space–time everything else arises, it becomes the absolute for Alexander. In the words of Radhakrishnan:

> There is no proof that at the beginning there was a primordial condition of space–time from which all the richness of concrete experience was absent, and from which it has somehow emerged. If space–time were the ultimate reality, we do not know what it is.[50]

The rise of matter from space–time is not logically tenable. Matter is not a piece of extension–duration. Matter is different from space and time. Alexander's evolution is without any idea of what evolution is and what it sets out to achieve. Why does space–time evolve at all? What is the inner spring of this evolution? How does it develop a nexus towards deity, unless deity is already concealed in it? Alexander could not answer these questions in a satisfactory way. The theory of evolution, propounded by Alexander, does not mark much progress over the naturalistic theories of evolution.

---

[47] S. Radhakrishnan, *An Idealist View of Life*, p. 225.

[48] Loc. cit.

[49] Loc. cit.

[50] S. Radhakrishnan, *An Idealist View of Life*, p. 256.

The superiority of Sri Aurobindo's position is beyond question. He has not only answered the "why" of evolution but also its "how". To him, evolution is nothing else than the inverse of the process of creation. One cannot understand evolution without linking it to creation. It is because the spirit has involved itself in matter, that matter can evolve into life, life representing something which has more of the spiritual element in it than matter. The same is true of the evolution of life into mind and of mind into the supermind. Evolution, in fact, is another name for the return of the spirit to itself. Alexander's theory of "emergent evolution" is superior to some others in so far as it asserts that mind is not the pinnacle of the evolutionary process. Sri Aurobindo shares his view that there are higher stages beyond mind that are to be attained by the evolutionary process. These higher stages of spirit unfold the hidden meaning of the evolutionary process.

Nature of Evolutionary Process

> All evolution is in essence a heightening of the force of consciousness in the manifest being so that it may be raised into the greater intensity of what is still unmanifest, from matter into life, from life into mind, from the mind into the spirit.[51]

The process of evolution is a triple one. It may be called a widening, a heightening and an integration. The widening of the field provides greater room for the operation of each principle as it emerges. The heightening is an ascent from grade to grade. The integration effects change in the lower grades so that at each step of the ascent, there is not merely an ascent to a higher principle but a lifting up and transformation of the lower principles by the higher one. Integration is an ascent through descent. Maitra observes:

---

[51] Sri Aurobindo, *The Life Divine*, p. 866.

> The usual view of evolution, which looks upon it as a mere ascent from the lower grade to the higher grade, may be compared to the march of an army which advances without keeping its lines of communication with the base intact. And we may compare Sri Aurobindo's conception of evolution with the march of an army which advances with the whole force, keeping all its lines of communication perfectly intact.[52]

The evolution starts in inconscience, travels through ignorance and culminates in knowledge. In the course of evolution, matter is modified into life and life into conscious substance. But the complete transformation is not effected. Life is fastened to death because it evolves in matter. Mind is also matter-bound and life-bound. It appears that neither mind nor life is the original creative energy. The original energy is higher than life or mind. This power is consciousness. It must be more potent than material energy. Since it is higher than mind, it must be something supramental. If it is a power more efficient than matter, life and mind, it must be a power of spirit. Neither material energy nor life-force or mind-force can effect a complete transformation of material substance. The transformation is possible when the spirit is postulated. The spirit transforms the inconscient into conscient. It implants the law of gnostic consciousness. It changes matter, life and mind into higher existence. The evolution culminates in spirit. It changes the ignorance into a movement of knowledge. This is the general nature of the "cosmic evolution".

Evolution is not only cosmic but also individual. It is compared to the triple eye of Lord *Śiva*. One eye is turned upward, another turned downward and one eye turned inward. The cosmic evolution is concerned with upward and downward movements. The inward is our soul. Evolution is

---

[52] S.K. Maitra, *An Introduction to the Philosophy of Sri Aurobindo*, p. 44.

as much individual as it is cosmic. The self as individual is no less real than the self as cosmic being or spirit, and both are powers of the eternal.

The Triple Transformation

In the course of evolution, we find a gulf between mind and supermind. Sri Aurobindo tries to bridge the gulf between mind and supermind. This is possibly done by the triple transformation.

> . . . there must first be the psychic change, the conversion of our whole present nature into a soul-instrumentation; on that or along with that there must be the spiritual change, the descent of a higher Light, Knowledge, Power, Force, Bliss, Purity into the whole being, even into the lowest recesses of the life and body, even into the darkness of our subconscience; last, there must supervene the supramental transformation, there must take place as the crowning movement the ascent into the supermind and the transforming descent of the supramental consciousness into our entire being and nature.[53]

The Psychic Transformation

The soul or psyche is the inner nature. It is by virtue of soul, we exist as individual beings. This permanent being employs mind, life and body as its instruments. But the soul remains unaffected by their operations. The development of soul is possible with the enhancement of our mind, life and matter in the higher light of the spirit. The psychic transformation marks the first stage of the integral transformation of man and of earthly existence. It will be possible by the descent of the higher grades of spirit and of supermind into earth consciousness. After psychic transformation, there will follow the spiritual

---

[53] Sri Aurobindo, *The Life Divine*, pp. 1061-62.

and supramental transformation. The passage of the supermind is through soul. The final stage of evolution is the supramental change. This effects a radical change in the whole of terrestrial existence — physical, vital and mental. The ascent to the supermind is made possible by the descent of the latter into the world of matter, life and mind. The supramental consciousness is at work in the whole of the evolutionary process. The transition from mind to supermind is a passage from nature to super-nature. Material, vital and mental stages of evolution are stages in ignorance. The supramental change cancels all ignorance and the evolution henceforth takes place in and through knowledge. The terrestrial nature, when it comes in contact with the super-conscient spheres, may give rise to an overmental transformation. In the long process of evolution, the superior race of mental beings, who think and act not by reasoning but by intuitive understanding, may emerge. This may lead to "overmentalization" which is the gateway to the region of the supermind.

The Spiritual Transformation

The spiritual transformation takes place as a result of the descent of the light and energy from the higher grades of spiritual existence — higher mind, illumined mind, intuition and overmind into earth consciousness. Sri Aurobindo observes:

> A highest spiritual transformation must intervene on the psychic or psycho-spiritual change; the psychic movement inward to the inner being, the self or Divinity within us, must be completed by an opening upward to a supreme spiritual status or a higher existence. This can be done by our opening into what is above us, by an ascent of consciousness into the ranges of overmind and supramental nature in which the sense of self and spirit is ever unveiled and permanent and in which the self-luminous

instrumentation of the self and spirit is not restricted or divided as in our mind-nature, life-nature, body-nature.[54]

Higher Mind

The higher mind is qualitatively different from mind and is free from its limitations. It is not subjected to the categories of thought or the rules of logic. It is a luminous thought-mind, a mind of spirit-born conceptual knowledge. It is the searchlight of intelligence. The spiritual consciousness has no cognition of isolated ideas. It is conceptual-cum-spiritual knowledge. The normal mind obtains knowledge through sense-experience, inference and other sources of knowledge. The higher mind apprehends totality at a single view. The relations of idea with idea and of truth with truth are not established by reason. It is pre-existent and experienced in the integral whole. Higher mind has cognitive, volitional and effective aspects. But the higher mind, by its descent, does not effect an integral transformation. Its knowledge is distorted by the mind, life and body. Higher mind may raise man to a higher status. It may permeate the whole being with a new and superior consciousness. It lays a foundation of change from the terrestrial to the spiritual. But it does not effect a total change.

> The power of the spiritual higher mind and its idea-force, modified and diminished as it must be by its entrance into our mentality, is not sufficient to sweep out all these obstacles and create the gnostic being, but it can make a first change, a modification that will capacitate a higher ascent and a more powerful descent and further prepare an integration of the being in a greater force of consciousness and knowledge.[55]

---

[54] Sri Aurobindo, *The Life Divine*, pp. 1083-84.

[55] Ibid., p. 1123.

Illumined Mind

This is a mind of spiritual light. It is a luminous inner force. It is a power which brings rapid transformation in comparison with the slow process of the higher mind. "The illumined mind," observes Sri Aurobindo "does not work primarily by thought, but the vision . . .."[56] Reason gives place to vision. There is vision of the truth itself and not merely of its image. The ascent to the illumined mind is followed by the descent of knowledge, power and joy or bliss from it. The personality is integrated into a higher order. It possesses a greater consciousness and superior dynamism. The knowledge and power of the illumined mind is not completely free from mental distortion. In the process of descent, it undergoes modification due to the resistance of the lower nature. As the integration of human personality is not yet complete, the evolution goes upward to a higher spiritual plane. This spiritual plane is called by Sri Aurobindo as "intuition".

Intuition

> Intuition brings to man those brilliant messages from the Unknown which are the beginning of his higher knowledge. Reason only comes in afterwards to see what profit it can have of the shining harvest. Intuition gives us that idea of something behind and beyond all that we know and seem to be which pursues man always in contradiction of his lower reason and all his normal experience and impels him to formulate that formless perception in the more positive ideas of God, Immortality, Heaven and the rest by which we strive to express it to the mind.[57]

Intuition transforms mind, heart, life, senses and even body. It brings radiant movement into will, feelings and emotions.

---

[56] Sri Aurobindo, *The Life Divine*, p. 1124.

[57] Ibid., p. 81.

Intuition is the result of the meeting of the subject consciousness with the object. Intuition is a power which leaps out direct from a concealed identity. Intuition sparks when the subject penetrates into the object. It visualizes and vibrates with the truth of what it contacts. Intuition is a flash of intimate truth-perception. The senses and reason conceive the forms or appearance of things. Kant, Śaṅkara and Sri Aurobindo believe that reality cannot be apprehended either by senses or reason. Sri Aurobindo says that the ancient Vedānta seized this message of the intuition and formulated it in the three great declarations of the Upaniṣads, "I am He", "Thou art That", "All this is the *Brahman*; this self is the *Brahman*".

Intuition probes into the realities underlying the appearance. "This close perception," says Sri Aurobindo "is more than sight, more than conception: it is the result of a penetrating and revealing touch which carries in it sight and conception as part of itself or as its natural consequence".[58] The Mind gets glimpses of intuitions coming from the higher level. The mind fails to intuitions coming from the higher level. The mind fails to experience intuition in their pure form. A pure intuition is "a rare occurrence in our mental activity". Intitutions are modified by our mental consciousness. The mind perceives in accordance with its own laws of perception and thought. The knowledge of intuition is modified by mental categories. In the process of modification, it loses it purity.

Sri Aurobindo points out the limited nature of reason but he does not decry the function of the same. He contends that reason must make scrutiny of intuitions. Intuition springs out from higher as well as lower level. It originates from subconscient as well as conscient sources. Reason is perfectly justified in discriminating properly between the truth and falsehood. It is right so far as it scrutinizes the inconscient

[58] Sri Aurobindo, *The Life Divine*, p. 1126.

and indistinct intuition. The tragedy with reason is that it sometimes distorts the intuition coming from higher sources. On mental plane, intuition has little significance. The mind rises to the higher mind and illumined mind. It is transformed by their knowledge and power. It gets rid of the shackles of space, time and categories. It becomes fit to receive spiritual truth. The ascent to the plane of intuition is followed by the descent of the power of intuition into the human organism. The integration of human personality is achieved on the higher plane of consciousness. Above intuitive mind, there is the overmind which is the supermind's delegate to the ignorance.

The Overmind

The overmind is the "first parent of ignorance". The supermind descends to the overmind. The overmind does not enjoy the integral unity of the supermind. The tendency of the overmind is towards separation. The supermind is not contaminated by ignorance. To supermind, *puruṣa* and *prakr̥ti*, conscious soul and executive force of nature are two-aspected single truth. The opposition between one and many, and being and becoming of the reality is dissolved in the supermind. The cleavage comes with the origin of the overmind. Overmind consciousness is global in its character. It attempts to reconcile differences. Like other mental grades, the overmind also is not able to effect an integral transformation of nature by its descent into the human organism. It cannot transform wholly the ignorance. The descent of the overmind does not change the basis of the terrestrial nature. The terrestrial evolution proceeds on the basis of ignorance. The overmind cannot transform the entire nature. It cannot guarantee against the downward pull of inconscience. Hence, to achieve integral transformation of the entire nature, the descent of the supermind is imperative.

The final ascent to the supermind is possible only by the

supramental descent. The psychical and spiritual changes are the preparatory stages for the supramental transformation. The four intermediary stages from mind to supermind are but stages of ignorance. The final stage of pure knowledge is only possible when there is a corresponding descent of the latter. The preparation from below and the grace from above are essential requisites for the radical transformation of the world-process into divinity. The supramental light radiates our being as we go on ascending. Sri Aurobindo, unlike Hegel, does not believe in the process of continuity but in emergence. He advances an emergent theory of evolution.

The Supramental Transformation

In Sri Aurobindo's scheme of evolution, the evolutionary process does not stop with the evolution of overmind. The overmind is an intermediary link between the supermind and the mind. The ascent from the overmind to the supermind follows the same principle as it does in the lower stages. In order to find out a link between the mind and the supermind, Sri Aurobindo develops the concept of intuition. But he contends that intuition cannot serve as an appropriate link, for it is not altogether free from mental influence. Maitra observes:

> . . . it is too flashy, too unstable, too much under the influence of masses of mental stuff that penetrate into it, to be able really to serve as a link between mind and supermind.[59]

The mind has its source in super-conscient cosmic mind. The super-conscient cosmic mind is called the overmind. The supermind communicates all its realities to the overmind, yet the latter is "a first parent of the ignorance". It lacks the integral and synthetic vision of the supermind. It takes each aspect or power of Supreme Reality independently and separately. Thus,

[59] S.K. Maitra, *An Introduction to the Philosophy of Sri Aurobindo*, p. 26.

the integrality of the supramental consciousness is missing in the overmind. In overmind, there is a cleavage between *puruṣa* and *prakṛti*, the conscious soul and the executive force of nature. In supramental consciousness, there is a complete harmony between *puruṣa* and *prakṛti*. The supermind is potentially present in nature. It emerges on account of a thrust in the evolutionary nature itself up to the stage of overmind, the evolution moves in the realm of ignorance. But the descent of the supermind brings a radical change in the original law of nature. The evolution now passes from the lower nature of *aparā prakṛti* to the higher nature of *parā prakṛti*. The result of this supramental descent is that the spiritual being is transformed into the gnostic being. The lower nature or *aparā prakṛti* is transformed into the higher nature or *parā prakṛti* or *cit-śakti*. The supramental transformation of human personality brings a radical change in the working of mind, life and body. The supramental evolution lifts mind, life and body to a higher and qualitatively different dimension altogether. They are not abolished but perfected; not suppressed but fulfilled. So, when the supramental consciousness emerges, discursive reason is not abnegated but absorbed and transformed into the spiritual reason. But, the working of the supermind remains beyond the ken of ordinary reason. Sri Aurobindo observes:

> As the summits of human mind are beyond animal perception, so the movements of the supermind are beyond the ordinary human mental conception: it is only when we have already had experience of higher intermediate consciousness that any terms attempting to describe supramental being could convey a true meaning to our intelligence; for then, having experienced something akin to what is described, we could translate an inadequate language into a figure of what we knew.[60]

From the above account it is clear that with the emergence of

[60] Sri Aurobindo, *The Life Divine*, pp. 1095.

the supramental consciousness, human being is transformed into the supramental being or what Sri Aurobindo calls it gnostic being. At the supramental stage, the process of knowledge undergoes a fundamental change. In the ordinary human personality, the senses and reason are important sources of knowledge. But in the gnostic personality, reason is supplemented by synthetic vision of unity or identity. Reason comprehends the phenomena as not-self which is totally different from and independent of the self. But to gnostic consciousness or supramental consciousness, the so-called not-self is not really opposed to the self but is only a part of the self. The phenomenal world is the projection of reality in the order of space and time. The gnostic consciousness will at once intimately and exactly know its object by a comprehending and penetrating "identification with it".

The evolutionary process does not come to a stop with the emergence of gnostic beings. Before the supramental consciousness dawns, the evolutionary process has to work through ignorance. But, after the emergence of the supramental or gnostic consciousness, it will continue through knowledge. After the supramental transformation, the evolutionary process will continue and manifest the bliss of *Saccidānanda* in the earth-consciousness. The supermind itself is in the involution or descent emerges from the *ānanda* (bliss), and the evolution or ascent merges into *ānanda*. The realization of self in supramental consciousness culminates in the bliss of *Brahman*. Sri Aurobindo says that with the dawn of gnostic consciousness, nature is transformed into super-nature. Nature or becoming will no more appear as something undivine and will no more suffer from darkness, ignorance and inconscience. On the other hand, it will shine with the light and consciousness of the Divine and will permanently enjoy in its movement and further evolution in knowledge, the powers and bliss of *Saccidānanda*.

The Gnostic Being

The being endowed with the supramental consciousness is called the "gnostic being". The possible destiny of man lies in his supramental transformation into gnostic being. The descent of the supramental consciousness does not imply the negation of the mental, vital and physical elements. It is simply the entire transformation of the total man into the Divine man. The supramental consciousness enters into our lower nature and divinizes it. Sri Aurobindo contends that the supramental consciousness illumines the terrestrial mind, life, bodily being and transforms the whole nature.

The supermind emerges on account of a push in the evolutionary nature itself. The descent of the supermind into earth-consciousness marks a radical change in the evolutionary process as well as terrestrial nature. It is seen that up to the stage of the overmind, the evolution proceeds through ignorance and through imperfect knowledge. But the descent of the supermind creates a radical change in this original law of nature. The principle of ignorance is now changed into that of knowledge. The evolution now passes from the lower nature to the higher nature. So, the result of this supramental descent is that the spiritual being is transformed into the gnostic being.

Sri Aurobindo observes:

> The gnostic individual would be the consummation of the spiritual man; his whole way of being, thinking, living, acting would be governed by the power of a vast universal spirituality.[61]

Further, he says, "He will be the perfected and complete individual . . .".[62] In the ordinary human personality, the sense and the mind are the chief sources of knowledge. But in the

[61] Sri Aurobindo, *The Life Divine*, p. 1156.

[62] Ibid., p. 1157.

gnostic personality, mind is replaced by a fundamental consciousness of unity or identity. Sri Aurobindo contends:

> Our normal perception or imagination or formulation of things spiritual and things mundane is mental, but in the gnostic change the evolution crosses a line beyond which there is a supreme and radical reversal of consciousness and the standards and forms of mental cognition are no longer sufficient: it is difficult for mental thought to understand or describe the supramental nature.[63]

To the mind, the world of objects appears to be totally different from and independent of the self. But to the gnostic consciousness, the so-called not-self is not really opposed to the self but is only a part of the self or a projection of it in the order of space and time. Sri Aurobindo remarks:

> Mental nature and mental thought are based on a consciousness of the finite; supramental nature is in its very grain a consciousness and power of the Infinite. Supramental nature sees everything from the standpoint of oneness and regards all things, even the greatest multiplicity and diversity, even what are to the mind the strongest contradictions, in the light of that oneness; its will, ideas, feelings, senses are made of the stuff of oneness, its actions proceed upon that basis.[64]

Gnostic consciousness knows objects in its entirety. It knows it by identification and oneness. A dominant principle of harmony will descend upon the life of ignorance.

> . . . the discord, the blind seeking, the clash of struggle, the abnormal vicissitudes of exaggeration and depression and unsteady balance of the unseeing forces at work in their mixture and conflict, would feel the influence and yield place to a more orderly pace and harmonic steps of the

---

[63] Sri Aurobindo, *The Life Divine*, p. 1148.

[64] Ibid., pp. 1148-49.

> development of being, a more revealing arrangement of progressing life and consciousness, a better life-order.[65]

Not only mind but life also undergoes a radical change in the personality of the gnostic being. Life is in reality nothing but the projection of consciousness force of spirit. Life is surrounded everywhere by the triple principle of death, desire and incapacity due to the limiting, dividing and ignorant mind. But when mind gets rid of its limitations and is transformed into the integral consciousness of the gnostic being, life also gets rid of its limitations of death, desire and incapicity.

In the gnostic personality, the relation between the spirit and body also undergoes a radical change. Ordinarily, the body is governed by the laws of the subconscious and the unconscious. But in the gnostic being, the will of the spirit controls and determines the movements and workings of the body. The physical, vital and mental laws that governed the body are replaced by the gnostic law of freedom.

The emergence of gnostic beings on earth will make a significant change in our attitude towards spiritual life. The spiritual life will no longer necessitate a rejection of the world. On the other hand, it will mean a free acceptance of it. The gnostic being will realize matter also as *Brahman*. But he will in no way be attached to the material or vital aspects of the reality. Nature or becoming will no more appear as something undivine. It will no more suffer from darkness, ignorance and inconscience. On the other hand, it will shine with the light and consciousness of the Divine. It will permanently enjoy in its movement and further evolution in knowledge the powers and bliss of *Saccidānanda*.

Now, a question may be asked: what is the place of personality in the gnostic being? Is gnostic being similar to

---

[65] Sri Aurobindo, *The Life Divine*, p. 1153.

other human beings in the form and appearance or quite different from them? In the Advaita Vedānta of Śaṅkara, there is no place for individuality and personality after the attainment of liberation. The individuality and personality are supposed to be constituted by the limited and separative ego. When the consciousness of the transcendent dawns, the ego is cancelled. Rāmānuja holds that the notion of individuality is not incompatible with that of salvation. The individual suffers from bondage due to ego and not due to his spiritual self or individuality. According to Rāmānuja, egoity is incompatible to salvation and not individuality. Sri Aurobindo agrees with Rāmānuja that liberation means only the annihilation of the ego and not that of the individuality itself. According to Sri Aurobindo, the liberation is attained by the individual in the present life and on this earth. According to Rāmānuja, though the individuality remains even after liberation, yet there no more remains any personality.

Now the question arises: is the gnostic being as viewed by Sri Aurobindo possessed of individuality like the liberated soul in Rāmānuja or of personality also? The gnostic being in Sri Aurobindo's view, is not devoid of body. It is possessed of personality. But the personality of the gnostic being will not be limited and restricted like that of an ordinary individual. The ordinary restricted personality can be grasped by an observation of the behaviour of the individual and by a description of the working of his inner mental processes. But such a description would be inadequate to express the character and personality of the gnostic being who has attained oneness in consciousness and power with the universal and the transcendent.

Now the question is: are gnostic beings alike in form and nature? Sri Aurobindo contends that as we find differences in the individuality and personality of mental beings, so there will be difference in the case of gnostic beings also. The principle of diversity will in no way be abolished by the emergence of the gnostic being. But unlike mental beings, there will be no ignorance in the case of gnostic being or superman. The gnostic being will be aware of their individuality, universality and transcendence. They will be aware of their outward differences as well as of the basic unity existing between them. "A supramental or gnostic race of beings," observes Sri Aurobindo, "would not be a race made according to a single type, moulded in a single fixed pattern; for the law of the supermind is unity fulfilled in diversity, and therefore there would be an infinite diversity in the manifestation of the gnostic consciousness . . .."[66] The moment ignorance is cancelled, the diversity and discord seem as nothing else but the manifestation of unity. So man, according to Sri Aurobindo, realizes his highest destiny not by sacrificing his individuality and personality at the alter of bare and abstract unity but by raising them to their highest status of development by the realization of his universal and transcendent nature. There will also emerge in human life a free play of intuition. Sri Aurobindo observes:

> A free play of intuition and sympathy and understanding would enter into human life, a clearer sense of the truth of self and things and a more enlightened dealing with the opportunities and difficulties of existence.[67]

Intuition and Integral Knowledge

The *ācāryas* of Vedānta (Śaṅkara, Madhva and others) as well as their Western counterparts (Spinoza, Bradley and Bergson) have regarded intuition as the supreme source of knowledge.

The question now is: is intuition the highest source of knowledge? To Sri Aurobindo, intuition is not the paramount

---

[66] Sri Aurobindo, *The Life Divine*, p. 1155.

[67] Ibid., p. 1153.

source of knowledge? It is relegated to "a rare occurrence in our mental activity . . .".[68] It occupies an intermediary and not the highest place in Sri Aurobindo's philosophy. This indicates a change in Sri Aurobindo's view from the traditional conceptions of intuition.

The term "intuition" has been used in various senses. Kant and Croce admit the validity of intuition in the aesthetic sensibility. The rudiments of aesthetic knowledge are supplied by the intuitive experience. They do not use it for the highest kind of knowledge. Spinoza apprehends intuition in the transcendental sense. For Bradley, intuition is a grasping of reality as a concrete system not only in its universal aspect but in its unique singularity and individuality. In immediate experience, according to Bradley, "what we discover rather is a whole in which distinctions can be made, but in which divisions do not exist".[69] Likewise, Sri Aurobindo holds:

> . . . the highest intuitive knowledge sees things in the whole, in the large and details only as sides of the indivisible whole; its tendency is towards immediate synthesis and the unity of knowledge.[70]

Bergson holds that reason bisects and fragments the whole and distorts the essential nature of reality. Intuition penetrates deep into the heart of reality. It is not mental consciousness. It gives us direct realization. It transcends the limit of reason. ". . . by intuition," observes Bergson "I mean instinct that becomes disinterested, self-conscious capable of reflecting upon its object and of enlarging it indefinitely".[71] Bergson further defines intuition as "the kind of intellectual sympathy by which one places oneself within an object in order to

---

[68] Sri Aurobindo, *The Life Divine*, p. 328.

[69] F.H. Bradley, *Appearance and Reality*, p. 128.

[70] Sri Aurobindo, *The Life Divine*, p. 84.

[71] Henry Bergson, *Creative Evolution*, p. 186.

coincide with what is unique in it and consequently inexpressible."[72] This definition makes intuition as an "elaborate intelligence". He gives other definitions of intuition as "intellectual expansion" or "intellectual auscultation". Bergson desires to distinguish between intellect and intuition. But, he is not very successful because his intuition remains as a dignified instinct being constantly influenced by intelligence. Maitra observes:

> This view of intuition, however, is not free from the difficulty, and raises a number of questions. In the first place, we may ask: do we get this intuition naturally, that is, without our seeking it, or does it require any effort on our part to get it? If it requires an effort, what is the nature of this effort? Secondly, are the intuitions of all persons of the same value, or even in the same person, are all the intuitions obtained at different moments of the same value? If not, by what criterion are the values of the different intuitions to be determined? Unfortunately, Bergson did not give any satisfactory answer to these questions.[73]

The above passage is dealt to pinpoint that intuition of Bergson is not free from ambiguities.

Further, Bergson speaks much about "the effort of intuition" in his, *Introduction to Metaphysics*. He characterizes it as "a laborious and even painful effort". This indicates that intuition is not natural but the outcome of the laborious effort. The nature of effort has not been specified. This effort makes it clear that intuition may vary according to the efforts put by the individuals. He recognizes like Sri Aurobindo levels of intuition. If there are grades, intuition cannot give the complete knowledge of reality. Bergson admits the grades of intuition

---

[72] Henry Bergson, *An Introduction to Metaphysics*, pp. 23-24.

[73] S.K. Maitra, *An Introduction to the Philosophy of Sri Aurobindo*, p. 24.

in his last book, *The Two Sources of Morality and Religion*. He distinguishes between ordinary intuition of human beings and the experience of mystic. To cite Maitra again:

> But while Bergson puts all the different strata of consciousness, from integral experience to the ordinary human intuition, under the same title "intuition", Sri Aurobindo has made a more thoroughgoing analysis of them and has differentiated the different layers, giving them different names. He has also very clearly shown why it is that human intuition falls short of the integral experience. Bergson, although he has based the whole of his philosophy upon intuition, has unfortunately not indicated, in a manner free from ambiguity, the nature of intuition and has not also shown on what principle the gradation of intuition can be made.[74]

Intuition as viewed by the different Vedāntic systems does not, according to Sri Aurobindo, give the integral and all-embracing view of Reality. The different systems of the Vedānta arrive at completely different views of reality, nevertheless, they recognize intuition as the source of knowledge.

Sri Aurobindo uses the word intuition in a restricted sense. He divides the higher knowledge into several grades. Intuition, according to him, is superior to mind, yet it is not to highest source of knowledge. It does not give us an integral and all-embracing view of reality. Sri Aurobindo agrees with the Kantian view and the Vedāntic views that reason can know only phenomena. It cannot comprehend being or the Absolute. Reason at its highest level is able to point to the transcendent but it cannot attain it. Thus, reason plays an important role in the cultivation of empirical knowledge as well as in paving

---

[74] S.K. Maitra, *An Introduction to the Philosophy of Sri Aurobindo*, p. 26.

the way for the realization of the Absolute. Though it cannot reach the Absolute by itself, yet it clears the way for the emergence and operation of intuitive and supramental consciousness in man which alone can realize reality in its entirety.

Intuitive knowledge, according to Sri Aurobindo, is not the highest source of knowledge or of spiritual experience. It does not comprehend reality in all its dimensions. It is possible only by the supramental consciousness or integral knowledge which is superior to intuition. Intuitive knowledge, according to him, is not altogether free from human subjectivity. This understanding of intuitive knowledge may be taken as an original contribution of Sri Aurobindo to our understanding of reality and our appreciation of the nature of knowledge. Reality, which is integral, can be apprehended, according to him only by integral knowledge and not by any other partial source of knowledge, whether it is sense-experience or reason or intuition. Sri Aurobindo succeeds in showing the logical necessity of supramental or integral consciousness by his analysis and criticism of the other sources of knowledge. Reason and intuition, according to him, find their fulfilment in the supramental or integral knowledge.

Integral reality can thus be realized by integral knowledge. In the philosophy of Sri Aurobindo, epistemology keeps in harmony with ontology. The integral knowledge is something inherent in the integral reality. It has to be discovered and is not something to be created. "The integral knowledge," observers Sri Aurobindo "is something that is already there in the integral reality: it is not a new or still non-existent thing that has to be created, acquired, learned, invented or built up by the mind; it must rather be discovered or uncovered, it is a truth that is self-revealed to a spiritual endeavour: for it is there veiled in our deeper and greater self; it is the very stuff of our own spiritual consciousness, and it is by awaking to it even in our surface self that we have to possess it. There is an integral self-knowledge that we have to recover and because the world-self also is our self, an integral world knowledge."[75] It means that integral knowledge apprehends things free from all discords. Further, Sri Aurobindo holds that integral knowledge gives an all-embracing view and comprehensive vision of reality, whereas intuition is not very successful. To Sri Aurobindo, even intuition is not the highest or the supreme source of knowledge. He adheres that intuition, as viewed by the different Vedāntic systems and some other systems, does not take us to the transcendent. Misra observes, "But intuition does not give us the integral and all-embracing view of reality".[76] Intuitional knowledge, according to Sri Aurobindo, is not altogether free from the limitations of mind or intellect. Intuition seems to be dominated by mind and fails to give us an integral view of reality. Maitra observes:

> For Sri Aurobindo there are various grades and types of intuition. The value of an intuition depends upon the source from which it originates. All intuitions that mankind has had so far, have suffered from this fundamental defect, that they are mind-controlled. All the defects of intuition — their flashy character, their particularity, their limited range, their lack of cohesion — are due to their being under the control of mind.[77]

Sri Aurobindo conceives that integral knowledge is supramental in nature, which absorbs the essence of sense-experience, reason and intuition, and remains free from their defects. Thus integral knowledge is in a position to comprehend integral reality.

---

[75] S.K. Maitra, *An Introduction to the Philosophy of Sri Aurobindo*, pp. 755-56.

[76] R.S. Misra, *The Integral Advaitism of Sri Aurobindo*, p. 25.

[77] S.K. Maitra, *The Meeting of the East and the West in Aurobindo's Philosophy*, p. 82.

Some philosophers confine experience to sense-experience, others to rational experience. In true sense of the term, the mission of philosophy is to have integral experience of the reality. It sets in order the manifold data provided by various means of knowledge. It arranges them into a coherent whole. It binds them to universal reality. Thus, philosophy becomes all-comprehensive, affirmative, synthetic and spiritual. Philosophy postulates the pursuit of knowledge of the Ultimate Reality. Sri Aurobindo maintains that reality is not mere "existence" but existence-cum-consciousness. To Sri Aurobindo, reality is integral because it includes existence, consciousness and bliss.

Integral knowledge is not of the nature of our sense-experience or mind or intuition. It is something supramental in nature. It links the highest grade of existence to the lowest through all the intervening terms and achieves an indivisible whole. The psychical, the vital, the mental and finally the physical, all participate in the achievement of knowledge. In integral knowledge, there are three steps of self-realization. The first is the discovery of the secret psychic entity: the second is the realization of the eternal self in all beings: the third step is to know the Divine Being who is the transcendental self.

Integral knowledge comprehends reality in entirety. It is one with the depth of existence. Integral consciousness eliminates the limited and separative knowledge. Sri Aurobindo envisages that in the course of evolution, gnostic being may emerge. He knows, as has been shown above, all the aspects of existence and consciousness. He avails integral knowledge and comprehensive vision of the whole of cosmic and supra-cosmic reality. He does not sunder existence into real and unreal, truth and falsehood. The integral philosophy of Sri Aurobindo is all-inclusive. Reason fails to have an all-embracing view of reality. Its approach is partial. It lacks a wholeness of the philosophical truth. If a philosophy seeks to explain all and reject the partial tendency, then it must stand on the basis of experience, larger, wider and more plastic than rational knowledge. Sri Aurobindo's philosophy embodies the spirit of integralism. It is monistic, all-inclusive and comprehensive. The more integral the experience, the more integral will be the philosophy based upon it. Philosophy should find a place for all types of experiences, sensual, religious occult, vital, spiritual, etc.

It is evident that reality can be realized by integral knowledge and not by any other means of knowledge such as sense-experience, reason and intuition. The sense-experience, reason and even intuition give us the partial aspects of reality. The integral knowledge is possessed by the supermind. But, it does not mean that integral knowledge rejects the knowledge obtained through other sources. Sri Aurobindo observes:

> The integral knowledge admits the valid truths of all views of existence, valid in their own field, but it seeks to get rid of their limitations and negations and to harmonize and reconcile these partial truths in larger truth which fulfils all the many sides of our being in the one Omnipresent Existence.[78]

Thus, Sri Aurobindo does not regard intuition as the highest source of knowledge. According to him, integral knowledge or supramental consciousness can alone have a direct vision of reality and realize it in entirety. Intuition, as has been shown above, is not altogether free from limitations. Man, at the present level of existence, cannot have the all-embracing knowledge of reality in entirety even on the attainment of intuition. As has been shown above, intuition is also conditioned by man's subjectivity. The fullest manifestation

---

[78] Sri Aurobindo, *The Life Divine*, p. 794.

of knowledge is possible only when man is freed every way from the limitation of nature and finitude. This is possible only after the descent of supermind in man and the supramental transformation of his entire nature. In this respect, Sri Aurobindo's conception of knowledge differs radically from the different schools of the Vedānta and the Western intuitionist philosophers.

The Higher Reason and the Fulfilment of Man's Destiny and of History

The philosophy of Sri Aurobindo is the most promising with regard to the destiny of man. *The Life Divine* and the other major works of Sri Aurobindo clearly emphasize the fact that there is going to be the fullest revelation of divinity in man and history. Therein lies the fulfilment of their destiny. Mankind is undergoing an evolutionary crisis in which is concealed a choice of its destiny. The destiny of man lies in the complete divinization of his nature. Man cannot fulfil his destiny so long as he is involved in the finitude of existence and is conditioned by his lower or finite reason. In this state man suffers from error, evil, suffering, etc. Sri Aurobindo believes that evil cannot be eradicated completely even by the knowledge of self. It may liberate the self of man from bondage, evil and suffering but cannot liberate his whole personality. Complete eradication of evils and sufferings is possible only by the supramentalization of man's personality. Similar is the case with the cosmic process or history. Sri Aurobindo takes the historical process as real and conceives its fulfilment in its complete divinization.

The march from nebulae to humanity marks a tremendous progress. If we admit that man started life as a jungle man or ape man, then we are prone to admit that he has not only changed but progressed too. According to anthropologists, "the cycle of human growth has undergone four such ages:

(i) the Old Stone Age, (ii) the New Stone Age, (iii) the Bronze Age, (iv) the Iron Age".[79] In the first stage, man started chipping a stone. Later on, he succeeded in fashioning and polishing a piece of stone. Again, in the Bronze Age, he liked not only a stone but a metal, and with the dawn of Iron Age man's arms and fingers attained a special deftness and conscious control over nature. This growing fineness and efficiency of the tool has served to develop and enrich man's external possession and dominion. In taking up his tool to chip a stone and fashion it in desired shape is an attempt to control external nature. Thus, man feels a sense of independence and agency. Man is precisely man because he has just the sense of self and not-self. The whole life is a series of conquest of the not-self by the self. This is, in short, the whole story of his evolution. Maitra observes:

> An idea of change from one condition to a better one, a growth, mental, moral or spiritual, seems to be implicit in almost all the above views on the march of man in history.[80]

Man has evolved from the biological to intellectual level. But this intellectual stage is not supposed to be the climax of the history of mankind. It has to transcend itself and reach the spiritual stage. So, according to Sri Aurobindo, the world as well as human race are heading towards fulfilment through evolution. So, not only the individual but the whole of cosmos and human race as a whole have to attain salvation. The history records the progress of man through the ages. The march of man and nature is the true concern of history.

> To depict the story of how evolutionary nature endeavours through the ages to prepare man for that glorious consummation will indeed be the truest function of history.[81]

---

[79] N.K. Gupta, *Human Progress*, p. 18.

[80] S.K. Maitra, *The Integral Vision of History*, p. 112.

[81] Ibid., p. 104.

History reveals how man as a race marches on in his pilgrimage towards the fulfilment of his destiny. History is not concerned with the life and work of a particular man but with the aspirations and struggles, the failures and victories of the entire humanity. To put in the words of Maitra:

> History therefore is a symphony of many tunes, an orchestra, as it were. It brings to light every effort of man to better and elevate himself both in his individual and collective life through the cultivation of the faculties that lie dormant in him.[82]

Then history is a combination of many tunes and presents a comprehensive picture.

> History is thus a comprehensive picture, an all-embracing panorama, epitomizing on its canvas the vast and variegated drama of man.[83]

It is concerned with the progress of humanity. Thus, with the progress of man, the idea of history also becomes wider and more clearly defined, but this history will achieve its crowning success when it will be able to interpret this march of man in the light of its ultimate destiny.

History is the mirror that reflects the various stages of progress of man from age to age. Man is the highest point so far reached by nature in her upward drive. She is preparing him for the fulfilment of his ultimate destiny which lies in his complete divinization.

> The animal is a living laboratory in which Nature has, it is said, worked out man. Man himself may be a thinking and living laboratory in whom and with whose conscious co-operation she wills to work out the superman, the God. Or shall we not say, rather, to mainfest God?[84]

---

[82] S.K. Maitra, *The Integral Vision of History*, p. 106.

[83] Loc. cit.

[84] Sri Aurobindo, *The Life Divine*, p. 4.

This is the obvious reason why there is always in man the urge towards perfection.

Sri Aurobindo conceives that in the upward march of evolution, man will be transformed into the superman. Man having completed the human cycle enters upon the new cycle of a divine living. A greater age of the spirit may dawn on earth. It will mark a fuller and progressive self-revelation of *Saccidānanda* in the human and cosmic history.

Comparison of Sri Aurobindo's and the Judaic Christian Conception of History

Sri Aurobindo's conception of the destiny of man and the fulfilment of history bears a close resemblance to the Judaic Christian conception of history, though there are radical differences also in their views in certain respects. The Judaic Christian view envisages the complete transformation or divinization of man's existence and the fulfilment of history. History, according to this view, is marching towards a goal. That goal lies in the complete fulfilment of the historical process. But this view holds that the fulfilment of history will be possible only at the end of time. It is not possible in the time process. The complete divinization of the world and history, according to the Judaic Christian view, will be possible only when the time comes to an end and the kingdom of God manifests itself fully in the timeless existence. It is only then that the earthly nature of man, according to the Christian view, will be completely divinized. Thus, the Judaic Christian view does not conceive the fulfilment of man's destiny and of history in the time process.

In this respect, Sri Aurobindo's view differs radically from the Judaic Christian view. He conceives the possibility of man's perfection and the fulfilment of history in time process itself. Thus, supramental descent, according to him, is to take place in time process itself. Time will not come to an end after the supramental descent. Evolutionary process will continue even after the supramental descent. The whole world will not be divinized all of a sudden by the supramental descent. This process of divinization will proceed gradually and will ultimately cover the whole world. Thus, Sri Aurobindo's conception of the possibility of man's perfection and the fulfilment of history marks an improvement over the Judaic Christian view in that regard. They also bear a close resemblance in so far as the Judaic Christian view as well as Sri Aurobindo believe in a goal or destiny, not only of man, but also of history.

In this respect, Sri Aurobindo's view of history differs from the ancient Hindu view of the cyclic conception of history. The ancient Hindu view believes in the destiny of man which lies in the attainment of liberation but not in the fulfilment of history. History, according to this view, moves in cycle. There is the evolution of the world and there is dissolution and this process goes on. The Hindu view does not believe in any goal for history. History, according to this view, is meaningful. But its meaning lies in its working for the freedom and liberation of man. So, the fulfilment of history, according to Hindu view, lies ultimately in man's spirit, in his attainment of spiritual freedom and liberation. History is meaningful not for itself but for spirit. It is due to this reason that the Hindu view does not believe in the onward march of history towards some remote fulfilment but in its cyclic movement which provides the proper field for the dynamic play of Spirit in the realm of nature.

Sri Aurobindo is one with the Hindu view in believing in the freedom and liberation of spirit or *ātman* but he differs from the ancient Hindu view in his conception of history as he does not believe in the cyclic view of history. In the same way, he comes very close to the Judaic Christian conception of history in so far as he believes in its onward march and fulfilment of the perfection of historical process. But, he differs in a radical way from that view by conceiving the possibility of the complete divinization of man and the fulfilment of historical process in the time order itself. This mystery of the working of the Divine in history can be fully understood and appreciated, according to Sri Aurobindo, only by man's higher reason or the integral knowledge. The higher reason is operating in man as well as in history and it can alone reveal the truth of man's life and of historical process and of their ultimate destiny.

3

K.C. Bhattacharyya
(1875–1949)

KRISHNA Chandra Bhattacharyya is profoundly original in his exposition of philosophical problems. The classical German philosophy and the traditional Advaita Vedānta exercised a major influence in shaping his philosophical views. The powerful impact of Kant on his philosophy is evident, though he does not subscribe to Kantian agnosticism. Bhattacharyya agrees with Kant in fixing the limits of reason, but he does not confine all knowledge to reason. The self, according to Bhattacharyya, can be known but it cannot be made an object of thought. Distinguishing his position from that of Kant in respect of self, he observes:

> With regard to the knowability of the self as a metaphysical entity, Kant holds that the self is a necessity of thought and is the object of moral faith but is not in itself knowable. My position is, on the one hand, that the self is unthinkable and on the other that while actually it is not known and is only an object of faith, though not necessarily only of moral faith, we have to admit the possibility of knowing it without thinking, there being a demand, alternative with other spiritual demands, to realize such knowledge. This is practically reopening the entire epistemological question of the meaning of thought and knowledge.[1]

---

[1] K.C. Bhattacharyya, *Studies in Philosophy*, vol. II, p. 100.

He makes a significant distinction between thinking and knowing. Though the self is unthinkable yet it is knowable. He observes:

> In taking the self to be unthinkable, I understand Kant's *Ideas of Reason* to be not only not knowledge, but not even thought in the literal sense. The so-called extension of thought beyond experience and the possibility of experience means to me only the use of the verbal forms of thought as a symbol of unthinkable reality, such symbolizing use not being thinking.[2]

For Kant, the self is a necessity of thought and is the subject of moral faith. It is not knowable in itself. But Bhattacharyya does not deny the possibility of knowing the self.

Though Bhattacharyya shows a considerable influence of Kant and the Vedānta on his thought, yet one finds a good deal of originality in his approach. According to Gopinath Bhattacharyya, K.C. Bhattacharyya's method of study is one of "constructive interpretation". He observes:

> . . . from a consideration of his actual procedure it would appear that by "constructive interpretation" the author means more of construction than of interpretation.[3]

His philosophy cannot be characterized in terms of any "ism". It is neither agnosticism nor Vedāntism; neither pragmatism nor existentialism. The appropriate description of his philosophy can be given by calling it "transcendental idealism". It is idealism in the sense of ideal-ism and not idea-ism. Idea-ism is mentalism. But Bhattacharyya's philosophy is not mentalism but idealism. Mentalism apprehends subject and object distinctly but idealism comprehends them in one whole.

---

[2] Loc. cit.

[3] K.C. Bhattacharyya, *Studies in Philosophy*, vol. I (Introduction by Gopinath Bhattacharyya), p. xi.

It is transcendental because no exact description of the ultimate reality can be given by human reason. Bhattacharyya relates everything to experience. Reality becomes the ultimate presupposition of experience. This experience of the ultimate is neither subjective nor objective. To relate the subject and object in knowledge is the function of reason. The ultimate reality transcends the duality of subject and object as it transcends reason. It is apprehended not by reason but by intuition or spiritual consciousness. Now we proceed to discuss Bhattacharyya's view regarding the nature of knowledge.

Nature of Knowledge

Bhattacharyya holds that "knowledge is a kind of awareness".[4] He contrasts knowledge with mere awareness According to Bhattacharyya, awareness is of two types: (i) awareness in the objective attitude, and (ii) awareness in the subjective attitude. The former is primarily awareness of physical objects. Here, we have distinction between the object of awareness (what one is aware) and the subject that has the awareness. The awareness in the subjective attitude is illustrated by one's awareness of oneself and of one's "knowing". In such awareness, there is no distinction between object of awareness and the subject that has the awareness. In other words, in the former, a distinction is made between the subject of awareness and the object of awareness; in the latter, it is difficult to make such a distinction. Gopinath Bhattacharyya says, "of the two types of awareness, it is one in the objective attitude that the author primarily takes to be what is signified by the term knowledge."[5] But he himself admits that even one's awareness of himself — an awareness in the subjective attitude — also

---

[4] K.C. Bhattacharyya, *Studies in Philosophy*, vol. II (Introduction by Gopinath Bhattacharyya), p. xvi.

[5] Ibid., p. xvii.

has been called knowledge at times.[6] Following this difference in attitudes, we understand awareness in the objective attitude and also that in the subjective attitude. Theories of knowledge and metaphysics of the subject usually fall under the former class. Bhattacharyya makes departure from this prevailing view. He holds that any study about knowing and the subject must be carried on in the subjective attitude. He speaks of a "cultivation" of the subjective attitude. Gopinath Bhattacharyya observes:

> He goes even further and appears to hold that awareness in the subjective attitude is far more authentic than the other kind of awareness. The subjective attitude, in his view, yields the self-evidencing truth.[7]

Bhattacharyya conceives that the term "knowledge" primarily signifies the awareness in the objective attitude. It does not mean that the other type of awareness is altogether denied of the name of knowledge. The awareness of the subject is an awareness in the subjective attitude. It is certainly taken to be a case of knowledge. According to Bhattacharyya, the awareness of knowing "function" and other functions of freedom like feeling and willing are definitely not knowledge. Knowledge is chiefly awareness in the objective attitude.

Bhattacharyya further makes a distinction between knowledge and belief. Knowledge involves belief but, it is, in one sense, distinct from mere belief. Belief may turn to be imaginative but knowledge is definite awareness. There is a distinction between knowledge and illusory apprehension and imaginative belief. Gopinath Bhattacharyya observes:

> Thus it appears that the word "knowledge" in the author's usage stands primarily (and not exclusively) for a valid

---

[6] Loc. cit.

[7] Loc. cit.

and certain awareness in the objective attitude, having intuition for one of its factors and involving the distinction of the object known from the knowledge itself. Primarily, because the author is quite categorical that one's awareness of oneself is an instance of knowledge, even though it is neither objective awareness nor intuitional in character.[8]

Further, he observes:

> One thing is not clear, however, and that is whether the author would agree to describe what he calls "knowledge" as a state or as "function". That would perhaps depend on whether he would like to designate awareness itself as a "state" or "function".[9]

If knowledge were to be regarded as a "state", it is required to come before the knowing function. If, however, it is a function, it becomes the function of knowing itself. There is not surely a knowledge function over and above the knowing function. "Certain trends," observes Gopinath Bhattacharyya, "in the author's mode of thinking would seem to favour the assumption that, according to him, knowledge and knowing function are one and the same thing. But editor is not at all sure on the point."[10]

Knowing, according to, Bhattacharyya, is a function and not a passive state of the subject. It is a sort of an activity. It is an activity of a free reference of the subject to the object. If this is the meaning of knowing, science cannot claim to know because it believes in facthood and the objectivity of the object. Function appears to be a sort of activity. To know is to act or to do something. But, it is activity neither in a physical nor in the volitional way. It appears to be *sui generis*. Bhattacharyya says that it is activity in a symbolic sense. Knowing activity is

---

[8] Loc. cit.

[9] Loc. cit.

[10] K.C. Bhattacharyya, *Studies in Philosophy*, vol. II, p. viii.

a "free reference of the subject to the object". It represents, according to Bhattacharyya, a "positive mode of freedom of the subject to relate to object without getting related to it".[11] The freedom of the subject lies precisely in the fact that it is known by itself and that in relating to the object, it does not get related to the latter. Such type of freedom of the subject is a matter of immediate certainty to Bhattacharyya. It might be suggested that the position is paradoxical, for if *A* relates itself to *B* (freely may be) it cannot but get related to *B*. To Bhattacharyya, this does not pose a paradox. The subject has an immediate feeling of relating itself to the object without having a feeling of getting related to it.

A free reference of the subject to the object might mean: (i) free reference of the subject to the object in the objective attitude or (ii) free reference of the subject to the subject as object. It means free reference of the subject to the object in the subjective attitude. In the former, the subject relates itself to the object freely without itself getting related to it. The subject is aware of his experiences and thoughts of the object without in any way identifying himself with them. This may be called knowledge in the objective attitude. The object of this knowledge may be either a physical fact or psychic fact. It may be a psychic fact because a psychic fact is not purely a mental event, but always an aspect of the object. The object has certain modes of relatedness to the subject, e.g. knownness and feltness. This relatedness viewed as a character of the object is a psychic fact. This knowledge may be called "awareness through psychological introspection in the objective attitude".

The Object of Knowledge

Knowledge is primarily of a definite object. It is to be

[11] K.C. Bhattacharyya, *The Subject as Freedom*, p. 13.

distinguished from the awareness of the indefinite. Bhattacharyya is positive that the indefinite is as much an object as the definite. It is exemplified by such entities as the aesthetic object, alternation, the image as being formed, the fringe of a psychic fact, etc.

Knowledge is a sort of cognition in the objective attitude. It is either cognition of the physical fact or of the psychic fact. Bhattacharyya accepts the ordinary view of the physical fact. But with regard to the nature of physical fact, he deviates from the usual view of the matter. The prevailing view is that a psychic fact is a purely mental occurrence. It is just anything that happens in the mind. It is accessible only to introspection. In Bhattacharyya's account, however, a psychical fact is never a pure mental event. It is not a pure mental entity, because it is always an aspect of the non-mental object. His psychic fact is neither non-mental as conceived by behaviourist nor it is only "experienced unity of subject and object". Psychic fact is an aspect of the non-mental object. This requires clarification. The object has certain "modes of relatedness" to the subject, e.g. knownness and feltness. This relatedness viewed as a character of the object is, according to Bhattacharyya, the so-called psychic fact. Knownness or relatedness is "a floating adjective like beauty".[12] A psychic fact constituted by this relatedness is a character of the physical object. It exists like the object, even apart from introspection. Two negative criteria are laid down in this connection. (i) What does not involve "knowledge" of object is no psychic fact. (ii) What introspection does not reveal is no psychic fact. It follows from the above that the following kinds of awareness, among others, do not come within Bhattacharyya's definition of a psychic fact:

(i) the awareness of the imaginary

---

[12] K.C. Bhattacharyya, *The Subject as Freedom*, p. 25.

(ii) the awareness of the illusory
(iii) the introspective state or process
(iv) objectless feeling
(v) belief in the past fear of some illusory object.

These are placed in a separate category and designed as "non-psychic fringe of a psychic fact". Though they are non-psychic, yet they are not for that reason physical entities. However, Bhattacharyya has not given us any hint as to the precise status which he ascribes to these fringe entities.

Presentation

Psychic fact is essentially presentation as embodying belief. It is not imaginary or non-factual. It is not completely accomplished as fact. It is only to be accomplished. It is not completely accomplished as fact in the sense that it is not isolated or freed from the object. It is necessary to explain, what does Bhattacharyya mean by the term "presentation". Knowledge involves belief. But it is also distinct from belief. It further involves the awareness of the distinction of the object believed from the belief. This distinction is something more than the object itself and is what Bhattacharyya calls "presentation" of the object.

Presentation as a psychic fact and object as a non-psychic entity are mixed up with each other in a peculiar way. The object is given as distinct from the presentation. The presentation, however, is not given as distinct from the object. It is only abstracted or distinguished from the object in introspection. It is in non-perceptual knowledge only that the object appears distinct from its presentation and not in perceptual knowledge. In perception, again, the presentation is not known as distinct from the object. It is believed and symbolized as what should be distinct.

Presentation is not necessarily perceptual. In addition to

external perception, we have presentation in the following modes:

(i) feeling of the body from within

(ii) immediate apprehension of absence

(iii) memory of an object as past

(iv) imagination of the object as formed or becoming formed to be perceptible object

(v) inference of the perceptible object as involving the unperceivable character of necessity, etc

Perceptual knowledge to Bhattacharyya is the actual standard of knowledge. The other modes of presentation imply in and involve a belief in something not yet known but which may be known in some ideal mode of realization.[13] Perception not only lends cognitive character to other modes of presentation. It prevents them from reaching their ideal completion contrasted to perception, the other modes are wanted to be so known.

Belief, Thought and Feeling

Bhattacharyya describes knowledge as:

> It is in introspection into knowledge . . . that we realize that we believed before we knew . . . and that there was thus no awareness of a distinction of the object believed from the belief. Knowledge as distinct from mere belief involves the awareness of this distinction.[14]

Here, knowledge has been described in terms of belief. It is true that nothing can be known unless it is believed. There is a difference between "belief" and the "object believed". The awareness of this distinction is also essential. Belief is the

---

[13] K.C. Bhattacharyya, *The Subject as Freedom*, p. 38.

[14] Ibid., pp. 56-57.

awareness of a fact as fact. Thought is a presentation that does not exclude belief in the object. Its object is presented as unpicturable meaning. Thought is a completed product and is about a definite object. It is complete in the sense of being dissociated from the forming or ideal timing that characterizes the image.

By "feeling" Bhattacharyya appears to mean the intuition of the intuitionists. It is non-sensuous, immediate and completely certain awareness, Bhattacharyya does not agree with the intuitionists in taking this feeling to be a superior type of knowledge. He does not regard it as knowledge in the literal sense. Knowledge involves a reference to an object while feeling is explicitly unobjective. It is a "positive subjective fact without any reference to any objective fact".[15] It is typically exemplified by the feeling of the body from within or of freedom. It is an awareness in which there is no conscious reference to the object even in the way of dissociation from it.[16] Feeling is not denied of content. But the content of feeling is unthought and unmeant. It appears to introspection as only distinct in itself and not as distinct from feeling. A psychic fact like thought is distinguished in introspection from its object. It is, accordingly, believed to exist outside introspection. But, as feeling is not thus distinguished from its content, it cannot be believed to exist outside introspection as a merely conscious fact.

In feeling, there is the positive consciousness of detachment from meaning. Bhattacharyya observes, "Feeling is the knowledge of the purely unknown as such the unknown that is not even meant."[17] It is only symbolized as knowledge of the unknown. It is to be noted that as the unknown here is

---

[15] K.C. Bhattacharyya, *The Subject as Freedom*, p. 101.

[16] Loc. cit.

[17] K.C. Bhattacharyya, *The Subject as Freedom*, p. 106.

the unmeant, the preposition "of" in the phrase "knowledge of the unknown" has no meaning and is used as a mere exigency of language.

Theory of Introspection

It is necessary at this stage to refer to Bhattacharyya's theory of introspection. Gopinath Bhattacharyya observes:

> Introspection is usually taken to be internal perception or the non-inferential awareness of a mental fact, and so far as its character of immediacy is concerned, it is placed on a par with the sense-perception of the physical object.[18]

It is quite pertinent to distinguish "psychological introspection" from "spiritual introspection". Spiritual introspection consists in distinguishing the functions of knowing as other than the character of knownness. A function, like knowing, represents a mode of freedom from the psychic fact of knownness. To Bhattacharyya, *The Subject as Freedom*, the consciousness of modes of freedom like knowing is as direct as that of psychic fact like knownness. This spiritual introspection is explained as the "enjoying understanding" of the subject or the "I". Here, introspection is awareness in the subjective attitude. Bhattacharyya, *The Subject as Freedom* is quite definite that "introspection proper is a form of theoretic consciousness that implies an abjuration of the objective attitude".[19]

According to Bhattacharyya, spiritual introspection is the introspection proper. It is an awareness in the subjective attitude. In other words, it is a free reference of the subject to the subject in an enjoying consciousness. In the psychological introspection, there was an awareness of a relatedness of the

[18] K.C. Bhattacharyya, *Studies in Philosophy*, vol. II (introduction by G. Bhattacharyya), p. xxi.

[19] Ibid., p. xxii.

object to the subject. In spiritual introspection, this has to be negated. This is understanding as knowing by enjoying. Bhattacharyya says, ". . . it is enjoying understanding of the subject 'I'."[20] This, therefore, is knowledge, in the realm of philosophy of spirit. That is why this knowledge is described as a free reference of the subject to the subject itself, in an, enjoying consciousness. But, if we analyse this enjoying consciousness still further, we find that in the act of enjoying itself, something over and above the self is also enjoyed. That something else may be either a body-physical or mental, or other selves with whom the self stands in some relationship. It may also be an overpersonal self to which a reference is made in religious consciousness. In the enjoying consciousness of "I" in which body is also enjoyed, there is, in a sense, an enjoyment of individuality. Such a consciousness is expressed in our saying. "I am such and such." The consciousness of individuality somehow gives to the self an objectivity; his subjectivity, therefore, becomes infected with objectivity and as such does not remain pure subjectivity. Likewise, when I am conscious of otherselves in my enjoying consciousness of "I", I am aware of myself in relation to others. This is not pure subjectivity.

A higher type of subjectivity would be the consciousness of an overpersonal reality. The reason is obvious. In the first two cases, subjectivity is affected either by the awareness of objects or by the awareness of other selves. It is true that in both these cases "the body" or "the other self" is a shadow of "I" because it is felt in the I-consciousness. This also is true that the shadow also does have its effects on the I-consciousness. But in the enjoying consciousness, the subject as "I" has an awareness of an overpersonal reality. The "I" itself becomes a shadow. Malkani has described "this

[20] K.C. Bhattacharyya, *Studies in Philosophy*, vol. II, p. xxii.

knowledge as knowledge by self-abnegation and not by self-denial".[21] When "I" is denied, we get pure subjectivity — the Absolute.

Now, before we proceed to discuss the metaphysical views of Bhattacharyya, we find it advisable to throw light on his philosophical method which helps us in having a correct understanding and appreciation of his approach to metaphysics and to the problem of man's ultimate freedom.

Philosophical Method of Bhattacharyya

Gopinath Bhattacharyya observes:

> Philosophy is the elaboration of different kinds of spiritual experiences. The abstractions of the high-grade metaphysics are based on spiritual experience and derive their whole value from the experiences which they symbolize. No metaphysical concept is entirely intelligible without reference to the spirit.[22]

Mere rational consistency is no guarantee for ontological certainty. The task before the philosopher is to develop a method for the realization of reality as well as appropriate logic to explain it. Bhattacharyya's philosophical method at best can be called "a method of cognitive inwardizing".[23] This method involves an analysis of the subject or different grades of human subjectivity. It enables one to go deeper from the surface to the deeper levels of existence and ultimately reveals the subject which is ultimate and free from all change and duality. The method of "cognitive inwardization" culminates in the attainment of spiritual consciousness or intuition. At

---

[21] G.R. Malkani, *Some Points in K.C. Bhattacharyya's Concept of Philosophy*, pp. 54-57.

[22] K.C. Bhattacharyya, *Studies in Philosophy*, vol. II (Introduction by G. Bhattacharyya), p. xvi.

[23] Ibid., p. 32.

this stage, man realizes himself as essentially free from all traces of objectivity. The goal of philosophy is reached when man attains spiritual consciousness and realizes himself as subject and as free from all objectivity.

Bhattacharyya conceives different grades of cognitional freedom. He proceeds to analyse the nature of the subject and explains bodily subjectivity, psychic subjectivity and spiritual subjectivity. Man realizes freedom when he attains spiritual subjectivity. The spiritual progress of man lies in the growing realization of the higher and higher grades of subjectivity. It results in the growing realization of man's freedom. Bhattacharyya observes, "spiritual progress means the realization of the subject as free".[24]

The method of cognitive inwardization attempts to dissociate the subject from the object. This ultimately results in the complete freedom of the subject from its relations to the object. According to Bhattacharyya:

> The subject is thus known by itself, as not meant but speakable and not as either related or relating to the object. It is, however, believed is relating to object and symbolized as such by the objective relations. The modes of relating are at the same time the modes of freeing from objectivity, the forms of the spiritual discipline by which, it may be conceived, the outgoing reference to the object is turned backwards and the immediate knowledge of the "I" as content is realized in an ecstatic intuition.[25]

The realization of self as free involves a specific activity of the subject. There is a demand for some kind of activity of the subject towards itself. There is the demand that the subjective function of knowing which is only believed and not known as fact has to be known as the self-evidencing reality of the subject

[24] K.C. Bhattacharyya, *Studies in Philosophy*, vol. II, p. 32.

[25] Ibid., pp. 31-32.

itself. Bhattacharyya says, "This would be the supreme method of cognitive inwardizing".[26] In the process of self-realization, one has to recognize a specific discipline or consecutive method of activity for such realization. The consciousness of perfection, freedom or salvation as the end is to them a demand for some kind of activity of the subject towards itself. Philosophical method involves the cult of the subject. It also involves an awareness of the subject as what the object is not. Bhattacharyya observes, "The specific activity demanded is primarily in the inwardizing direction".[27] Further he states:

> The cult of the subject par excellence, a spiritual discipline of the theoretic reason, a method of cognitive inwardizing, the possibility of which, as indeed of any method of realization, is not ordinarily recognized.[28]

A philosophical method implies a series of consecutive steps for the realization of an end. The steps in Bhattacharyya's philosophical method correspond to a gradation of subjective functions, of modes of freedom from the object. We usually identify ourselves with body, our freedom from the perceived object is actually realized only in our bodily consciousness. This bodily consciousness is also imperfectly realized. The next stage of freedom is suggested by the distinction of the perceived object including the body from the ghostly object in the form of the image-idea and meaning which may be all designed "presentation". Consciousness as undissociated from such presentation, but dissociated from the perceived and felt body may be called presentational of psychic subjectivity. The dissociation of the subject or consciousness from this presentation conceived as a kind of object would be the next

---

[26] K.C. Bhattacharyya, *Studies in Philosophy*, vol. II, p. 7.

[27] Ibid., p. 32.

[28] Loc. cit.

stage of freedom which may be called non-presentation or spiritual subjectivity. According to Bhattacharyya,

> The elaboration of these stages of freedom in spiritual psychology would suggest the possibility of a consecutive method of realizing the subject as absolute freedom, of retracing the felt positive freedom towards the object into pure intuition of the self.[29]

In Bhattacharyya's philosophy, a great emphasis is put on the subject. He deals elaborately with "the cult of subject" and "the subject as freedom". The cult of the subject involves abstraction from the object. The way to understand the word "subjective" is to call it "non-objective". Bhattacharyya observes, "The modes of subjectivity are the modes of freeing oneself from the modes of objectivity."[30] The cult of the subject involves a feeling of dissociation of the subject from the object. It is a sort of an awareness of the subject as what the object is not. The most important characteristic of subjectivity, therefore, is the subject's awareness of its distinction from the objects.

Subject as Distinct from Object

There are two basic terms in ontology — subject and object. Subject and object involve each other. Bhattacharyya makes it a point that the subject has always an awareness of its distinction from the object. The object, at best, is defined as "what is meant". The object has always a "meant content". The awareness of the subject is definitely different from meaning awareness. The meaning awareness involves relation. It is exclusively the function of reason to give meaning awareness. the subject awareness entails withdrawal from the object. It is a sort of "cognitive inwardization". This "cognitive inwardization" is a sort of consciousness which may be taken here as "intuition". It is not meaning awareness but realization.

[29] K.C. Bhattacharyya, *Studies in Philosophy*, vol. II, p. 33.

[30] K.C. Bhattacharyya, *The Subject as Freedom*, p. 29.

The meaning of awareness involves duality but the cognitive inwardization is a sort of self-realization. Bhattacharyya observes:

> Object as meant is distinguished from the subject or the subjective of which there is some awareness other than the meaning awareness.[31]

At best, the subject can be termed as "significant speakable". The object can be pointed as "this". The subject can be indicated by the word "I". Bhattacharyya suggests that the word "this" is the symbol of the object. Bradley also holds that "this" can stand for the object. Every object can safely be called "this". But the subject can call itself as "I". The pronouns "he" and "you" can claim to stand for the subject. Bhattacharyya has given original definition of the subject. The word "I" stands for the subject "I" appears to be more basic because "he" and "you" can also call themselves "I". Two speakers may use the term "this". "This" may stand for the same object. But two speakers cannot use the word "I" in the same sense. The word "this" as used by speaker means primarily what he perceives. The hearer may use "this" of some other object as well as he can use it of the same object. One speaker uses it for the object that he perceives. Another may use it for a different object. He can also use "this" for the same object. This is possible because in the realm of objects, "what the speaker means by a word must be capable of being meant by the hearer if he were to use it".[32]

This is not the case with the word "I". If I use this word, I mean myself and if anybody else uses it, he uses it for himself and not for me. This clearly shows that there is a basic difference between the subject and the object. There is again a difference

---

[31] K.C. Bhattacharyya, *The Subject as Freedom*, p. 1.

[32] Ibid., p. 2.

between object consciousness and self consciousness. Object consciousness is to understand through the meaning of the word. Object consciousness involves meaning of the word and self consciousness is enjoying understanding of the subject or I. The meaning awareness involves relation. Reason can serve as an efficient instrument to give meaning awareness. For example, when somebody from a control room reports that "a fighting jet" is approaching, it is "jet" as approaching that is understood and the self as speaking. In case, self consciousness is communicated, it is not only the self that is understood, but the self as speaking "communicating or expressing itself is understood". Therefore, "what then is meant is expressible as this is not what is conveyed by the word 'I'".[33]

Object may be an individual object or a group or a class. Object may be described as individual or general. But subject can neither be described as singular nor general because the word "I" is neither singular nor general. On the other hand, in some sense, it is singular and in other sense, it is general. It is singular because everybody uses it for himself only. It is general in the sense that everybody uses it. As used, the term has a uniquely singular reference. But as understood, it is general in the sense the term "unique" is general.

Sometimes, subject may be spoken of as the object though not meant as object. But the object can never be spoken of as subject. Suppose one say, "I am a leader". There is an objective reference of the subject here, in so far as the subject appears to be something. Here "I" appears to be "this". In other words, "I" appears to be an object. But no object can ever be referred to as a subject. Bhattacharyya makes this point clear when he says, "The statement 'this is I' is false, while the statement 'I am this' cannot be denied".[34] This leads to one controversial

[33] K.C. Bhattacharyya, *The Subject as Freedom*, p. 2.

[34] Ibid., p. 5.

point concerning subject and object. The question arises: when the subject is spoken of as an object, why should it be not treated as an object? Bhattacharyya says that even when subject is objectified, that objectification is not a determination of subject. That the subject is spoken as the object, is no argument for assuming that there is a similarity between the two. Even while the subject is referred to as "this" or "that", it does not become object. On the other hand, the subject is felt to be dissociated from the object as being prior to object logically. Bhattacharyya defines object as "what is meant". The "meant" involves doubt, where the question of doubt is involved, the question of its correction is also involved. This derives one to the point that object can always be doubted. The "meaning awareness" cannot be taken for granted. If the nature of object is doubtful, it cannot be known with the same assurance as the subject. The subject is not the meant content. Therefore, it is not subject to doubt. It is known more intimately than the object. Its knowledge is more assured than the object only because its awareness is direct and not through the medium of a meaning or reference to something outside itself.

The above distinction between subject and object has been drawn with a significant purpose. Metaphysics, according to Bhattacharyya, is primarily a study of these two basic concepts. Its essential function is to distinguish subject from object and know the reality which transcends them both. This "negative function" is done by reason. Reason negates what is not real. It points ultimately to the subject. In the Advaita Vedānta, ontology is taken as the science of Being. Reason, as conceived by the Vedānta, does not give the knowledge of Being. It gives the knowledge of what is non-being. Bhattacharyya, like the Advaita Vedānta, conceives that the real subject cannot be apprehended by reason. It is "cognitive inwardization" or "intuitive vision" which realizes subject as free from subjectivity.

Now, we proceed to discuss the concept of philosophy, propounded by Bhattacharyya.

Concept of Philosophy

"Philosophy starts in reflective consciousness . . .."[35] Reflection is a sort of awareness of a content as to a mode of consciousness. The phrase "as to" indicates some relation. In philosophy, we start with the relation between content and consciousness. Before we come to be reflectively conscious of a relation between content and consciousness, we must know the relation between content and content. The relation between content and content is given in objective consciousness. The relation between content and consciousness is given in reflective consciousness. First we get objective consciousness and then the question of reflective consciousness comes. Philosophy starts at the level of reflective consciousness. Bhattacharyya observes, "Reflective consciousness is definite consciousness of something".[36] Philosophy or reflective consciousness gives us understanding of the problem and not its solution. He further observes, "Reflection understands the problem but does not see the solution".[37] Reflective consciousness or rational consciousness cannot give the true nature of reality. It can help to understand reality in different dimensions but it cannot fathom its depth. The indefinite remains beyond the grasp of reflective consciousness. Metaphysics or philosophy, including logic and epistemology, does not give actual knowledge. It is also known as even literal thought. Its contents are contemplated as true in the faith that it is only by such contemplation that the Absolute can be known.

"Philosophy", according to Bhattacharyya, "presents beliefs that are speakable or systematically communicable and is like

---

[35] K.C. Bhattacharyya, *Studies in Philosophy*, vol. II, p. 125.

[36] Ibid., p. 130.

[37] Ibid., p. 140.

science, an expression of the theoretic consciousness."[38] This definition contains three factors. First, philosophy presents beliefs. Second, beliefs are speakable. Third, it is an expression of theoretic consciousness or reason. He observes, "Theoretic consciousness at its minimum is the understanding of a speakable".[39] Both science and philosophy are expressions of theoretic consciousness or reason; because both deal with the judgements that are speakable or systematically communicable. He says, "What is spoken must be in the first instance believed".[40] This can be illustrated with the help of examples like "a square circle" or "golden mountain". "A square circle" is neither believed nor disbelieved. Even when it is spoken, it seems as if it has not been spoken. Therefore, it cannot form part of theoretic consciousness or reason. On the other hand, speakables, which are believed, constitute the part of theoretic consciousness or reason. For example, even a lie will be a part of theoretic consciousness or reason because it has a content that is believed. When we speak, we try to express and communicate some belief. But when a man speaks a lie, he surely does not believe what he says. Is he then not speaking? Bhattacharyya says that even a lie is to be understood with the universal and generally understood, "prefix of all speech, viz. the imperative believe me".[41] The liar apparently impresses his hearer to believe what he says. Here, we find the formulation of a belief which is not held by the speaker but sought to be imposed on the hearer. A lie is not really or truly spoken. When one speaks lie, one does not speak truly but falsely. Bhattacharyya, contends that everything true or false, real or unreal, subjective or objective is speakable. Philosophy starts with speakables. He observes:

---

[38] K.C. Bhattacharyya, *Studies in Philosophy*, vol. II, p. 101.

[39] Loc. cit.

[40] Loc. cit.

[41] Loc. cit.

> The three believed contents or the subject, the positive freedom of the subject and the meant object — are all speakable and it is from the speakable that we have to start in philosophy.[42]

The grades of thought or reason are really grades of speaking. Fact in science is spoken of as information. It is understood without reference to the spoken form. It is what need not be spoken to be believed.

> Speakability is a contingent character of the content of empirical thought, but it is a necessary character of the content of pure philosophic thought.[43]

If the content of philosophic thought is not spoken, it would not be intelligible. So, Bhattacharyya says that in philosophy, the content that is spoken, is not intelligible except as spoken.

The philosophical contents are speakable and are also self-evident. It means that they are not dependent on the individual mind. He holds that philosophical content is believed to be self-evident. According to Bhattacharyya, there are four grades of speakable. There is the primary distinction between what is only symbolically speakable and what is literally speakable. The literally speakable comprises what is spoken of as information and what is only spoken and not spoken of. Of these, what is only spoken is spoken either as symbolized or as meant. Truth is only symbolically spoken, reality is literally spoken as symbolized and the self-subsistent is literally spoken as meant. None of these is spoken of as information. But, fact is spoken of as information.

This classification simply shows, how the contents of theoretic consciousness or reason are spoken or expressed through speech. Fact is what is spoken of, self-subsistent is

---

[42] K.C. Bhattacharyya, *The Subject as Freedom*, p. 24.

[43] K.C. Bhattacharyya, *Studies in Philosophy*, vol. II, pp. 102-03.

spoken, reality is spoken as symbolized and truth is symbolically spoken. Fact is spoken of means that a fact is related to other facts. It can be expressed in the form of judgement, e.g. "*A* is thus related to *B*". This judgement is expressed about the relation between two facts "*A* and *B*". Bhattacharyya observes, "Fact is always expressible as a judgement of the form "*A* is thus related to *B*", this being the only judgement form that is literally intelligible".[44] According to Bhattacharyya, the relation between two facts "*A* and *B*" is embodied in real judgement. He further holds that fact is always a fact in relation to some facts. To quote him:

> Fact is always a fact related to facts. If anywhere "*x* is" means something other than the relational assertion, it means that *x* is self-subsistent, real or true, which is only an apparent judgement.[45]

All the judgements about facts are always related to other facts. A fact can never be conceived apart from the relation with other facts or in isolation. According to him, only facts can be expressed in real judgements. In philosophy, the real judgement is not possible. All judgements are apparent. In a judgement proper, the word "is" expresses only objective attitude of the subject; but in this apparent judgement "is" means an objective content which is self-subsistent but not fact. To express or formulate this content is still to retain the objective attitude. The objective attitude is dropped in saying "I am". The content here also is spoken and not spoken of, but it is explicitly understood as not objective and as only apparently objective or symbolized by objectivity. What the word "am" means is not contemplated in the objective attitude but is subjectively enjoyed and only spoken as though it were objectively contemplated. Bhattacharyya says:

---

[44] K.C. Bhattacharyya, *Studies in Philosophy*, vol. II, p. 103.

[45] Loc. cit.

> If fact is spoken of and the self-subsistent object is only spoken, both being spoken as meant, reality is spoken not as meant but as only symbolized.[46]

The judgement "object is" is not a judgement about facts, because it does not express relation with other facts. It is a judgement about the self-subsistent. "I am" is a judgement of reality. Reality is spoken as symbolized. Here, "am" is the symbol of "I". So, "am" is the symbol which symbolizes the reality "I". Therefore, reality is always spoken as symbolized and not as meant. Here "am" itself is not a fact, but only a symbol which refers to the subject or reality. Truth or Absolute is symbolically spoken. It cannot even be symbolized. Like the Vedāntists, Bhattacharyya admits that truth is expressed or proved always by negations or negative judgements. In the judgement "I am not", the "I" points towards the existence of Absolute. If there is no "I", there must be something higher than the real. So the Absolute can never be spoken actually as symbolized. It can only be pointed out and all the affirmations and negations are the symbols which point to the Absolute. Philosophy is not a body of judgement but self-elaboration of self-evident. Bhattacharyya observes, "Philosophy is such self-evident elaboration of the self-evident and is not a body of judgements".[47]

Grades of Theoretic Consciousness or Reason

According to Bhattacharyya, the function of theoretic consciousness becomes the elaboration of the self-subsistent principles. He has made four grades of theoretic consciousness or reason. They are:

(i) Empirical thought
(ii) Pure objective thought

---

[46] K.C. Bhattacharyya, *Studies in Philosophy,* vol. II, p. 104.
[47] Ibid., p. 103.

(iii) Spiritual thought

(iv) Transcendental thought.

Bhattacharyya recognizes empirical thought as actual thought. The content of empirical thought is fact which is studied in science. It is also known as literal thought. Fact, which is the content of empirical thought, is spoken of and not simply spoken. Empirical thought has always a reference to the object. This reference to the object constitutes its meaning. Here, the object is understood as fact. There is no need of referring it to thinking. Bhattacharyya observes:

> Empirical thought is the theoretic consciousness of a content involving reference to an object that is perceived or imagined to be perceived such reference being part of the meaning of the content.[48]

Pure objective thought can also be called contemplative thought. The content of pure-objective thought or contemplative thought is self-subsistent. It is studied in philosophy. It is also known as symbolic thought. It is spoken in the objective attitude. The difference between the pure objective thought and empirical thought lies in the fact that whereas the latter makes a reference to sense-perception as revealing the object as fact, in the former, such a reference is not necessary. In the latter, there is no reference to the subject, but in the former the consciousness is self-subsistent. Bhattacharyya observes:

> There are contents that are objective but have no necessary reference to sense-perception and the consciousness of such contents may be called pure objective or contemplative thought.[49]

Spiritual thought is a consciousness which refers neither to fact nor to the objectivity of fact. Its content is reality which is

---

[48] K.C. Bhattacharyya, *Studies in Philosophy*, vol. II, p. 102.

[49] Loc. cit.

appreciated in enjoying attitude. This enjoying attitude or spiritual thought is subjective one. It is spoken in the subjective attitude. Bhattacharyya observes:

> The content of spiritual thought is no object, nothing that is contemplated in the objective attitude, being subjective in the sense of being appreciated in a subjective or "enjoying attitude".[50]

Transcendental thought or reason makes reference neither to the objective nor to the subjective content, but it transcends both. The content of transcendental thought is truth. It is symbolic thought. It is spoken in the transcendental attitude. Bhattacharyya says:

> Transcendental thought is the consciousness of a content that is neither objective nor subjective, the further characterization of which will come later.[51]

It is required to be mentioned that the purpose of grading theoretic consciousness under four grades is to pinpoint that thought or reason can be used in the lower as well as in higher senses. The empirical thought or lower reason is successfully operative in science but other grades of thought come under philosophy. Bhattacharyya opines:

> Theoretic consciousness is embodied in science and philosophy. Science alone speaks in genuine judgements, the content of which is fact intelligible without reference to speaking and is alone actually known and literally thought. Philosophy deals with contents that are not literally thinkable and are not actually known but are believed as demanding to be known without being thought.[52]

---

[50] K.C. Bhattacharyya, *Studies in Philosophy*, vol. II, p. 102.

[51] Loc. cit.

[52] Ibid., p. 107.

Literal thought refers to science and symbolic thought relates to philosophy. Bhattacharyya also uses terms "secular reason" and "metaphysical reason". Here, we can understand "secular reason" in the lower sense and "metaphysical reason" in the higher sense. Seculare reason is finite, which is successful in the realm of science and technology. Metaphysical reason is a higher one and operates in philosophy or metaphysics. Secular reason is literal thought but metaphysical reason operates through symbols. Literal thought gives expression to fact but symbolic thought deals with self-subsistent, reality and truth. Bhattacharyya observes:

> Science deals with fact, the content of empirical thought. Philosophy deals with the last three, the contents of pure thought in the objective, subjective and transcendental attitudes.[53]

In Bhattacharyya's scheme, we have already seen four grades of theoretic consciousness or reason. Corresponding to these grades, there are four type of contents of consciousness and forms of speakability.

Table 3.1: Grades of theoretic consciousness, contents of consciousness and forms of speakability

Sl. No.	Theoretic Consciousness	Contents of Consciousness	Forms of Speakability
i	Empirical thought	Fact	Spoken of
ii	Pure objective thought	Self-subsistent	Spoken
iii	Spiritual thought	Reality (I)	Spoken as symbolized
iv	Transcendental thought	Truth (Absolute)	Symoblically spoken

Science, Metaphysics and the Philosophy of Object

Bhattacharyya takes philosophy in the sense of metaphysics.

[53] K.C. Bhattacharyya, *Studies in Philosophy*, vol. II, p. 102.

Metaphysics is the science of being or reality. Science is empirical. It is solely concerned with facts. Malkani observes:

> Metaphysics might study the nature of matter as such. What is a material substance? Science does not ask such a question. It merely studies the phenomena of matter. Matter as such is no sensible phenomena. Similarly, it studies the phenomena of life, not what is life. Questions about the nature of life may be left to metaphysics. Similarly, the question, what is mind, as distinct from the phenomena of mind, is a metaphysical question. We have in this way certain questions about the object which science cannot study, but metaphysics can and should.[54]

For Bhattacharyya, there is a fundamental distinction between science and philosophy. Science is interested in phenomena. It studies them without reference to the subject. But, philosophy discusses the concept of the object only in relation to the subject. To Bhattacharyya:

> Metaphysics elaborates the concept of the object in reference to the subject. The rationale of any distinction of metaphysical contents is to be found in an introspectively appreciable distinction within spiritual experience. Even the crude division of the object into matter, life and mind is not intelligible as an inductive classification of fact. That, there are all that is can at least never be known by induction.[55]

Matter, life and mind are the symbols of an introspective or enjoyed content. The fundamental experience is that of the simple or unitary consciousness of oneself living in body. In other words:

---

[54] G.R. Malkani, *Some Points in K.C. Bhattacharyya's Concept of Philosophy*, pp. 49-50.

[55] K.C. Bhattacharyya, *Studies in Philosophy*, vol. II, p. 111.

> No metaphysical concept is intelligible without reference to the subject or spirit which itself goes beyond metaphysics.[56]

Further he observes:

> Metaphysical reasoning is only the systematic exposition of symbolic concepts, concepts that are implicitly taken as symbols of contents that are enjoyingly believed.[57]

Philosophy and science both deal with the object which is known in the objective attitude. But, the object in science is understood as fact and not as self-subsistent. Philosophy deals with the object as self-subsistent and not as fact. By "fact" is meant something perceivable or has necessary reference to the perceivable. "Fact" is speakable in the form of a literal judgement. It is believed without reference to the speaking of it. So "fact" has three characteristics. First, it is perceivable. Second, it is expressed in the form of literal judgement. Third, it has no necessary reference to speech. It is evident that all the facts are perceived. Science does not believe in any unknowable object. It always deals with what is known and can be known. Facts of science are always the objects of perception. They have necessary reference to the perception of senses. "Fact" can be expressed in the form of affirmative and negative judgements. Fact remains a fact whether we speak of it or do not speak. In other words, facts are not necessarily related to the subject or speaking of it.

The self-subsistent is neither perceived nor has reference to the perceivable. It is not expressed through literal judgement. It is believed only as it is spoken. If it is not spoken, it will not be believed. The self-subsistent object is necessarily related to speech or the subject. It is known as an object in contrast to the subject. The self-subsistent is not an object or

---

[56] Loc. cit.

[57] K.C. Bhattacharyya, *Studies in Philosophy*, vol. II, p. 112.

fact though it is objective. The self-subsistent is a concept of philosophy. It is not a concept of science.

According to science, the object must be knowable or usable. Science believes that the object is knowable and usable. This belief is questioned in philosophy. Philosophy deals with object that is intelligible only in reference to the subject or the "I". The object is called "fact". It is dealt in science. The difference between the fact and object is that the latter has got larger connotation than the former. Fact is exclusively dealt in science but this is not the case with the object. The object, that has necessary reference to the speaking of it, is the self-subsistent object for philosophy. Philosophy formulates and elaborates the concept of the self-subsistent object. The common factor between self-subsistent and scientific fact is objectivity. Objectivity itself is no fact. It is only understood in the objective attitude. Philosophy elaborates the concept of the object in reference to the subject. Philosophy rises from the self-subsistent object to self and ultimately to the Absolute. In this sense, the religious consciousness is said to outgrow all empty subjectivity and to be the enjoyed fullness of being.

Philosophy of the Spirit

The contrast of logic and metaphysics suggests the distinction between the self-subsistent and the real. The distinction between self-subsistent and reality is verified in the "enjoying" consciousness of a content. In enjoying consciousness, one experiences reality and not self-subsistent. The content of this "enjoying" understanding is understood neither as fact nor as the self-subsistent object. It is understood as what object is not. It is understood as the speaking subjectivity as "I". Gopinath Bhattacharyya observes, "The study of all contents enjoyed in explicit reference to the subject 'I' may be called 'philosophy of the spirit'."[58] The "enjoying" understanding is

[58] K.C. Bhattacharyya, *Studies in Philosophy*, vol. II, p. xv.

called introspection. Its content is not understood as fact nor even as the self-subsistent object. Bhattacharyya observes, "Introspection proper is a form of the theoretic consciousness that implies an abjuration of the objective attitude".[59] The content of introspection is neither fact nor self-subsistent object but "I" or reality. It implies "I" which is understood as what object is not. Introspection, in the proper sense of the term, is to speak in the first person actually or ideally — with the consciousness of the "I" as what the object is not. When such speaking involves the consciousness of being what is spoken, it may be called spiritual introspection. In spiritual introspection, the subject "I" is never enjoyed by itself. Something else is always enjoyed along with the subject and enjoyed in reference to it. It is always enjoyed: first, as unaccountably embodied; second, as having personal relation to other selves; and third, as having identity with the over-personal self. The over-personal self is enjoyingly understood not only in reference to the subject "I" but as implying the specific experience of communion. Bhattacharyya mentions:

> The consciousness of the over-personal self as thus one with the "I" is the religious form of the spiritual consciousness.[60]

Spiritual consciousness is not mere consciousness of reality but is reality itself. It involves some consciousness of reality as distinct from what may be called empty objectivity. In the enjoying consciousness of the self as embodied or symbolized by the object, the object is conceived not as self-subsistent, but only as a shadow or symbol of the "I". The experience of religious communion or worship is the consciousness of the over-personal reality as symbolized by "I". Bhattacharyya points out, "Religious experience is consciousness of being and,

---

[59] K.C. Bhattacharyya, *Studies in Philosophy*, vol. II, p. 113.

[60] Ibid., p. 114.

as simple, it admits of no variation within itself." The conscious, symbolized by "I", is a non-theoretic experience of self-abnegation. It is consciously being nought and not conscious of "I" as nought. Consciousness is the over-personal reality alone. In this sense, the religious consciousness is said to outgrow all empty subjectivity and to be the enjoyed fullness of being.

Religious experience is simple consciousness of being. Bhattacharyya observes:

> Religious experience as consciousness of being is simple and admits of no variation within itself.[61]

It is clear that it does not admit variation within itself. There is, however, an infinite plurality of unique religious experiences. Their relation is determined by themselves and not by any external reflection. Each experience, by its self-deepening, gets opposed to or synthesized with other experiences. One experience may enjoy another as a stage outgrown or as in absolute conflict with it. A third experience may emerge as adjusting them to one another. There is no possiblity of systematizing them by "secular reason" or "technical reason". As far as they systematize themselves, they present themselves in many alternative systems. We believe in a system only in so far as it is actually revealed.

The theoretic form of religious system is a philosophy of religion. There being as many forms of this philosophy as there are religious systems. This form expresses itself in the lower grades of philosophy — in the theory of the sub-religious spirit, in the metaphysics of the object and even in logic. Every system of religion has its distinctive theory of the spirit, metaphysics and logic. The fundamental differences within logical theory are, as has been suggested, implicitly metaphysical. Those in

---

[61] K.C. Bhattacharyya, *Studies in Philosophy*, vol. II, p. 115.

metaphysics are implicitly religious. Religions may indefinitely multiply and indefinitely get synthesized. There is enough scope for differences and synthesis in philosophy. There is no question of philosophy progressing towards a single unanimously acceptable solution. All philosophy is systematic symbolism and symbolism necessarily admits of alternatives.

Philosophy of Truth

While discussing the philosophy of truth, we come to the point that in religious consciousness, there is no theoretic denial of the subject "I". According to Bhattacharyya, there is a theoretic consciousness of "I am nought". The denial of "I" or subject is possible because we believe that the Absolute is. The Absolute or truth is positively believed entity. It is only negatively understood as what the subject "I" is not. Bhattacharyya points out:

> The denial of the "I" is possible because we already believe that the absolute is. The Absolute is not the same as the over-personal reality that is enjoyed in religion. It means what the subject "I" is not, but the reality of religious experience while it is enjoyed and symbolized by I does not mean such theoretic negation of I.[62]

The positive character of the Absolute is expressible only by the negation of "I". This is not literally speakable at all. Reality as expressed in religion is symbolized by "I". It is also expressed as a self. It is expressed literally. The positive character of truth or the Absolute is not literally expressible because it is expressible only by the negation of "I". "Reality is enjoyed but truth is not."[63] The consciousness of truth is neither understood in the objective nor in the subjective attitude. It is not literally speakable at all but speakable only in the purely symbolistic way. The consciousness of truth is

---

[62] K.C. Bhattacharyya, *Studies in Philosophy*, vol. II, p. 116.

[63] Loc. cit.

extra-religious of transcendental consciousness. Truth is self-revealing. Bhattacharyya observes, "Truth is believed or revealed as independent of it, as self-revealing."[64]

The Concept of the Absolute

Bhattacharyya points out:

> The Absolute may be generally defined from the standpoint of reflection as what is free from the implicational dualism of content and consciousness.[65]

Though the Absolute can be reached only through relation, yet in itself it is free from any kind of relation or from the dualism of content and consciousness. In order to clarify the meaning of "implicational dualism", let us quote Gopinath Bhattacharyya:

> Consciousness is always the consciousness of a content and we are reflectively aware of the content as distinct from and in necessary reference to consciousness. The peculiar relation between content and consciousness is described as "implicational dualism". An entity that is free from such dualism would be an entity that is distinct but not in reference to consciousness. Such an entity seems to be what the writer designates as the absolute.[66]

The dualism of content and consciousness is grasped at the level of reason. Bhattacharyya defines the word "reflection" as follows:

> Reflection is the awareness of a content as to a mode of consciousness. The phrase "as to" means some relation and it is in reference to this relation that the concept of the absolute has to be understood.[67]

---

[64] Loc. cit.

[65] K.C. Bhattacharyya, *Studies in Philosophy*, vol. II, p. 141.

[66] Ibid., pp. xxix-xxx.

[67] Ibid., p. 125.

According to Bhattacharyya, philosophy starts at the reflective or rational level. A philosopher reflects over the problems, and tries to understand the meaning behind the ideas, whereas the common people are satisfied only with the ideas. So the reflective consciousness is possible only in an advanced state of human mind and philosophy starts with the reflective consciousness or reason. The term "implicational dualism" implies the relation between subject and object, consciousness and content. It is in reference to this relation that the Concept of Absolute has to be understood.

Reason reflects and grasps relations. It apprehends relations subsisting between content and consciousness. Bhattacharyya conceives of "objective consciousness" and "reflective consciousness". "Objective consciousness" conceives relation between content and content, whereas "reflective consciousness" conceives relation between content and consciousness. Objective consciousness can establish relation between two existing contents. It cannot establish relation between contents which are absent. Reflective consciousness or reason conceives the concept of relation as such. Hence, we can know a relation of two contents only through reason. The difficulty is that the relation of content and consciousness is not explicitly of self-evidently appreciated as an identity-in-difference by reason itself. It is claimed to be so appreciated only in a higher or supra-reflective consciousness. Bhattacharyya observes:

> The possibility, however, of this supra-reflective consciousness may be disputed and if is necessary in the first instance to show it and how reflection points to it.[68]

Reflection or reason seems to be the chief instrument of philosophy. Reason gives an awareness of a content which

---

[68] K.C. Bhattacharyya, *Studies in Philosophy*, vol. II, p. 121.

has a relation with consciousness. The relation between consciousness and content is known as "implicational dualism".

The implicational relation of content and consciousness is slightly different from the usual relation of implication. In ordinary cases of implication, as in the example of "*A* implies *B*", the relation is between a term that is definite and independent of implication and a term that is implied. Unless that definite term is there, the relation cannot be one of implication. But in implicational relation of content and consciousness, no such definite term is there. Therefore, in this case, we have only an indefinite relation between content and consciousness. Within reflection consciousness and content are somehow distinct, yet their identity cannot be denied. Their relation is indefinite. But, whatever appears as indefinite in some respect demands to be definable in that respect, and if such indefiniteness necessarily appears to a stage of consciousness, that stage demands a higher stage where the indefinite is defined. The demand is for a "supra-reflective consciousness" or intuition. The concept of absolute belongs to such supra-reflective consciousness. It need not involve identity of consciousness and content. It is hypothetically understood within reflection simply as a completely definite distinction of content and consciousness.

This shows that the implicational dualism of content and consciousness is not final to reflection and is itself indefinite. Therefore, there is a demand for this indefinite distinction to be defined. That would be possible only through a consciousness that would be supra-reflective and from where this distinction can be visualized. Reason or reflection lands us in the vortex of relation or implicational dualism. It suffers from limitation. So there is a pressing necessity on the part of reason to transcend itself. Reason moves in the realm of implicational dualism. Intuition of supra-reflective consciousness can transcend reason and realize absolute as free from the relation of implicational dualism of content and consciousness. That is why Bhattacharyya defines the Absolute as "what is free from the implicational dualism of content and consciousness".[69]

In this, the reflective implication of content and consciousness turns into a "non-implicatory distinction". This should not lead one to suppose that here there is a consciousness of identity, between content and consciousness. If there is any consciousness of identity, it would be only in a symbolic or metaphysical sense and not in a literal or logical sense.

Reflection is the consciousness of the contents. Theoretic consciousness or reason reflects over certain things and those things are called the contents of consciousness. So, reflection is possible when man is aware of a content in relation to a mode of consciousness.

The Absolute is something which is free from the implicational dualism of content and consciousness. According to Bhattacharyya, implicational dualism as has been said above, consists in the relation of content and consciousness. He holds that the content and consciousness appear to be related by way of implicative distinction. There cannot be any relation between the two things which are identical. Relation is only possible where there is distinction. And so when we say that the content and consciousness are related, it proves that they are distinct and not identical. Though they are separate and distinct, they are related. The relation between them is the relation of implicative distinction.

An object is an object only for the subject. The object is not an object-in-itself but for the consciousness. Consciousness is always of a content, so a content is a content for a consciousness but consciousness is never the content of itself. Consciousness is always the consciousness of the content. Consciousness

---

[69] K.C. Bhattacharyya, *Studies in Philosophy*, vol. II, p. 128.

cannot be conscious of itself. It is always conscious of some content or object. Thus, it is this relationship of content and consciousness which is called the relationship of implicative distinction. Though there is a state where consciousness can be absolutely free from content and content from consciousness. But this state is not possible as long as we remain at the reflective or rational level.

Bhattacharyya says that if we have to reach the Absolute, then this implicatory distinction should be changed into non-implicatory distinction. This means the consciousness is freed from content and to say that the content is freed from consciousness means that content becomes unrelated to consciousness and to say that consciousness is freed from content is to reach the state of Absolute. Consciousness becomes or turns into the Absolute because it is the characteristic of the Absolute, that it is independent, self-existent, free from everything.

Theory of the Trinal Absolute

The Absolute is free from the implicational dualism of content and consciousness. The implicatory distinction varies according to the nature of consciousness. Consciousness is generally taken to be consitituted of knowing, feeling and willing. Implicational distinction is, accordingly, of three types. Bhattacharyya thinks that there are three ways in which freedom from this distinction can be understood. First, the content may be freed from its reference to consciousness and we have truth — the Absolute for knowing. Second, consciousness may be freed from the content and we have freedom of the will — the Absolute for willing. Third, the implicational relation of content and consciousness may be freed from their distinction as a unity and we have value — the Absolute for feeling. Implicational dualism may be in the realm of knowing or in the realm of willing or in the realm of feeling. Bhattacharyya observes:

> The content may be spoken of (a) as unconstituted by consciousness or (b) as constituted by consciousness or (c) as along with consciousness constituting some kind of unity.[70]

It is evident that implicational distinction of content and consciousness will vary in accordance with the three aspects of consciousness — knowing, willing and feeling. So the implicational distinction (or the relation) between content and consciousness is not the same from all points of view of knowing, willing and feeling. Each of these views gives different variety of understanding of the Absolute. Bhattacharyya believes that the Absolute is ultimately free from the implicational dualism of content and consciousness.

How there is the implicational distinction between content and consciousness, in respect of knowing? Bhattacharyya says that though content is distinct from consciousness, yet it cannot be created by consciousness. Knowing an object does not mean creating the object.

The word implicative distinction simply gives an idea about the situation of content and consciousness, but it does not explain the exact relation between them. The implicational distinction is to be resolved into non-implicational distinction, which is the state where there will be complete distinction without any relation. There will be no necessary reference between content and consciousness. In the state of non-implicational distinction, the consciousness becomes free from content and so it becomes the Absolute and the consciousness ceases to be the consciousness of the content.

Relation Between Content and Consciousness

According to Bhattacharyya, there are three kinds of relations:

(i) Relation between content (object) and consciousness (subject)

[70] K.C. Bhattacharyya, *Studies in Philosophy*, vol. II, p. 122.

(ii) Relation between content (one object) and content (another object)

(iii) There can be a third kind of relation where both unifiedly are related to the absolute.

This can be explained as follows:

		Content	Consciousness
		A	*B*
I	(i)	*B*	Constitutes *A*
	(ii)	*A*	Completely different from *B*.
	(iii)	*A* and *B*	Are unified in *C*.
II	(i)	*A*	Is constituted by *B*.
	(ii)	*A*	Is unconstituted by *B* (completely independent).
	(iii)	*A* and *B*	Constitute *C*.
III	(i)	Content is unconstituted by consciousness.	
	(ii)	Content is consituted by consciousness.	
	(iii)	Content and consciousness are somehow unified.	

The first view (III (i)) is that of the realists like the Nyāya-Vaiśeṣika philosophies, who hold that content is unconstituted by consciousness. Object exists independently of the perceiving mind. The second view (III (ii)) is that of the idealists like the Vijñānavādins who hold that the content is the manifestation of consciousness. The third view (III (iii)) which believes in the unification of content and consciousness, and their relation to the Absolute is best represented by Hegel. The Absolute, therefore, being free from the threefold implicational dualism has to be conceived in a triple way.

The Absolute for Knowing

The first is the Absolute for knowing. This need not be any content of knowing, because content here has been freed from any reference to knowing. It is completely unrelated to knowing, that is to say, it cannot be known. Bhattacharyya describes this character of the Absolute as knowing in this way, "It may accordingly be (loosely) called a known no content. It is explicitly known as what known content is not".[71] Bhattacharyya says that in reflection or at rational stage, we arrive at this relationship through knowing. When we approach through knowing, we come to the conclusion that content is unconstituted by consciousness. Bhattacharyya is not a realist but an absolutist. He says that, in reflection, what knowledge does is that it reveals the objects and does not create the objects. Knowing function does not constitute the object as the idealist would have us believe. Though in dreaming, there is the distinction between content and consciousness, the objects or contents of dream are the constructions of consciousness, and have no existence apart from a perceiving mind. But in the waking state, this does not hold good, for when we see a table or a man, we are aware that they exist independently of us. So, the content is to be taken as unconstituted by consciousness. The realists say that the table exists, even if nobody perceives it. So, knowledge is an accidental factor. It does not in any way affect the existence of the object.

In any act of knowledge, we cannot say definitely that the content is absolutely unconstituted by mind. This is Bhattacharyya's point against the realists. He says that only that content which is self-revealing is absolutely unconstituted by mind. The content which is free from consciousness (the individual ego) becomes the truth itself. This truth is the Absolute of Knowing. Reason points to a supra-reflective state. The concept of the Absolute in any form points out to supra-reflective consciousness, according to Bhattacharyya. Reason

---

[71] K.C. Bhattacharyya, *Studies in Philosophy*, vol. II, p. 123.

can only act as a pointer to the Absolute. Bhattacharyya is definite in his approach that the Absolute is beyond reason. Reason lands us in "indefinite relation". For every implying term, it is necessary to find such a non-implying term, if possible, and until and unless it is found, the implication has to be taken as an "indefinite formulation of factual relations (or units)"! To reflective consciousness or reason, there is implication between the content and the consciousness of it and the implication points to a factual relation of which one of them at least is not really a term. Intuition of supra-rational experience can alone reveal the Absolute. Bhattacharyya observes, "The concept of the Absolute in any form is taken to belong to a supra-reflective consciousness".[72] But the role of reason cannot be minimized as it alone shows the self-contradictions inherent in itself and in the phenomenal experience and the necessity to transcend itself and reach the Absolute through the higher or supra-rational consciousness. Bhattacharyya points out:

> The possibility and nature of this consciousness have to be understood is reflection as a necessary problem.[73]

The implication is resolvable in the different ways in these three spheres and the Absolute is understood in the reflective stage in terms of the mode of resolution in each case. Knowing, feeling and willing will then each have its own formulation of the Absolute truth, value and reality (or freedom), namely, respectively, as will be discussed subsequently. In the reflective stage or at the rational level, these formulations of the Absolute will be found to be un-unifiable and to be in a sort of alternation. Whether a mystical identity of the Absolute can be reached in the supra-reflective consciousness does not concern us. Reason can separate content from consciousness,

---

[72] K.C. Bhattacharyya, *Studies in Philosophy*, vol. II, p. 128.

[73] Loc. cit.

but it is only in the supra-reflective consciousness that this separation is realized or appreciated. The relational experience points to the non-relational experience of the Absolute.

The Absolute for Willing

The Absolute for willing is absolute freedom. Will means free will or freedom. The implicative distinction is resolved in willing. "Consciousness may be freed from its content and we have freedom of the will — the Absolute for willing".[74] Consciousness in the sense of willing is free from content or act of willing, and as such the Absolute for willing is contentless in that sense. It is difficult for reason or reflection to understand as to how willing is freedom. Bhattacharyya observes:

> We will an act in order to get rid of the being of the act, to get rid of the self-complacent will to continue in this being — what may be called the will to indolence.[75]

Here, willing is a willing itself and completely free from the act of the will. In this, the Absolute is taken as freedom or reality.

The content of willing is something alien to it and is, thus, a limitation to itself. At the stage of reflection or reason, this limitation is not realized as a self-limitation or the free limitation of the will to realize itself. Reflection or reason demands that the limitation should be realized as self-limitation in this sense. The relation between two contents willed suggests the relation between the willed content and willing. Two contents are willed at once when one of them is a means to the other. This relation of means and end has to be understood as the relation between the willed content and willing. It is difficult to understand how one can be said to act

[74] K.C. Bhattacharyya, *Studies in Philosophy*, vol. II, p. 124.

[75] Ibid., p. 138.

in a particular way to act freely. Reason or reflection indicates that it is to be understood by contrasting "I will this act" with "I will this act that I ought to will". This contrast points out that willing as represented by the former is itself a being that is to be superseded by willing. We will an act in order to get rid of the being of the act. Reason or reflection cannot understand this willing or freedom at its limit.

According to Bhattacharyya, the act of willing and the end of willing are the contents of willing. Will plays a great role in life, not only in secular life but also in the religious life. In his philosophy, both the will and the way are the contents of willing. Though the object of knowledge is independent or unconstituted by knowledge, the content of willing is constituted by willing because the goal is determined by the will and also the way. So, the content of willing is distinct from willing, but it is not independent of willing because apart from willing, the content will have no existence. So, the content of willing is constituted by willing.

The will may work in a natural way or in a free-way. At the natural level, everyone is willing something and doing something. So, will is directed towards something which one wills, for example, the moral values. In this situation, man crosses the natural level of will and his will ceases to be the natural will and becomes freewill. In the natural state, will is conditioned or limited and this limitation means that man wants to attain that which he lacks. But reason points to a state where the will limits itself or reaches the state of self-limitation. Bhattacharyya observes, "Reflection indicates the way but cannot understand willing or freedom at its limit".[76] Sri Aurobindo says that God consciously puts Himself under limitation. It means that He puts His will under self-limitation. This act itself is indicative of His absolute freedom. Reason

[76] K.C. Bhattacharyya, *Studies in Philosophy*, vol. II, p. 138.

points to the state where every act of will is free will, and this, is the state of the absolute. So, the content of willing is not unconsituted by willing. To say that God created the world means that it is the will of God, and the will of God means that it is distinct from God but at the same time dependent on God or constituted by God.

The Absolute of willing is called the Absolute of freedom or reality. Here, we reach the state where consciousness as will resolves the content altogether or transcends the content or becomes free from the content. Consciousness as will is no more the consciousness of content, it is consciousness in itself. Bhattacharyya says, "Reflective willing is consciousness of the act willed as being distinguished by the willing from itself".[77] This willing is utter freedom. As in Mahāyāna Buddhism, the Absolute is contentless and is realized as utter freedom, so in this way, the implicational dualism of content and consciousness is resolved. It is simply the freedom of consciousness from the content. In the Absolute of knowing, the content is altogether freed from consciousness, and in the Absolute for willing, consciousness is altogether freed from content. Bhattacharyya observes:

> Consciousness that is free from its content (in the sense that it solely constitutes its content, makes the content a content, creates its distinction from itself) is freedom of the will — the Absolute for willing.[78]

The Absolute for Feeling

Reflection or reason feels the demand for the unity of the content felt and its feeling, but does not understand it. Bhattacharyya observes, "Reflection accordingly demands such a unity of felt-content and feeling but cannot itself understand

---

[77] K.C. Bhattacharyya, *Studies in Philosophy*, vol. II, p. 129.

[78] Ibid., p. 141.

it".[79] Such a unity which has been freed from the duality of content and consciousness is the Absolute for feeling. It may be understood as "content that is indefinitely other than consciousness or as consciousness that is indefinitely other than the content".[80] It should be understood, therefore, as that from which known being is distinct; that is, it is indifferent to both being and non-being.

Here also, the implicational dualism has to be resolved. In the relation of feeling, the content is "feeling content" and the consciousness is "feeling consciousness". In feeling, we find unity between content and consciousness. To reflection, the distinction of content and consciousness is present even in feeling. In other words unity of content and consciousness does not mean their identity. If they are taken as identical, then there can be no distinction. It means that there is place for distinction of content and consciousness even in their unity. Though there is distinction, there is unity too. Bhattacharyya observes:

> In appreciating a beautiful object where we feel the object as a whole as well as the parts, the parts that appear neutral — are together felt to be distinct from the whole that appears beautiful.[81]

Bhattacharyya says that the unity of content and feeling is called value. Unity between felt-content and feeling consciousness is value. In other words, the felt-content and feeling are united in value. Beauty is the value in our feeling of the beautiful rose.

The question is: where this value (beauty) resides in the object or in the subject. This question is difficult to answer.

---

[79] K.C. Bhattacharyya, *Studies in Philosophy*, vol. II, p. 138.

[80] Ibid., p. 139.

[81] Loc. cit.

Because, it cannot be said to exist solely either in the object (realists) or in the subject (idealists). Value is something which is on the one hand with the object and on the other hand with the subject. So, it seems that in value, there is a sort of unity between object and the subject.

At the level of reflection, the content and consciousness of feeling cannot be distinguished from value in a perfect way. The content and consciousness both are unified in value. So, the value represents the unity of content and consciousness. In self-subsistent unity, the implicational relation is freed from its terms, content and consciousness. But to reflection, unity means an imperfect distinction of content and consciousness. It does not appear to be self-subsistent unity to reflection, though it is demanded. The Absolute is the self-subsistent unity, where the content and consciousness are distinguished altogether, in a perfect way. Implicational relation is freed from their terms, i.e. from content and consciousness. The self-subsistent unity is free from implicational relation of content and feeling. It also represents the non-implicational relation of content and consciousness. They are perfectly distinguished.

The self-subsistent unity is called value. Bhattacharyya says that in this state the value will exist in itself. It will have no reference to contents. Thus, the value shines, in isolation, as a self-subsistent unity, it will be independent of valuation. Bhattacharyya observes, ". . . the demand is for the concept of a value that is independent of valuation, of its reference to a known object".[82] It means that it will have no reference to the objects or contents. According to this view, beauty or value can be enjoyed without the beautiful objects in this state (here is the idea of universal beauty or goodness). In reflection there is only an imperfect distinction between the content and

---

[82] K.C. Bhattacharyya, *Studies in Philosophy*, vol. II, p. 140.

consciousness. Implicational dualism is resolved and the self-subsistent unity is attained only in the supra-reflective consciousness, in the Absolute, the Absolute for willing.

So, the implicational dualism is resolved in three ways — through knowing, willing and feeling. Accordingly, we find a triple formulation of the Absolute — the Absolute for knowing called truth, the Absolute for willing called freedom and the Absolute for feeling called value.

It is difficult to determine the mutual relation of truth, freedom and value. In Absolute, their mutual relation is called "alternation" and each one of these is called an alternative form of the Absolute. Bhattacharyya says:

> In one direction their identity and difference are alike meaningless and in another direction their identity is intelligible but not assertible. Truth is unrelated to value, value to reality and reality to truth, while value may be truth, reality value and truth reality. The Absolute may be regarded in this sense as an alternation of truth, value and reality.[83]

The Absolute is not a known content. It is meaningless to try to describe the character of the Absolute. It is futile to say that there are three absolutes or that there is only one Absolute. Such questions of one or many are raised only with respect to the known and not in the case of the Absolute.

Bhattacharyya says that the Absolute is only a possibly believed entity that is only negatively understood. It is only speakable in terms of symbols, in itself, it is "indefinite". Truth, freedom and value are only the symbols of the Absolute. They are not three absolutes. The Absolute is beyond the distinction of one and many. It is experienced only in supra-reflectional state. Truth, freedom and value are also not the three aspects of the Absolute. Each of them is the Absolute. They are the

---

[83] K.C. Bhattacharyya, *Studies in Philosophy*, vol. II, p. 143.

symbols of the Absolute. The Absolute represents freedom from the implicational distinction of content and consciousness. Value represents the self-subsistent unity of content and consciousness.

In the end, it may be mentioned that implicational dualism of content and consciousness is apprehended at the level of reflection in the act of knowing, willing and feeling. Reason demands the resolution of the implicatory distinctions into non-implicatory distinction. This is not possible at the level of reflection itself. Dualism between content and consciousness is inevitable at the reflectional level. But reason becomes conscious of it and demands its resolution at a supra-reflective level. It points to this supra-reflective consciousness or the Absolute. This resolution is possible in knowing, willing and feeling, the three ways of reaching the Absolute. The Absolute is free from the implicational dualism of content and consciousness. The implicational dualism of content and consciousness is inevitable at the reflectional or rational level and it is resolved in the supra-reflectional or spiritual level. Man has to transcend reason and attain a supra-reflective consciousness in order to realize the Absolute which is free from the implicational dualism of content and consciousness. This realization results in man's enjoyment of absolute freedom. In this state, the subject is freed altogether from its relations to the objectivity.

Now we proceed to discuss the concept of freedom, and the process which help man attain the supreme state of freedom.

The Concept of Freedom

GRADES OF SUBJECTIVITY

According to Bhattacharyya, freedom lies in the gradual abstraction of the subject from the object. The cognition of subject or self as different from the object or meant entity is the first mark of subjective freedom. This awareness of the distinction from the object is due to the subject's awareness of his body. I know that there is a book before me because I can see it through my eyes and touch it with my fingers. The awareness that the eyes and fingers — sight and touch — are distinct from the object — the book, might produce in me the awareness of the subject being distinct from the object. But even this is not pure subjectivity. If the subject is identified with the body, it is not the pure subject. There, subjectivity involves an awareness of the subject's distinction from the body also.

This awareness might make the subject identify itself with the psychic activities. It is believed that when anything is known by a self, the self as knowing is also known. When an object is known or felt, there is also an awareness of the knownness and feltness. This is psychic subjectivity. Bhattacharyya holds that the subject proper cannot be identified with knownness, feltness, etc. The notion of subjectivity proper involves an awareness of the subject's distinction from psychic activities also. In brief, the subject proper is neither body nor psychic fact. It means that the subject should be understood as "what is expressed by the word 'I'". The next stage to psychic subjectivity is spiritual subjectivity.

Let us consider the above three stages of subjectivity in some detail.

Bodily Subjectivity

There is a distinction between "man as a subject" and "man as an embodied person". Man as an embodied person is an individual. The subject proper cannot be individual. In Bhattacharyya's analysis, we find a distinction between "body" and objects also. Though body is not free from objectivity, yet it is not object in the crude sense of the term. It is closer to the subject than the objects. In a particular sense, even body appears as subjective. Objects are external in relation to the body. Body is not external in that sense. Body does not belong to the world of perceived objects. One may perceive his half portion of the body. He takes the help of imagination and the rest of the portion of his body is eked out by imagination. In this sense also, the awareness of his body is uniquely different from other perceived objects and has no place in the objective world that he conceives to be presentable to him. On the other hand, one becomes aware of the body in a somewhat subjective way. Even if the subject is taken as nothing but the body, it involves knowledge of something that cannot be understood in terms of perceptible objects. It implies an awareness that the body is distinct from the objects and in that sense it enjoys subjectivity. Bhattacharyya observes:

> What is intended by the word I cannot be characterized even in the lowest stage of subjectivity as simply this object.[84]

Moreover, body awareness is definitely sensuous but it cannot be called sense-perception. Bhattacharyya holds, "The awareness of the body from within is, indeed, sensuous but it can hardly be called sense-perception".[85] In sense-perception, there is no feeling of the object. The object is known from outside. To quote Bhattacharyya:

> One's own body is not only perceived from outside. One is immediately or sensuously aware of it also from within in what is called feeling of the body.[86]

One is aware of the body from outside as well as from inside. The body awareness is certainly different from perception of an object. The former is "a feeling of the body", whereas the

---

[84] K.C. Bhattacharyya, *Studies in Philosophy*, vol. II, p. 51.

[85] Ibid., p. 52.

[86] Ibid., p. 51.

latter is perception and not feeling. Bhattacharyya observes, "Subjectivity apart from spiritual discipline is rooted in bodily feeling".[87] When the felt body is distinguished from the perceived body, we have a feeling of freedom and that is the initiation of the subject's efforts to realize subjectivity.

It is clear that Bhattacharyya does not consider body an object among other objects or a meant entity. True, the subject is primarily intended by the word "I". The body is partially identified with "I". It is partially identified because "I" constitutes more than the body. So, it is not legitimate to identify body completely with "I". The term "I" which, indicates body as a particular person which is unique in itself, may be treated as subjective. Hence, it is permissible to speak of the "bodily subjectivity". The bodily stage has three sub-stages:

(i) the body as externally perceived
(ii) the body as internally felt
(iii) the absence of object known as a persent fact.

The body as abserved and felt is the subject in relation to the environment. A question may arise: what is the distinction between "body as externally perceived" and other objects perceived? Bhattacharyya makes it clear that "body as externally perceived" cannot be equated with other perceived objects. Though the body represents a stage of being of the subject, yet one's own body, even as a perceived object, has a unique singularity. The emphasis is on the "unique singularity" of the perceived body. The objectivity of other perceived objects is constituted by their space–position relatively to the percipient's body. This is not the case with the percipient's own body which is in this sense dissociated from the external

---

[87] K.C. Bhattacharyya, *Studies in Philosophy*, vol. II, p. 54.

world. A person's own body cannot be classed under other perceived objects. Gopinath Bhattacharyya observes:

> A person's own body is uniquely different from other perceived objects and has no place in the objective world that he conceives to be presentable to him.[88]

Bhattacharyya points out the distinction between percipient's body and perceived objects. First, contends that there is an element of subjectivity in externally perceived body. It is characterized by unique singularity. Second, there is the awareness of the body from within in the "feeling of the body". The perceived body may be treated as object existing in space and time. The "felt-body" cannot be taken as an object among objects in that sense. The felt-body indicates a sense of awareness. This feeling of detachment from the object is the feeling of freedom. The first hint of this freedom is reached in the feeling of the body. Third, there is such a thing as a sense-conditioned cognition of an absent object, or of the absence of an object. The absence of object is not ordinary perception. The absence of object is ligitimately known as a present fact. According to Bhattacharyya, there is the facthood of a perceived absence. For example, a tree was observed in a field in the past, later on it was cut down. Now, when the observer, who does not know that the tree has been cut down, observes the field, he notices a difference without knowing the tree is no longer there. This is a case of perceived absence.

Then, there may be the facthood of absence known by conscious non-perception. For example, a person looks at the table and perceives that a certain book is absent. This sort of knowledge is similar to *anupalabdhi*. It is a kind of imaginative perception conditioned by conscious non-perception of that which is cognized. Gopinath Bhattacharyya observes:

---

[88] K.C. Bhattacharyya, *Studies in Philosophy*, vol. II, p. xxvi.

> The subject that imaginatively perceives the absence of an object is, dissociated from the perceived body; but the subject that knows absence through conscious non-perception is consciously dissociated from it. Conscious non-perception is thus a transitional stage between body-feeling and imagination with which the psychical stage begins.[89]

In Bhattacharyya's analysis of the subjective life of the subject, subjectivity begins with a realization of freedom even from the felt-body. The body perceived externally is the "perceived body". The body felt from within is the felt-body. The distinction between the two is only imagined because even the felt-body does not belong to the subjective activity in so far as it is not a psychic fact. It is with psychic fact that subjective activities begin. Therefore, the subject must be abstracted even from the felt-body. That is why Bhattacharyya says, "The realization of this freedom from the felt-body is the pre-condition of all distinctively spiritual activity".[90] Man or subject is not only not the object, but also not the body. Any attempt to identify man with the body is nothing but reducing the subjective character of man to a sort of an objectivity.

Psychic Subjectivity

It has already been made clear that the subject is distinct from psychic subjectivity. A psychic fact is ordinarily understood as a mental event. But, according to Bhattacharyya, it is not purely a meant entity because it comprises an aspect of the non-mental also. The psychic stage begins when attention is withdrawn from the objective fact of absence to the psychic image and thought. There are certain modes of relatedness of the object with the subject. These modes are psychic facts. In brief, it can be said that psychic facts include "images" and "thoughts".

---

[89] Loc. cit.

[90] K.C. Bhattacharyya, *Studies in Philosophy*, vol. II, p. 105.

It is clear that conscious non-perception is a transitional stage between body-feeling and imagination with which the psychical stage begins. The image of the object, whose absence is known in conscious non-perception, marks the transition to the psychic stage. According to Bhattacharyya, the image is substantive something from which the object is distinct. The image appears as the forming of a form, the process and the product being presented at once. Image is a fact in a non-objective sense. There is the facthood of a perceived object which is determined in relation to the percipient's body. Bhattacharyya thinks that there is the facthood of the perceived body, the felt-body and a perceived absence. The facthood of image is similar to the facthood of absence known by conscious non-perception, because the image is not known as having space–time position. Now, subject has to be distinguished from the mental image. First, it can be said that the image "appears as a ghostly object that does not consciously imply belief, much as the half-perceived body appears when an object is perceived to be there. The awareness of the image is still bound up with the perceiving attitude and is not introspective".[91] This shows that it is character of psychical object, even though not an object of perception itself. But that is sufficient to prevent it from being subjective. It has not been able to free itself completely from the contacts of the objective. Therefore, it cannot represent the essential nature of man which has to be essentially subjective. Second, an image is a form of "presentation". In every awareness, there is an element of belief. But often a distinction is made between the object believed and the belief itself. Bhattacharyya calls this distinction, "the presentation of the object". The image is also a sort of an awareness of a distinction between the object on the one hand and its knownness, feltness, etc. on the other.

---

[91] K.C. Bhattacharyya, *Studies in Philosophy*, vol. II, p. 66.

Therefore, it is not also a type of presentation. Actually, presentation is not given as completely distinct from the object. It is to be abstracted from the belief in the object. Therefore, again, it is not free from a kind of a relatedness with the object and cannot represent the nature of the subject.

Thought or idea is the next psychic activity. Bhattacharyya defines thought in this way:

> . . . there may be idea of something in the object that cannot be defined or concreted into image at all. Such an idea is thought proper that is definite in itself and is not defined in meaning but at best fixed or detained in the mind by the images it may still call up.[92]

Thought is also a presentation but unlike image, it has an "attained meaning". The image implies a belief in its possible objectivity. But, thought utilizes images in such a way that it transcends time and becomes eternal. It is still about the objects. It suggests a detachment from objectivity. Thought moves in the realm of universals, abstractions and significances. Therefore, it appears as completely detached from the substantive nature of the objective.

Man or subject cannot be identified with thought also. First, thought is also about the object and, as such, still retains contact with the objective. Second, in thought, a distinction is made between thought and its contents. Thought appears to be completely detached from and indifferent to its objective content. But, the very fact that such a distinction is made in thought, prevents man from being identified with his thought-process. In the truly subjective state, this distinction between content and consciousness is not maintained. The subjective is always and at once both the "content of its consciousness" and the "consciousness of its content". Therefore, the subject cannot be reduced to thought.

---

[92] K.C. Bhattacharyya, *Studies in Philosophy*, vol. II, p. 69.

This examination of the nature of "images" and "thoughts" shows that subject cannot properly be represented by or identified with psychic activities.

Spiritual Subjectivity

Spiritual subjectivity is the next stage to psychic subjectivity. In the states of bodily subjectivity and psychic subjectivity, there is a definite connection with the object that is meant. When one enters the realm of spiritual subjectivity, this connection is transcended. Psychic subjectivity is characterized as presentational subjectivity. The non-presentational subjectivity is characterized as spiritual subjectivity. If the term "subjectivity" is taken in a wide sense, then even bodily subjectivity or psychic subjectivity would come under it. But the true nature of man is revealed in spiritual subjectivity. Pure subjectivity must be completely free from all traces of objectivity. It must be spiritual. Subject in the spiritual sense has been viewed in three different senses — subject as feeling, subject as "I", and subject as complete freedom. Let us consider them separately and determine the nature of freedom.

Subject as Distinct from Feeling Subjectivity: The first expression of spiritual subjectivity is feeling. Bhattacharyya says about feeling,

> The positive consciousness of detachment from meaning which is the last residium of the object is feeling. Feeling is the knowledge of the purely unknown as such, the unknown that is not even meant. It is symbolized as knowledge of the unknown, though the unknown being unmeant, the preposition "of" has no meaning.[93]

In feeling, there is no meaning awareness. In the psychic stage the process of detachment from meaning is not complete. In

[93] K.C. Bhattacharyya, *Studies in Philosophy*, vol. II, p. 76.

feeling, there is an awareness of this detachment. This awareness is "positive". Let us make a distinction between "feeling" and "thought". Thought is the final grade of psychic subjectivity and feeling is the first expression of spiritual subjectivity. Feeling is immediately next to thought.

In thought, the content of thought appears to be distinct from thought. In feeling, there may be a content — a distinct content — but that is only "distinct-in-itself" and not distinct from feeling. Feeling-awareness itself appears as feeling. Bhattacharyya observes:

> In introspection into feeling, the distinction of feeling from its presentative content is appreciated as definitely not known but only felt and symbolized.[94]

Thought appears to exist outside introspection. Feeling does not appear to be distinct from its content. It does not appear also to exist outside introspection. Thus, we find that thought, in spite of its efforts to keep unity, maintains a separation between content and consciousness. In feeling, there is identity between content and consciousness.

As a matter of fact, subject cannot be completely identified with feeling. Feeling is the first mode of spiritual consciousness. It is only by superseding this mode that subject proper can be realized. There are two grades of feeling of which the first admits of two sub-grades. We know now that feeling is a felt awareness of a detachment from even thought. This freedom may be freedom from actual thought (the first sub-grade) or freedom from possible thought (the second sub-grade). In the second grade of feeling, there is a "feeling of not having a feeling". Bhattacharyya observes:

> The feeling of not having a feeling is not an uncommon

[94] K.C. Bhattacharyya, *Studies in Philosophy*, vol. II, p. 155.

> experience. The awareness of wanting a feeling — whether sense-enjoyment, aesthetic satisfaction or spiritual serenity — is itself a feeling.[95]

Further he says:

> It is not simply one feeling due to the want of another feeling but the feeling of the want of its own being or actuality.[96]

This is what Bhattacharyya calls "feeling" of a feeling.

Bhattacharyya asserts that the subject proper cannot be a "meant content" like the object. The subject can be either "unmeant" or "unmeaning". It can either be a content that is unmeant or just a function. If man is conceived as feeling, it will become unmeant. An unmeant feeling has still some association, positively negative with meaning. The unmeant is meant as unmeant. The case is different with "unmeaning" because it is merely a function having no content, not even a content that is unmeant. If man is identified even with the purest form of feeling, a complete detachment from the felt-content will not be possible; and unless that is possible, the pure subjective nature of man cannot be expressed. Bhattacharyya observes:

> We are aware of the unmeanable. The unmeanable here refers to the pure subject as completely dissociated from the objective — that is to the subject as Introspection in two stages — as the meant unmeanable and as the mere function of meaning or speaking. The knowledge implied in the former is of a contradiction, while that implied in the latter is not anything, being merely knowing.[97]

The feeling of feeling is the former kind of awareness, while the latter is just introspection.

---

[95] K.C. Bhattacharyya, *Studies in Philosophy*, vol. II, p. 78.

[96] Loc. cit.

[97] K.C. Bhattacharyya, *Studies in Philosophy*, vol. II, p. 79.

Introspection: the Nature of Subject as I: Introspection seems to have been conceived by Bhattacharyya in a very special sense. Ordinarily, introspection is used in psychological sense. Psychological introspection is almost an "internal perception". It is a sort of "looking within". It is an awareness of what is happening inside. In that sense, introspection is merely "a process of abstracting from the object of its character of relatedness to the subject".[98]

But this sort of introspection is not introspection proper. It is introspection in the objective attitude. Introspection proper is introspection in the subjective attitude. Introspection is a pure knowing function. It is only enjoying understanding of the subject as "I".

In introspection, there is not only a "conscious absence of all meaning", but also an impossibility of meaning. Introspection is not the "meant unmeanable". To say that a thing is unmeanable is also to mean something. That is, merely admitting that that thing is indescribable or that that is a negation that cannot either be asserted or denied. Introspection cannot be conceived in that manner. Bhattacharyya observes, "Introspection is a subjectivity that is detached both from being and from negation".[99]

This subjectivity must be the "I". The speaking of "I" is neither giving a meaning to "I" nor is making any denials. Bhattacharyya has explained this point in the following passage:

> Introspection is the function of believing or meaning which is not itself meant even as the unmeanable and is, therefore, not actually doubtable. It is just the first person "I", the speaker who is not an object to introspection but is simply

---

[98] K.C. Bhattacharyya, *Studies in Philosophy*, vol. I (editor's introduction), p. xxii.

[99] Ibid., vol. II, p. 81.

the function of speaking. Introspection is not believing in the "I" : it is the "I". . .[100]

Beyond Introspection: In our attempt to bring out the true nature of subject, we have undertaken the discussion of spiritual subjectivity. In that discussion, we have so far arrived at the stage of introspection which is the function of speaking "I". According to Bhattacharyya, man's true nature is exhibited in this I-function. He says, ". . . the self is known in the form 'I am I', which is an analytic self-identity".[101] The true subject is expressed in the spoken word "I" because the spoken word "I" is the best expression of subjectivity. In this sense, man alone may be called a subject. It is in terms of subjectivity that man's nature can be expressed. The best expression of man will be in the form of pure-subjectivity. Therefore, it is expressed in the spoken word "I". In his *Studies in Vedānta,* while commenting upon the Vedāntic conception of self, Bhattacharyya says that waking life, dream, dreamless sleep and ecstasy are attempts to represent gradation of existence in terms of subject–object.

Now, we come to the central point that the subject is what intends himself by the word "I". It may be variously named. It may be called man or self, or subject or introspection. It is a sort of a self-intuition and yet it is self-revealing and self-expressing. It is not, in any way, the understanding of the meaning of the word "I". The word only reveals it to different selves.

But this should not create the impression that Bhattacharyya has reduced subject almost to the status of naught. Bhattacharyya observes, "It is not unmeanable in the sense that it presents no problem of meaning".[102] It is not the

---

[100] Loc. cit.

[101] K.C. Bhattacharyya, *Studies in Philosophy,* vol. I, p. 195.

[102] K.C. Bhattacharyya, *Studies in Philosophy,* vol. II, p. 83.

understanding of the meaning of the word "I". First, the self is not an object of knowledge. Second, it has no meaning content. It is not an object of knowledge because it is self-revealing. He says, "My self-consciousness is not the understanding of the meaning of the word 'I' — the word only reveals it to another".[103] It has no meaning content because it has no "rigidity" or "fixity" or "distinctness of meaning" attached to it. No two persons would use the word "I" of the same thing. In case of any awareness having a meaning-content, there is the possibility as has been shown previously of the same word being used for the same thing by two persons at the same time. All such persons who know that particular meaning content may use the same word for the same meaning. That is not the case with "I". Everybody uses it in his own particular sense.

When we further analyse the introspection of the subject as "I", we find that "possible introspection" or "actual introspection" is implicitly social. The spoken word "I" has also a reference to some hearer because it is self-revealing to others. Bhattacharyya says:

> Neither self-knowing nor other-knowing is through thinking or the meaning of the word and both might be called "intuition" in this negative sense. There are thus two cases — self-intuition with other-intuition implicit in it and other-intuition with self-intuition implicit in it.[104]

The self-intuition with other-intuition means that the subject in expressing itself in "I" is self-evidencing to others. This possibility of the subject's reference to others takes us to a very subtle and important consideration — there is the possibility of man's transcendence of this stage of subjectivity as well. It is a fact that man's true nature is expressed in this

[103] K.C. Bhattacharyya, *Studies in Philosophy*, vol. II, p. 84.

[104] Loc. cit.

stage of subjectivity. It also implies a possibility of the transcendence of this stage — which is still an unrealized possibility of subjectivity in the realization of which lies the ultimate human destiny.

This possibility of the subject going beyond his I-consciousness can be analysed still further. Man in expressing himself to others, is also aware that the other self is aware of him. Likewise, the other self is aware that the former self is aware of him. Now, it can be said that the former self is aware that the other is aware that he (the former self) is aware of him (the second self). That shows that he can conceive of a possible introspection beyond his actual introspection. Here, Bhattacharyya arrives at the same conclusion by analysing, what he calls, "the illusion of the subjective state". Therefore, the subject does have the possibility of going beyond his introspection.

Bhattacharyya arrives at the same conclusion in a different way also. If we examine the various grades of subjectivity carefully, we would notice that in each stage, there is an inherent demand to go beyond that stage. Up to the stage of reason, the object appears as alien to the subject, which necessitates a transition to the next stage of intuition. Intuition is free from every thought-content and every meant-content. Intuition is also free from the felt-content. The introspective subject is free from felt-content but it is not complete freedom. At the level of introspection, "I-consciousness" persists. In spiritual consciousness, this I-consciousness should vanish. Therefore, even in the introspective level, there is a demand for self-transcendence. This demand is fulfilled when intuition arises. Bhattacharyya has made this point clear when he says:

> The introspective subject is, indeed, free from this being or possible objectivity and is thus freedom itself but it is still a distinct individual though only unconsciously. It knows itself not as itself but as a distinct subject that

> is only possibly identical with itself. It is thus aware of a demand to know this subject as actually itself, to annul its possible distinction from itself and, therefore, also its actual distinctness through the word "I". The demand is for the intuition of the subject as absolute freedom.[105]

Subject as Freedom

The legitimate destiny of human being, according to Bhattacharyya, is self-transcedence or the realization of subject as freedom. The fulfilment of human destiny lies in the realization of the Absolute or utter freedom. According to Bhattacharyya, man cannot realize utter freedom on rational plane. Reason moves in the realm of duality between content and consciousness. This duality can be resolved in higher consciousness. The higher consciousness is spiritual realization of pure-subjectivity. Freedom can be realized when the subject is completely dissociated from the object. In the states of bodily subjectivity and psychic subjectivity, there is a definite connection with the object that is meant. When man enters the realm of spiritual subjectivity, this connection is transcended. It is seen that there is no connection with the object as meant even in feeling, which is the first and the lowest expression of spiritual subjectivity. At the stage of feeling, if there is any reference to meaning, it is only to meaning as felt. This shows that "spiritual", according to Bhattacharyya, means detachment from the objective. The cult of the subject involves dissociation of the subject from the object. The subject is self-evident. Bhattacharyya observes:

> The intuited subject is not only revealed but revealing: it is directly known as self-expressing in the spoken word I without being meant by I.[106]

---

[105] K.C. Bhattacharyya, *Studies in Philosophy*, vol. II, p. 88.

[106] Loc. cit.

Spiritual consciousness is fundamentally different from rational knowledge. Spiritual consciousness transcends both meant-content and felt-content. Spiritual life lies in "inwardness". The objects and animals of the world do not have any "inwardness". The inner or conscious life of man is much more fundamental and basic than his outward life. Bhattacharrya says that man, in the way of the realization of his true nature, steadily moves away from the external and objective to the inner and subjective. This progress toward inner life has been given a name "spiritual progress". Spiritual progress implies the realization of the subject as free. The demand is for the intuition of the subject as absolute freedom. Freedom lies in dissociation of the subject from the object.

Bhattacharyya believes that freedom is the basic nature of man. Pure freedom, which has no definite content, is the goal of man. In intuitive experience or spiritual consciousness, man gets awareness of freedom from all "contents". He realizes a state of freedom in intuitive awareness of the subject as free from the object. Bhattacharyya's account of the progression of man is an account of the gradual realization of freedom. While discussing Kant's view as freedom and morality, Bhattacharyya thinks about two kinds of freedom, the freedom of the elective will, which is more or less the freedom of choice, and the noumenal freedom. The noumenal freedom characterizes the true nature of man. Man has got power to realize the indefinite. Reason cannot realize the Absolute. Intuition transcends reason and resolves the duality between content and consciousness. Man has got power to go beyond reason and realize the Absolute in intuition.

The possibility of self's transcendence of the introspective self shows that man's destiny lies in the realization of that possibility. The subject as "I" is, somehow, aware of an urge, almost an absolute demand, to go beyond itself. This shows that in the satisfaction of that demand, he will attain his final status. To make it more clear, Bhattacharyya makes a distinction between "subject being free" and "subject as freedom". According to him, subject as freedom is the destiny of man. This sort of freedom can be attained by the denial of "I" or subject. Bhattacharyya observes, "I am never positively conscious of my present individuality, being conscious of it as what is or can be outgrown . . .".[107] By "subject being free," it is meant that there is a relation between individual and his freedom. The individual seems to be aware of his freedom. This awareness points to a state that is beyond individuality. In the final stage of subject as freedom, freedom does not belong to subject. In the words of Bhattacharyya, ". . . freedom . . . is de-individualized . . .".[108] In this state, subject and freedom are not related to each other. Subject itself is freedom and freedom is the subject. It is complete freedom. That is the final stage of subjectivity. Here, the I-consciousness vanishes. The individual subject of "I" is negated. The true subject is unrelated and absolute. There is no awareness now of an actual introspector or even of a possible introspector. This is what Bhattacharyya calls, "a de-individualized freedom" or "the subject as absolute freedom". The negation of "I" leads to the real and transcendental subject. In the introspective stage, man has an awareness of freedom from all content — meant or felt. In the final stage of subjectivity, this consciousness is no longer there. There is freedom without any consciousness of it.

This may be remembered that the final stage of subjectivity — the stage of the subject as absolute freedom — is only a possiblity to be realized. Man, with his present capacities, cannot have an idea of this stage, because this is not yet an actual stage of his subjectivity. In a sense, this stage is completely indefinite, because it is beyond comprehension.

[107] K.C. Bhattacharyya, *Studies in Philosophy*, vol. II, p. 92.

[108] Loc. cit.

Bhattacharyya says that "what is neither contemplated in the objective attitude, nor understood subjectively in the enjoying attitude"[109] can only be the self-revealing subject to which no attitude is possible.

Spiritual consciousness cannot give us any idea of the "subject as freedom". This is possible only in a transcendental consciousness. In spiritual consciousness, there is enjoying consciousness of "I". At this stage, individuality is not completely transcended. There is a relation between subject as free and freedom itself. In transcendental consciousness, "I" is negated. In this stage, even the enjoying of consciousness "I" or subject is negated. There remains pure-consciousness. Man is the inner subjective self that expresses itself in the speaking of "I". The subject always strives to realize the stage of complete freedom which is its legitimate destiny.

[109] K.C. Bhattacharyya, *The Subject as Freedom*, p. 58.

4

Sarvepalli Radhakrishnan (1882–1975)

Reason: Its Nature and Function

REASON is an essentially human phenomenon. It distinguishes human existence from the rest of living creation. Reason is the capacity to use universal concepts and in this respect man alone can claim reason. In the absence of reason, he cannot abstract and formulate scientific principles of universal nature. S. Radhakrishnan tries to use the word "reason" in a wider sense. According to him, reason is not mere abstract or formal in nature, but it is higher and synthetic. He undertakes the task of transforming the faculty of reason into something fuller and richer than is ordinarily connoted by the term intellect. Reason operates through the whole of mind. It is not one faculty along with others. Radhakrishnan observes:

> But reason is not a faculty co-ordinate with others. It is the whole mind in action, the indivisible root from which all other faculties arise.[1]

He also draws a distinction between reason and intellect. According to him, the mind as a whole can know things which are beyond the purview of intellect. Intellect is abstract and partial, but reason is comprehensive and synthetic.

---

[1] S. Radhakrishnan, *An Idealist View of Life*, p. 134.

The term "reason" has derived from the Latin word *ratio.* Its synonym German is *Vernunft*. For Kant, it is a specific mental faculty, distinct from sensibility and understanding. Radhakrishnan thinks that reason is superior to understanding or intellect. It is a sort of contemplation. Reason is such a principle which admits the distinction but also apprehends the underlying identity. According to Hegel as well as Radhakrishnan, reason is the principle of the identity of opposites. It comprehends the object as distinct from the subject, yet it unifies them. Here, intellect is understood as analytic or discursive faculty of human mind and reason as a synthetic one. This distinction bears a close resemblance to Hegel's "speculative reason" and theoretical reason. Speculative reason differentiates as well as assimilates, whereas theoretical reason abstracts and analyses. Theoretical reason is analytic, whereas speculative reason is synthetic. Whitehead has also mentioned two functions of reason in his book, *The Function of Reason*. He makes a significant distinction between practical reason and speculative reason. Practical reason operates for our pragmatic purposes and speculative reason operates in logic and mathematics. Here, it may be pointed out that Whitehead is not conscious of the deeper and richer meaning of reason as we find in Paul Tillich, Sri Aurobindo, K.C. Bhattacharyya and S. Radhakrishnan. Reason of Whitehead remains confined to technical or finite level and does not extend to ontological or higher level of human knowledge.

Radhakrishnan does not agree with Hegel's view that the "real is rational". He makes departure from Hegel and his followers in so far as they ". . . make thought not merely revelatory but constitutive of reality".[2] One may arrive at this point when one follows the rationalist procedure to its logical

---

[2] S. Radhakrishnan, *An Idealist View of Life*, pp. 118-19.

end. "For some Hegelians, if not for Hegel", observes Radhakrishnan, "thought alone, in and by itself, is the creative of all existence. Reality becomes thought incarnate, the idea made flesh."[3] He holds that reality is something more than thought and that it cannot be apprehended by thought in entirety. In order to have a direct and fuller comprehension, of reality, one has to transcend reason and attain a higher level of knowledge or spiritual comprehension, called intuition or *aparokṣānubhūti*. Though reason is a higher activity of mind, intellect is formal and abstract. Yet, we find that reason is not free from objectivity. Intuition is a subjective experience. It is a higher source of knowledge than reason. Reason does not give immediate knowledge. Reason works under the limitations of senses and categories of mind, whereas intuition is free from all these influences. Intuition is integral knowledge which absorbs sense-experience and reason, and transcends their limitations. Intuition is the activity of the whole being. Radhakrishnan says:

> The intuition which is an activity of the whole being cannot be gained by mere intellectual effort, though it is equally true that it cannot be gained without it. Intellectual inaction seems to be the prelude to the intuitive flash. To allow the non-intellectual and yet rational part of our mind to play on the object, relaxation is necessary.[4]

Intuition is the very basis of reason. Reason is not discarded but thoroughly subordinated to intuition. In the philosophy of Radhakrishnan, words like reason, intellect and logic are used in dual sense, as excluding and including intuition. Arapura, very significantly, observes:

> Apart from the context, there is another very simple but sure

[3] S. Radhakrishnan, *An Idealist view of Life*, p. 119.

[4] Ibid., p. 141.

> test for finding out the sense in which he uses these words, which is this: if he uses them with approval then the sense is inclusive, if with disapproval, it is exclusive. It looks like an oversimplification, but in fact it is a good rule. Sometimes these words are used not merely as implying intuition but as forms of intuition.[5]

Now, it is clear from the above discussion that when reason is used by Radhakrishnan as including intuition, it is certainly ontological reason of Tillich and higher reason of Sri Aurobindo.[6] In case, it excludes intuition, it is no better than technical reason or finite reason. It may also be pointed out that there is no opposition between reason and intuition in his philosophy. He makes it very clear that the seeming opposition remains between intellect and intuition and not between reason and intuition.

Reason functions within the limits of time–space and other mental categories. Like Kant and the Vedānta, Radhakrishnan believes that reason cannot fathom the depth of reality. Reason plays a very important role in man's life and is necessary for knowledge of man and the world. It also enables man to realize the limits of the phenomena and makes him aware of reality or the transcendent. But it is inadequate in so far as it fails to realize the transcendent or the absolute. The inadequacy of reason is something which he had recognized from his early days, even when he was extolling it in his early works like *The Reign of Religion*. But the growing tendency of distrust becomes quite evident in his book: *An Idealist View of Life*. In his *Indian Philosophy*, he writes:

> To the concrete life of experience our intellects are quite inadequate. Nay, they are made for each other, practically the parallel manifestations of one process. If Śaṅkara regards

---

[5] J.G. Arapura, *Radhakrishnan and Integral Experience*, p. 63.

[6] See pp. 34-39 of the present book.

> intellect as not the highest mode of man's consciousness, it is because the completed world of intellect still leaves us with a riddle. The completed world of logic is not the completed world of life and experience. The triumph of thought is the triumph of the concrete, but the most concrete thought is abstract in the sense that it is incapable of apprehending reality as it is.[7]

According to Bergson, conceptual analysis yields not the component parts of the object but its varied expressions. It does not give us a split sunset which has its own beauty, but a conceptual notation that it has qualities of gold, light, etc. A set of qualities is not a sunset. We really persuade ourselves that by setting concepts besides concepts, we are in a position to reconstruct the whole of the object with its parts. It is a wrong notion that we can form a faithful representation of duration by setting in line the concepts of unity, multiplicity, continuity, finite or infinite divisibility, etc. Reason ascertains what is essential and unique in the reality. The concepts laid side by side never actually give us more than an artificial reconstruction of the object of which they can only symbolize certain general and impersonal aspects. It is, therefore, useless to believe that with them we can grasp a reality of which they represent only shadow. Radhakrishnan remarks:

> Partial notations are not real parts. If the conceptual analysis gave us real parts, then perhaps we might try to fit them together so as to obtain the original object but such a procedure is impossible with a mere notation. Intellect finds it easy to distinguish and separate, but when it synthesizes it is artificial in its methods and results. It gives us a patchwork and a harmony.[8]

Bergson contends that reason objects as static and, therefore,

---

[7] S. Radhakrishnan, *Indian Philosophy*, vol. II, pp. 523-24.

[8] S. Radhakrishnan, *An Idealist View of Life*, pp. 107-08.

dead. Concepts remain the same for ever. For instance, a flower may blossom and fade away, but the idea of flower is a permanent concept. The concept, obtained by reason, cannot do justice to the changing things. To comprehend motion, it tries to assemble states of rest; to comprehend life, it tries to catch fixed units of laws. Reason operates on immobile and the lifeless. As such *elan vital* of Bergson, which is fluid and living, cannot be fully grasped by reason. Reason is viewed as giving us partial and imperfect knowledge of reality, but according to Bergson, it has no ontological or metaphysical significance. According to Bradley, reason separates the "what" from the "that" and, then by a kind of rational synthesis, tries to restore the unity of the two. It may be mentioned that no amount of conceptual synthesis can restore the original integrity of reality. Thus, reason is not the primary or original source of knowledge. It works on the materials supplied by sense-experience. Hence, if any view of reality is to be based on rational cognition, it would have to presuppose not only reason but sense-experience also. Reason is only an aspect of life. Feeling, conation, etc. are other equally important aspects. A complete comprehension of reality requires a satisfaction of all these aspects of life. Radhakrishnan observes:

> The phenomena of life cannot be squeezed into the rubrics of reason. Life eludes logic. Philosophy must be intuitive while science may be intellectual.[9]

Reason gives external knowledge of an object. In other words, it approaches an object from outside. To know a thing by way of its likeness to something else is to know it in relation to that other thing. It is also to know it in relation to the interest. It means that every concept or class represents a "point of view". For example, the publisher's concept of "the thesis" is a commodity having good or bad sale after publication. He

---

[9] S. Radhakrishnan, *The Reign of Religion*, p. 193.

does not pretend to know "thesis" as it is, but only in relation to certain interest. A publisher is not interested with the intrinsic, but with the market value of the "thesis". But, for scholars, it has got its intrinsic value. They view it as it is. So, this brings us to conclude that reason clings to certain interest and gives a relative and not an absolute knowledge of objects.

Further, knowledge obtained by reason is abstract and partial. Any point of view is one among many possible points of view. If the truth is obtained from any one of them, it is likely to be a part of the whole truth. A scientist may conceive a rose as a flower from the point of view of a botanist. But for a man of aesthetic sense, it may be a beautiful piece of decoration and a thing of joy. To a small kid, it may be a patch of colour. But rose is all of these things and something more. Any one of these concepts gives incomplete knowledge of the rose.

Reason analyses a whole into parts. It cannot restore the living whole. Radhakrishnan observes that reason, ". . . cuts out cross-sections of this flow, sharpens their outlines and solidifies their contents".[10] Reason distorts and mutilates reality. Reality is required to be grasped without the intervention of formulas construed by reason. Reason cannot grasp reality as it is. It can only arrest it, break it up, schematize it. Reason reconstructs only a symbolic image of the real. The essence of things escapes the grasp of reason. He observes:

> Intellect gives us interpretations, formulas and symbols, and not the experiences or the objects symbolized. It is the function of a sign to signify, but for this it need not resemble or reproduce the thing signified. Its function is only to symbolize and not to photograph.[11]

Reason struggles hard to know the real, to seek the truth, but

[10] S. Radhakrishnan, *The Reign of Religion*, p. 154.

[11] Ibid., p. 199.

it can attempt to know the real only by relating it to some thing other than itself. The real is neither true nor false. But in our knowledge, we attribute this or that characteristic to it. All knowledge, whether perceptual or conceptual, attempts to reveal reality in a limited, partial and symbolic way. Radhakrishnan contends that the limitations of reason is due to its dualistic and existential attitude. Reason bifurcates subject and object, and views them separately. This difficulty is solved by a higher mode of consciousness known as intuition (*aparokṣānubhūti*). Intuition transcends the limitations of reason and views things in its integral whole. Intuition gives a specific answer to the confusions arising from the "relativity of knowledge". It dispenses with points of view. Radhakrishnan contends that above reason, there is intuition which springs from the spiritual level. Intuition resolves the conflict of reason and fathoms the depth of being by entering into its heart.

Intuition

It has been shown in the preceding pages that reason of Radhakrishnan is equivalent to ontological reason of Paul Tillich and intellect can be used in the sense of technical reason. Reason used in ontological sense is more than discursive reasoning. Intellect may appear to be at conflict with intuition but reason prepares the ground for intuitive grasp of being. Reason finds its fulfilment in intuitive knowledge. In intuitive experience, ". . . feelings are fused, ideas melt into one another, boundaries broken and ordinary distinctions transcended".[12] Intuition according to Radhakrishnan, presents a unifying vision of reality. In this respect, it presents a marked contrast to intellectual knowledge which remains involved in multiplicity and fails to have all-embracing knowledge of reality or of the oneness of things. To put in the words of Radhakrishnan:

[12] S. Radhakrishnan, *An Idealist View of Life*, p. 72.

> Intellectual knowledge is a scattered, broken movement of the one undivided infinite life which is all-possessing and ever-satisfied. Intuitive knowing is un-imprisoned by the divisions of space, successions of time or sequence of cause and effect. Our intellectual picture is a shadow cast by the integral knowledge which possesses the object truly and securely.[13]

Reason gives symbolic representation of an object, whereas intuition brings about an identification between subject and object. It penetrates deep into the very nature of things. Intuition probes into the essential nature of being. To quote Radhakrishnan:

> By employing intuitive consciousness we know the object with less distortion and more actuality. We get close to perceiving the things as it is.[14]

According to Radhakrishnan, intuitive knowledge reveals the real and not merely appearances of things. Śaṅkara regards *anubhava* (integral experience) as the supreme spiritual experience. Buddha puts emphasis on *bodhi* (enlightenment). *Buddhi* is not able to apprehend the reality. The knowledge of reality is to be obtained by spiritual efforts. In early Buddhism, *prajñā* (intuitive insight) represents the highest activity of the mind. Murty observes:

> Buddha resolves the conflict by an intuitive perception of the Real as non-dual (*advaya*), the Mādhyamika does it by turning Reason against itself, through the dialectic.[15]

The categories are so many conceptual devices (*vikalpa, prapañca*) by which reason tries to apprehend the real. Reality cannot be categorized and made relative. Reason (*buddhi*) is,

---

[13] S. Radhakrishnan, *The Principal Upaniṣads*, p. 98.

[14] Ibid., p. 96.

[15] T.R.V. Murty, *The Central Philosophy of Buddhism*, p. 9.

therefore, condemned as falsifying the real (*saṁvṛti*). Relativity is the mark of the unreality. Hegel takes mutual dependence or inherent dependence of things as the dialectical necessity of reason working through the opposites, differentiating and, at once, unifying them. For Hegel, mutual dependence is the mark of the real. This is due to the fact that he does not go beyond reason. Reason and the real are identical for Hegel. For the Mādhyamika, dependence marks the lack of inner essence. *Tattva* (the real) is something in itself, self-evident and self-existent. Reason, which understands things through distinction and relation, is a principle of falsity, as it distorts and thereby hides the real. Bradley observes:

> The conclusion to which I am brought is that a relational way of thought — any one that moves by the machinery of terms and relations — must give appearance, and not truth.[16]

The unconditioned or the Absolute can be realized in intuition. Murty observes:

> The unconditioned (*paramārtha*) is transcendent to thought; it is certainly accessible to us in intuition.[17]

Kant is aware of the subjectivity of reason because it gives us only the knowledge of phenomena. He thoroughly exposes the transcendental illusion in his *Dialectic*. Kant in his *Critique of Pure Reason* denies that the illusion can ever disappear. He holds that transcendental illusion does not cease even after it has been detected and its invalidity clearly revealed by transcendental criticism. For the Mādhyamika, the complete disappearance of thought is intuition of the real. To quote Murty, "The death of thought (*dṛṣṭijñāna*) is the birth of *prajñā*, knowledge devoid of distinction (*jñānam advayam*)."[18] The intuition of the

---

[16] F.H. Bradley, *Appearance and Reality*, p. 28.

[17] T.R.V. Murty, *The Central Philosophy of Buddhism*, p. 140.

[18] Loc. cit.

Mādhyamika (*prajñā*) has nothing in common with sensory intuition. Sensory intuition is a transitory act with a limited content. *Prajñā* is not a transitory state. In the words of Murty:

> Intuition must be viewed as that generic and invariable form of knowledge of which other modes of apprehension are species.[19]

Intellectual intuition (*prajñā*) of the Mādhyamika is required to be distinguished from the Bergsonian view of intuition. According to Bergson, reason spatializes things; it freezes reality which is movement, *elan vital* — the life principle. The real can be apprehended by intellectual sympathy. Bergsonian intuition is instinctual in nature. On the other hand, *prajñā* of Mādhyamika is not instinct. It is supra-rational and not infra-rational. According to Radhakrishnan, the *prajñā* (insight) is superior to *vijñāna* (logical knowledge) and *sṁñjñā* (perceptual knowledge).

Kant's *Critique of Pure Reason* prepared the way for voluntarism of Schopenhauer and Nietzsche, the intuitionism of Bergson, the pragmatism of William James and the existentialism of Jean Paul Sartre. Bergson's intuition is a mark of protest against Kant's agnosticism. Radhakrishnan thinks that Kant himself has taught us to use intuition although he did not grasp its full implications for ontological knowledge. As Radhakrishnan observes:

> The self-evidencing and underivative character of intuitions is the lesson of Kant's Philosophy, though he was himself not conscious of it.[20]

"The ideas of reason" which Kant declared to be unknown and unknowable, are for Radhakrishnan, "most objects of logical knowledge but intuited certainties".[21] Logical or rational

---

[19] T.R.V. Murty, *The Central Philosophy of Buddhism*, p. 219.

[20] S. Radhakrishnan, *An Idealist View of Life*, p. 130.

[21] Ibid., p. 134.

knowledge remains valid till intuition arises. Intuition is the knowledge of things-in-themselves. Radhakrishnan designates it in the Vedāntic fashion by the term *aparokṣānubhūti* which stands for the non-sensuous immediate apprehension of reality. Intuition arises from an intimate fusion of mind with reality. It is a sort of awareness of truth of things by identity or coincidence. The knowledge of the self is a definite example of such intuitive apprehension. We are aware of our own self, as we become aware of love or anger directly by a sort of identity with it. Self-knowledge is inseparable from self-existence. It is not right to continue intuition to the narrow region of one's self. It is more comprehensive. It grasps the Ultimate Being or reality.

Radhakrishnan tries to remove certain misgivings that centre round intuition. As he observes:

> Intuition is not used as an apology for doctrines which either could not or would not be justified on intellectual grounds. It is not shadowy sentiment or pathological fancy fit for cranks and dancing dervishes.[22]

It is distinguished from fancy or imagination. Intuition is often confused with irrationalism or anti-rationalism. Bergson and Bradley are being charged of being anti-rational. According to Radhakrishnan, intuition is not anti-rational but supra-rational. It is safe to say that it is non-rational and not anti-rational. Reason and intuition are not inconsistent and incompatible, but are two fundamental ways of knowing and apprehending reality. Radhakrishnan observes:

> Intuition is beyond reason, though not against reason. As it is the response of the whole man to reality, it involves the activity of reason also.[23]

---

[22] S. Radhakrishnan and J.H. Muirhead (eds.), *Contemporary Indian Philosophy*, pp. 486-87.

[23] Ibid., p. 486.

Reason and intuition must co-operate with each other. He states:

> Intuition and intellect are not two opposed methods of grasping reality, for only a comradeship between the two can help us to knowledge of reality as it is.[24]

Reason, emotion and will are the fragmentary manifestations of the spiritual energy of man. Cognitive, conative and emotive aspects of man's life are not cut-off and separated from one another. They flow into one another, modify, support and control each other because all spring from the same spiritual fountainhead. Intuition makes man one with the spirit. It reveals the integral whole into which all the aspects of mind are properly cultivated, developed and merged. The religious life consists in the culture of intuition through the harmonious perfection of emotion, reason and will. Radhakrishnan observes:

> . . . intuition is not crude perception. It is the exercise of consciousness as a whole, it is mind penetrated by the heart, knowledge suffused by feeling, intellect transfigured by emotion. Intuitive experiences are the moments of deepest wisdom which give us glimpses into the ultimate essence, or the whole which is the true and the real. Intuition is always viewed as the perfection of rational experience, since the demand of reason becomes a fulfilment in it.[25]

Radhakrishnan conceives that intuition is the wisdom gained by the whole spirit or integral being which is above mere feeling or reason. In order to know the inner nature of reality, we must resort to the whole personality of which reason is only a part. Radhakrishnan uses intuition in a deeper and integral sense. His main contention regarding intuition is that, it should not be regarded as an alternative to reason. It must

---

[24] S. Radhakrishnan, *The Reign of Religion*, p. 164.

[25] Ibid., p. 188.

not be regarded as a way of knowledge adopted in mystical experience as against philosophical enquiry. Radhakrishnan removes the limitations of Advaita Vedānta by establishing the relationship between intuition and reason on a solid footing. The Vedāntins, following Śaṅkara, created a gulf between reason and intuition by confining reason to the domain of appearances and extending intuition to the realm of reality. P.T. Raju observes:

> But they did not take the trouble to show clearly that this direct experience is a form of knowledge involved in and presupposed by the discursive knowledge of the intellect, and that the intellect is not necessarily opposed to this higher experience but is absorbed in and completed by it.[26]

Though Radhakrishnan gives intuition the supreme place in the realm of knowledge, he hardly uses the same to designate mystical experience. Intuition, according to Radhakrishnan, is integral knowledge, whereas mystical experience cannot be characterized as an "integral experience". Mystical experience is prone to be cut-off from sense-experience and rational experience, whereas intuition includes and transmutes all these experiences and transcends their limitations. However, there is an ambiguity in Radhakrishnan's exposition of the term "intuition". He is himself conscious of this fact. "It is unfortunate," he observes, "that we are obliged to employ the single term 'intuition' to represent scientific genius poetic in sight, ethical conscience as well as religious faith. Though these diverse movements represent the integrated activity of the mind, the activity is oriented towards knowing in some cases, enjoyment or creation in others."[27] Intuition is dynamically continuous with reason. Both intuition and reason

---

[26] P.T. Raju, *Radhakrishnan and Indian Thought* (Tudor Publication), p. 536.

[27] S. Radhakrishnan, *An Idealist View of Life* (see footnote), p. 157.

are valid in their respective fields and one does not preclude the autonomy of the other.

In order to know things in their uniqueness, we must transcend reason and seek fulfilment in intuition. Radhakrishnan emphasizes the fact that intuition transcends reason, it does not reject it. He thinks that intellect, which is discursive reason, and reason, which is synthetic in nature, must be linked and integrated in intuition. Thus, Radhakrishnan's conception of intuition is rightly called by Arapura as "integral experience".[28] George P. Conger also holds that if his theory of intuition as integral experience:

> . . . were to be widely accepted, it would probably need to be freed from any implications of a super-consciousness, and rendered really integral, as a total reaction or total adjustment of the whole man, physiologically as well as psychologically and/or spiritually, to the total situation confronting him.[29]

It is not correct to exalt intuition at the cost of other modes of knowledge. It is a wrong notion that mind is a conglomeration of separate faculties. The human mind "does not function in fractions. We need not assume that at the sense-level, there is no work of intuition or at the level of intuition, there is not the work of intellect. When intuition is defined as integral insight, the suggestion is that the whole mind is at work in it."[30] We find similar expression when Radhakrishnan says:

> The mind of man does not function in fractions. It cannot be split up into a few sharply defined elements, as the intellect, the emotion and the will.[31]

---

[28] J.G. Arapura, *Radhakrishnan and Integral Experience* (Preface), p. vii.

[29] George P. Conger, *Radhakrishnan's World* (Tudor Publication), p. 105.

[30] S. Radhakrishnan, *Reply to Critics*, pp. 790-91.

[31] S. Radhakrishnan, *The Hindu View of Life*, p. 24.

The purpose of the above citations is to emphasize the totality of the knowing process. Knowing process is one whole. One can only theoretically analyse it into different mental components but it cannot be actually split up into such fragments. It becomes fully evident to man in intuitive knowledge which bring into clear light the unitary nature of things. This brings Radhakrishnan's theory of intuition very close to the view of Gestalt psychology that perception is of the whole and not of parts of things.

Radhakrishnan uses intuition in various senses. We will discuss this point in the subsequent pages of this thesis under the heading, "types of intuition". Here, we can understand that in spite of different connotations assigned to the word "intuition", we find that intuition, according to Radhakrishnan, is the integral knowledge. He observes, "Personally I use intuition for integral knowledge".[32] Radhakrishnan emphasizes the all-inclusive and all-comprehensive nature of intuition. "All dynamic acts of thinking," he says, "whether in a game of chess or a mathematical problem, are controlled by an intuitive grasp of the situation as a whole".[33] It make's clear that intuition operates at all levels of human experience. It is involved in simple thinking as well as in the most complex methods of logical reasoning. To quote Radhakrishnan:

> In every logical proof, there is a grasping of the intellectual togetherness as a whole, an intuition of the whole as sustained by the different steps. Not only creative insight but ordinary understanding of anything implies this process.[34]

Intuitive knowledge is the grasping of the whole. In his scheme of knowledge, reason is not relegated to an insignificant place. It enjoys supreme place in its own realm, the realm of

[32] S. Radhakrishnan, *Reply to Critics*, p. 791.

[33] S. Radhakrishnan, *An Idealist View of Life*, p. 117.

[34] Ibid., p. 181.

phenomena or time-conditioned existence. He often uses phrases like "rational intuition" and "integral experience". It implies that reason should not be discredited but harmonized with intuition. If we undermine the role of reason, it will be sheer exaltation of feeling or instinct. Intuition, if not adequately supported by reason, will "lapse into self-satisfied obscurantism".

Hegel might charge intuition as something infra-rational and cut-off from the rest of mental life. Immediate knowledge dispenses with mediation and interdependence. Intuitive knowledge which excludes mediation cannot for Hegel, possess a content which is true. He regards intuition as something unrelated to reason. Radhakrishnan observes:

> Even as the bare category of being requires to be filled with the wealth of the concrete world, so is the intuition to be sustained by the other parts of mental activity. As a warning against views which oppose intuition to intellect and identify it with crude fancy or mere feeling, Hegel's criticism is justified.[35]

It seems that Hegel is prone to miss the integral nature of intuition. His criticism is based on the:

> . . . misapprehension that the intuitive power is something cut-off from the rest of mental life, and the reality which it apprehends is equally abstract and isolated from the rest of existence.[36]

Radhakrishnan is in full agreement with Bergson and many other philosophers in recognizing the value of feeling in integral knowledge. The main difference between Radhakrishnan and Bergson with regard to intuition is that, according to the latter, we feel ourselves away into the world, into the primitive underived stream of life, the *elan vital*, while

---

[35] S. Radhakrishnan, *An Idealist View of Life*, p. 116.

[36] Loc. cit.

the world of objects itself is taken up into one's own self, going by the former. For Bergson, it is the life-force of the universe that persists through changes, being the very soul of change itself. For Radhakrishnan, it is the self that persists. This is the fundamental difference between Radhakrishnan and Bergson. For the point of similarities, we find that both tend to agree to the directness, objectivity and authority of intuition.

While Bergson subordinates the passive and receptive side of the experience to the active and the dynamic, and finds the completion and consummation of it in voluntary participation in the onward creative movement of the *elan vital*, while going by the former Radhakrishnan finds its consummation in the sense of rest and salvation that come with the consciousness of unity with the whole, as something beyond the reach of time and movement. Radhakrishnan differs with Bergson for his anti-intellectual bias. In his book, *The Reign of Religion*, he joined the issue with Bergson. His critical attitude to Bergson was softened in his later work, *An Idealist View of Life*. Bergson emphasizes life-force rather than the self as the essential reality of consciousness. Bergson is not taking sufficient consideration of the self-conscious self in his doctrine of intuition. His intuition is of vital level, whereas Radhakrishnan's intuition originates from spirit. In *Time and Free-will* and *Creative Evolution*, Bergson seems to suggest that the knowledge of reality, as revealed by intuition, is that of a pure flow, of a spontaneous movement, to which Bergson has given the name, "Time". But this is far from integral experience what Radhakrishnan suggests by the term intuition. In pure flow, there is no integration at all. There is no cohesion at all between what goes before and what comes after. Bergson points out that in his philosophy for life implies some stability and some cohesion. We see that integral experience remains vague in Bergson's philosophy, whereas in Radhakrishnan, it assumes clear-cut and central-meaning of intuition.

Further, it may be pointed out that intuition, being the faculty of human knowledge has got certain limitations. But, its limitation does not undermine its bright aspect and successful operation in empirical as well as ontological knowledge. It is generally said that intuition is subjective and personal. It lacks public character. It is an incommunicable experience. Radhakrishnan observes:

> It transcends expression even while it provokes it. It is just what it is and not like anything else. There is no experience by which we can limit it, no conception by which we can define it.[37]

Conceptual substitutes for ineffable experiences are inadequate. They are product of rational thinking. Radhakrishnan holds, "Any attempt to describe the experience falsifies it to an extent".[38] Intuition also bears the stamp of individuality. Radhakrishnan observes, "If individuality is lost all is lost".[39] It is also said that intuitive knowledge is unverifiable and incommunicable. Logical positivism holds that true knowledge is what can be verified in terms of sense experience. It may be pointed out that unverifiability and incommunicability simply mean that intuitive experience cannot be adequately explained in terms of sense-experience or categories of thought. It has been described by men of the deepest insight as, ". . . self-established (*svatassiddha*), self-evidencing (*svasaṁvedya*), self-luminous (*svayam-prakāśa*)".[40] Far from being of doubtful authenticity, intuition can give "pure comprehension, entire significance, complete validity".[41] It may be objected, what proof can we offer for the validity of

---

[37] S. Radhakrishnan, *An Idealist View of Life*, p. 75.

[38] Ibid., p. 76.

[39] S. Radhakrishnan, *Religion and Society*, p. 77.

[40] S. Radhakrishnan, *An Idealist View of Life*, p. 73.

[41] Loc. cit.

intuition? Radhakrishnan's answer is that since intuitive knowledge is proved on our pulse, and it is a matter of faith, Radhakrishnan remarks:

> Intuitive knowledge is proved on our pulses. It is the only kind of absolute knowledge. It is possible only when the individual is fully alive and balanced. We can see truly only when our inner being is harmonized. Intuition is the ultimate vision of our profoundest being.[42]

Ordinarily, we cannot deny it. Intuitive knowledge, being self-knowledge, is itself a legitimate proof of its authenticity. Radhakrishnan observes:

> The proof of the validity of the intuitive principles is somewhat similar to Kant's proof of apriori elements. We cannot think them away. Their opposites are inconceivable. We cannot disbelieve them and remain intellectual. They belong to the very structure of our mind.[43]

Thus, the validity of intuitive knowledge, according to Radhakrishnan, cannot be questioned. It is the supreme knowledge. It is, according to him, "higher than discursive process from which it issues and on which it supervenes".[44]

Intuition: Śaṅkara and Radhakrishnan

Śaṅkara's "Advaitism is a system of great speculative daring and logical subtlety".[45] His doctrine equals in rank to Plato and Kant, and has won him "a place among the immortals". Śaṅkara's contribution is important in the growth and development of Indian thought. Whitehead in his book, *Process*

---

[42] S. Radhakrishnan, *The Idealist View of Life*, p. 114.

[43] Ibid., p. 123.

[44] S. Radhakrishnan, *The Spirit in Man*, p. 486.

[45] S. Radhakrishnan, *Indian Philosophy*, vol. II, p. 445.

and Reality, speaking of Plato, says that the safest general characterization of the European philosophical tradition is that it consists of series of footnotes to Plato. Likewise, we can say that the post-Śaṅkara Vedānta consists of a series of footnotes to Śaṅkara. Even the theistic schools of Vedānta which show great hostility to Śaṅkara also portray a mighty impact of Śaṅkara's thought, if not positively, at least negatively. This impact of Śaṅkara is clearly witnessed even in the philosophies of the recent and contemporary thinkers like Sri Aurobindo, Bhattacharyya and Radhakrishnan.

Radhakrishnan's intuition is akin to *anubhava* of Śaṅkara. Both characterize it as *aparokṣānubhūti*. Nevertheless, Radhakrishnan's intuitive experience differs from the *anubhava* of Śaṅkara. Radhakrishnan establishes integral relationship between reason and intuition, whereas Śaṅkara seems to create a gulf between the two by confining reason to the domain of illusion and extending intuition to the realm of reality. Radhakrishnan's theory of knowledge implies certain significant departures from Śaṅkara's doctrine of identity of knowledge, knower and known. It also marks a notable difference about the nature of self-evidence as presented in Śaṅkara's Advaita Vedānta. Radhakrishnan takes integral experience both in the ontological as well as in the epistemological senses; for, according to him, integral experience is not only a mode of knowing but also a mode of being. Being is to be taken in the sense of both knower and the known. Integral experience is that of the reality as a whole, which involves the knower as well as the known. Integral experience is the fullest comprehension of reality in all its dimensions — the individual, the universal and the transcendent, the cosmic and the supra-cosmic, and the time-conditioned and the timeless existence. The integral reality as conceived by Radhakrishnan transcends the duality of transcendence and immanence without rejecting either of the two. Śaṅkara's thought shows a powerful tendency to reject the phenomena ultimately speaking and to proclaim the truth of the non-dual Absolute which is realized in and through intuition. Reason in Śaṅkara's view comprehends phenomena while intuition realizes the non-dual and transcendent Absolute. No close link can be established in his philosophy between intuition and reason and, thus, intuitive experience of Śaṅkara cannot legitimately be called integral as it fails to comprehend phenomena. But, Radhakrishnan's intuitive experience can be called integral as it attempts to comprehend Reality in all its dimensions as has been stated above.

The question of integral experience pre-supposes the "unity of being". The unity of being includes two things — (1) the unity of the Absolute "beyond" and the universe, and (2) the unity of "the other" and the self or object and subject. The "beyond" implies a contrast with the world; the "other" implies a contrast with the self of man. It may be noted that what Radhakrishnan sets out to do is not to bind "the beyond" and the universe together by reducing them both to a common neutral reality and to combine the objective "other" and the subjective self in a common ego. He thinks of the possibility of transcending the duality of transcendence and immanence. He also desires to transcend the duality of objectivity and subjectivity. Radhakrishnan gives a unity of "the beyond" and the universe, and a unity of the "other" and the self. The two aspects are to be regarded as perspectives of the same unity. This unity can only be called by the term "spirit".

Radhakrishnan is not satisfied with any cleavage between the "beyond" and the "universe". He conceives the universe as spirit which connects the "beyond" and the universe in a coherent whole. Now the question is: whether the materiality of the universe is in harmony with the spirituality of the "beyond"? Radhakrishnan thinks that the materiality of the world does not contradict the spirituality of God. As a matter of fact, spirit comprehends matter. To apprehend universe as "matter" is a partial view. In its fullness, the universe or world is the manifestation of the spirit. Thus, spirit is not opposed to matter, rather it includes the latter. This poses a problem. If the universe is essentially spirit, how do we account for its appearance as non-spiritual? If integral experience is the awareness of the universe as harmony, how do we explain the tension and discord existing in the universe? Śaṅkara solves it by negating the universe or world as illusory. Radhakrishnan's position becomes clear from the following lines:

> The world of science and common sense seems so different from freedom of the self. Is it an illusion or is it a reality? Those who are pragmatically inclined take the practical life as the reality and treat spiritual experience as a mere dream, so deep seems to be the division between them. Some of the more careful trace the appearance of the multiple universe to the limitations of human intelligence, *avidyā*, nescience. The human mind being what it is, tries to reconstruct the universe from the intellectual point of view into an organic whole. For the intellect, the unity is only a postulate, an act of faith. For the spirit, the harmony is an experienced reality.[46]

We view things partially because we use reason which is only a part of our self in apprehending the universe. The integral experience will show that the universe is essentially spirit. Then:

> . . . the earth and the sky, the world and animals — all become suddenly strange and wonderful. For our eyes are opened and they all declare the presence of the one supreme. The universe seems to be alive with spirit, aglow with fire, burning with light.[47]

Radhakrishnan makes a distinction between the universe as apprehended by the scientist and as apprehended by the

---

[46] S. Radhakrishnan, *An Idealist View of Life*, pp. 86-87.

[47] Ibid., p. 68.

mystic. The former apprehends only through reason and sense and, therefore, remains on the surface.

> The truth of the universe is not a mathematical equation or a kinematical system or a biological adjustment or an ethical individualism but a spiritual organism.[48]

The view that the universe or world is material seems clear to reason. The world as spirit seems mysterious. But, ". . . this mysterious, unclear and inarticulate knowledge brings us closest to reality".[49] In truth, the pulse of the spirit throbs through nature. In his view, all the grades of being are conscious. It is this fact that underlies our rational and sense-intuition of empirical realities. "All being is consciousness and all consciousness is being".[50] The standpoint of integral experience from which Radhakrishnan proceeds makes his view of nature distinctive. To him, the Absolute is not just the immanent totality of the universe conceived as spirit. It is also "the beyond". The transcendent and the immanent aspects of reality are woven together in his integral knowledge or integral experience.

Radhakrishnan and Rudolf Otto

Otto as well as Radhakrishnan conceive intuitive experience or religious experience as non-rational. Non-rational is neither anti-rational nor irrational but suprarational. Radhakrishnan and Otto, like Tillich and Śaṅkara, tone down the agnosticism of Kant and realize the unknown by non-rational religious experience. According to the Vedāntins, Otto and Radhakrishnan, though the Absolute or Unconditioned is unknowable to reason, yet it is comprehended by the higher modes of experience like "intuition" and "numinous

48 S. Radhakrishnan, *An Idealist View of Life*, p. 247.

49 Loc. cit.

50 S. Radhakrishnan, *The Idealist View of Life*, p. 72.

experience". Radhakrishnan, like Tillich, believes that reason is a limited faculty but its role in religion and theology cannot be minimized.

Religion is profoundly based on experience whether it is intuitive or revelatory. Religious experience, according to Otto and Radhakrishnan, is at its deeper levels, mainly non-rational. In contemporary literature on religion, a distinction is often made between non-rational and rational. In ordinary parlance, non-rational is equated to passion, will, desire and volition. Otto as well as Radhakrishnan take non-rational in the sense of supra-rational and not infra-rational. In his introduction to *The Idea of the Holy*, John W. Harvey, the English translator writes:

> The "feelings" Otto has to explore are, he seeks to show, though a non-rational sort of apprehension, in no sense an anti-rational element in human experience. In religion at its highest, the rational and non-rational are (in a favourite metaphor) intimately woven together.[51]

Religious experience is technically known as "numinous experience" in Otto's thought and "intuitive experience" in Radhakrishnan. These experiences are not irrational. Otto observes:

> The "irrational" is today a favourite theme of all who are too lazy to think or too ready to evade the arduous duty of clarifying their ideas and grounding their convictions on a basis of coherent thought.[52]

Radhakrishnan contends that religious experience is not of the nature of sense-experience or mind. It is supra-rational in nature. The integral religious experience is not based on any empirical source of knowledge whether it is sense-experience

---

[51] Otto Rudolf, *The Idea of the Holy*, p. 10.

[52] Ibid., p. 13.

or reason. These different sources of knowledge cannot give us an integral and all-embracing view of reality. "Intuitive experience" is similar in certain respects to "numinous experience", for both are non-rational, but differ in the sense that the former is integral, while the latter is, in some sense, mystical. Here, it is to be mentioned that intuition can be taken into a lower as well as a higher sense. Radhakrishnan's "intuitive experience" and Otto's "numinous experience" are taken in higher sense and not in the lower or restricted sense. As philosophers of religion, Otto and Radhakrishnan find out the limits of reason and point out its role in religion. Like Kant, Otto and Radhakrishnan seem to be conscious of the limitations of reason, for it is time-conditioned. Kant declared the Absolute to be unknown and unknowable. Reason fails to unveil the nature of reality. Kant's contention gets serious challenge from other thinkers like the Vedāntins. The "unknown" to them is not the unknowable. According to the Vedāntins, Otto and Radhakrishnan, the unknown becomes known through non-rational experience like "intuition" and "numinous experience". Otto, Tillich, Śaṅkara and Radhakrishnan attempt to break through the limits of agnosticism and realize the unconditioned or the unknown by the non-rational religious experience or intuitive experience or revelation. Tillich contends in his book, *Systematic Theology* (vol. I), that reason is limited and suffers from inherent difficulties. But, he does not undermine the role of reason in theology. Reason serves as a pointer to the Holy. Tillich tries to resolve the contradictions of reason in "revelation" which is certainly supra-rational experience. With the Hegelians, Radhakrishnan accepts the value of reason to purge religion of its infra-rational elements, but unlike them, he subordinates reason to supra-rational or intuitive experience.

In spite of the fact that religious experience is non-rational for both Otto and Radhakrishnan , there are striking contrasts in their expositions. Radhakrishnan's intuitive knowledge absorbs sense-experience and reason, whereas Otto's "numinous experience" creates a gulf between the rational and the non-rational, though Otto admits the rational element also in religion along with the non-rational. G.D. Hicks observes in his book, *The Philosophical Bases of Theism,* that Otto's non-rational and the rational as consisting merely of concepts, involve an abstraction which precludes him even from so much as indicating any middle term by which to bring them into union. Otto treats "numinous" as strictly non-rational and it is simply incomprehensible how it could be clothed with the ideas of goodness, mercy and love. H.J. Paton in his book, *The Modern Predicament,* points out that the relation of the non-rational to the rational element in Otto's account of religious experience is precisely the most baffling aspect of it. Otto, on the one hand, speaks of a "unique original feeling response" and the "numinous feeling" as non-rational and non-conceptual. It is the inmost core of religion at all its levels. On the other hand, he attempts to relate this "numinous feeling" to human reason. There seems to be a cleavage between the rational and non-rational in Otto's religious experience. Though Otto and his followers may not accept it, yet we find some justification in this criticism. Since Otto's "numinous experience" is mystical in nature, it is prone to be cut-off from the rational experience. Śaṅkara also fails to reconcile intuition with reason, for the former comprehends reality, the latter gives appearance. Otto's numinous experience is concerned with the category of the "holy" which is "wholly other" and according to Hicks and Paton, Otto undermines the empirical reality of the rational level. Being a mystic by temperament and in his approach, Otto, like Śaṅkara, fails to bridge the gulf between the rational and the non-rational in religious experience. Here, we find a sort of improvement in Radhakrishnan's religious experience, which is intuitive and integral in nature. The integral vision of Radhakrishnan removes, to a great extent, the limitations of non-rational experience of Otto and Śaṅkara.

Otto's religious experience is a sort of feeling which is technically known as "creature feeling". It is the feeling of a creature when he confronts God and experiences the *tremendum*, as Otto says, from the depth of his heart. Creaturefeeling, according to Otto ". . . is the emotion of a creature submerged and overwhelmed by its own nothingness in contrast to that which is supreme above all creatures".[53] This creaturefeeling arises in man only when he confronts God.

According to Otto, religious experience is the experience of the "wholly other". It is the feeling of the creature directed towards God. One confronts the "holy" which is "the wholly other" in his numinous experience. It presents man's most intimate relationship with the Divine, the I–Thou relationship. While the fullness of spiritual being transcends our reason, we are sure that its nature is akin to the highest kind of being; we are aware of in ourselves. Radhakrishnan observes:

> If the real were utterly transcendent to the self of man, it would be impossible for us to apprehend even dimly its presence. We would not be able to say even that it is "wholly other".[54]

This difficulty is solved by Radhakrishnan as he does not believe in any gulf existing between man and the Divine. Radhakrishnan conceives that the self of man is a portion of the Divine and is, thus, one with it. Man is eternally one with the Divine and at the highest level of his spiritual experience has an all-embracing and luminous vision of the Divine. As he puts it:

---

[53] Otto Rudolf, *The Idea of the Holy*, p. 24.

[54] S. Radhakrishnan, *An Idealist View of Life*, p. 81.

> There is in the self of man, at the very centre of his being, something deeper than intellect, which is akin to the supreme.[55]

Otto thinks that "the wholly other" completely transcends man and the world. Radhakrishnan's position in this respect seems to be opposite to that of Otto and no reconciliation seems possible. If "the other" is wholly transcendent to the self, it becomes impossible for us even to say that God is "the wholly other". "Otherness" needs to be absorbed into the self. Self is so conceived as to include itself and "the other", if the sense of "the other" or "numinous awareness" is to be regarded as legitimate. It is true that in spiritual experience as such the polarity between the self and "the other" is felt to be real and valid. But in the higher order of ontological experience, which is here presented as integral experience, it is transcended. Radhakrishnan maintains the position that all knowledge is through identity in which the knower and the known are one. If this position is accepted, the apprehension of "the other" would require that, that which knows it must be identical with it, and so logically speaking "otherness" is cancelled.

Radhakrishnan observes:

> God's revelation and man's contemplation seem to be two sides of one fact . . . There is a real ground in man's deepest being for the experience of reality.[56]

This fact is the apriori basis of all spiritual experience.

> The consubstantiality of the spirit in man and God is the conviction fundamental to all spiritual wisdom. It is not a matter of inference only. In the spiritual experience itself, the barriers between the self and the ultimate reality drop away. In the moment of its highest insight, the self becomes

---

[55] Loc. cit.

[56] S. Radhakrishnan, *The Idealist View of Life*, p. 81.

> aware not only of its own existence but of the existence of the omnipresent spirit of which it is, as it were, a focusing.[57]

This, he feels, is the meaning of the great text of the Upaniṣad, *Tattvamasi* (That art Thou).

Types of Intuition

Determining the types of intuition is an extremely vexing problem because mind does not function in fraction. Sense experience, reason and intuition work together in any mental activity. As such, the problem of intuition has become a complex one. Archie J. Bahm observes, "Intuition is at once simple, extremely simple and complex, infinitely complex".[58] Now the question arises: if intuition is simple, consisting merely in immediacy of apprehension, how can it be at the same time complex? If all intuitions are alike, in being merely immediate, how can there be types of intuition? The question of the types of intuition arises because intuition operates at different stages of human knowledge and apprehends different kinds of objects. According to Bahm, a man is involved in as many kinds of intuition as there are kinds of things apprehended. Thus, the classification of intuition may be complex and various. This results in the use of the term intuition in various senses by the philosophers. J.L. Stocks observes:

> One of the strangest of many strange habits of philosophers, which mark them out of the Ishmaels of the scientific world, is the refusal to agree as to the precise meaning of the word, they may use. No philosopher, it seems, is bound to the definitions given by his predecessors or contemporaries of even the most central terms, each has to define his terms for himself.[59]

---

[57] Loc. cit.

[58] A.J. Bahm, *Types of Intuition*, p. 1.

[59] J.L. Stocks, *Reason and Intuition*, p. 1.

Kant and Croce confine intuition for aesthetic apprehension. Bradley and Śaṅkara use it for higher knowledge. The intuition of Kant and Croce is lower because it is confined to aesthetic and sensory level. The intuition of Śaṅkara and Bradley is a higher one because it is involved in the knowledge of self and Being. The lower and higher intuitions and operate at the infrarational and superational levels, respectively. The higher intuition of Śaṅkara as well as of Bradley is vitiated by a serious defect of keeping away from rational and empirical realities. Radhakrishnan's conception of intuition comprehends the lower as well as higher intuitions and links them in a complete harmony which is called "integral experience". On the one hand, integral experience connects the lower and higher intuitions, on the other, it absorbs different sources of knowledge — sense-experience, reason and intuition — into a harmonious whole.

Browning's Classification of Radhakrishnan's Intuition

In order to have a clear picture of Radhakrishnan's various types of intuition, let us consider Robert Browning's classification of his intuition. Browning has made an exhaustive classification in his article, *Reason and Types of Intuition*. He points out that Radhakrishnan's conception of intuition denotes different meanings and is assailed by certain confusions. He uses it in a number of senses. Prof. Browning observes:

> Sometimes it intimates what cannot be known in other ways; sometimes it names a fuller "realization" of what may be already abstractly known in symbols; sometimes it is attached to the drawing, in the mind of the discoverer, of what will be, after confirmation, a powerful, scientfic generalization; sometimes it denotes a knowledge of individual things in their concreteness; sometimes it is

> referring to unitive knowledge of The One Real. Sometimes it is accenting the dynamism of thinking as against the results; sometimes it is emphasizing a spontaneous dynamism as against movements which may be automatic or mechanical.[60]

The above passage points out that the meaning of intuition in Radhakrishnan's philosophy is extermely vague. The classification of intuition is required so that it may help:

To spot gross importations and misinterpretations, and to fill up lacuna in our account. A wide variety of "intuitions" may be placed under five heads:

(1) Sensory intuition

(2) Rational intuition

(3) Descrying of complex structures of fact and possible fact (including connections between unarticulated logical structures).

(4) Valuational intuition

(5) Integral experience.[61]

Sensory intuition gives the outer characters of objects. It is capable of perception but is innocent of interpretation. Radhakrishnan does not call it true intuition because it is affected and surrounded by sensible phenomena.

Rational intuition conceives about meanings and relations of meanings. These relations are required to be intuited. For instance, in working out a mathematical problem, one gives the product of the multiplication of two numbers of several digits without conscious efforts or application of memorized shortcuts. In a chain of reasoning, intuition comes as a flash.

---

[60] R. Browning, *Reason and Types of Intuition* (Tudor Publication), pp. 177-78.

[61] Ibid., p. 180.

Radhakrishnan does not deny but rather recommends such intuitions. He recognizes them but does not call them true intuitions, for they seem to him to be associated with mechanical and routine operations as against the spontaneous and creative insight of intuition. He appropriately labels it as the "logic of proof".

The third category of intuition is describing of complex structures of fact and possible fact. By this, Browning understands that by the use of intuition "a wealth of unco-ordinated detail falls into proper order and becomes a perfect whole".[62] It is certain that amid much that is entangled and confused, "we have flashes of wondrous insight which appear less the product of reasoning than of revelation".[63] When a region of blurred facts becomes suddenly lit up, illumined, as it were, to what do we owe this enlightenment? Radhakrishnan observes:

> It is due not so much to a patient collection of facts as to a sudden discovery of new meaning in facts that are already well known. Apples had been falling to the ground a long time before Newton worked out the law of gravitation.[64]

The genius discovers the meaning which binds the facts which remain distinct and separate for the ordinary understanding. "It is the intuitive grasp of the dynamic principle which enables one to organize the facts successfully."[65] This category of intuition does not specify the range of what we would like to bring within it. Scientific facts and enquiry relating to them proceeds with hypothesis which is based on intuition. In order to ascertain facts or possible facts, we assume certain hypothesis. Browning gives instances such as, "Is this

---

[62] S. Radhakrishnan, *An Idealist View of Life*, p. 138.

[63] Loc. cit.

[64] S. Radhakrishnan, *The Idealist View of Life*, p. 139.

[65] Loc. cit.

grandfather's lever watch? Is this a time bomb?" The describing or making out such possibilities or hypothesis may be called intuitive. Such intuition apprehends the relevance of the parts in some complicated logical or mathematical consequences.

The fourth category is concerned with valuational intuition. It is related to the intrinsic values of life, such as (a) moral, (b) aesthetic, and (c) religious. Radhakrishnan observes:

> In our ethical life also, intuitive insight is essential for the highest reaches.[66]

Mechanical observance of moral codes or imitations of models will not take us far. Virtue, according to Socrates, is knowledge. It is not merely intellectual knowledge which is teachable but springs from the deeper level of man's being. Radhakrishnan observes:

> It is acquired by the raising of one's mind, the growth of one's consciousness. The deeper a man is rooted in spirit, the more he knows directly.[67]

It means that moral intuition, for Radhakrishnan, is not what is found in routine, mechanical or formalized rational ethics. The certainty of moral judgements springs from the very self. Aesthetic values are also a form of self-expression but the self that is expressed in and through them is not the narrow particular one. Artistic vision bears the mark of individuality. Art is the expression of the whole self, for no two men can ever produce the same work of art. Religion is at its deeper levels an expression of the whole being, a response of the whole personality. Religious insight or experience is not an emotional thrill. It is required to be distinguished from the intellectual view, aesthetic forms and moral valuations.

---

[66] S. Radhakrishnan, *The Idealist View of Life*, p. 155.

[67] Ibid., p. 156.

Integral experience is the fifth type of intuition. It is all-embracing vision of reality in all its dimensions and includes within it and transforms the cognitive, aesthetic, moral and spiritual experiences of man. In integral experience, these are not apprehended in the same way as they are in the normal mental level but they transformed and raised into a higher order of experience.

The above classification is pretty exhaustive but it is not free from ambiguities. Browning seems to be conscious of this fact that there is a "great danger in tearing what may be seamless". But, such a classification helps to differenciate one intuition from another. When we analyse the above classification in the light of Radhakrishnan's usage of intuition, it is found that the first three classifications can be grouped together and may be taken as empirical or lower intuition. The lower intuition works at the empirical level and serves our pragmatic purposes. Radhakrishnan does not deny lower or empirical intuition but confines it to the realm of phenomena. Browning seems to be fully aware that the first three classifications fall under empirical or lower intuition. They do not serve any useful purpose for man's religious and spiritual life. To quote Browning:

> It is likely — that Radhakrishnan never refers to the first two (possibly the first three) as 'intuition'; but even then — in addition to our own ulterior purposes — these will be useful (as perhaps we have already seen) in the way of saying that what our author's intuition is not.[68]

Further, he observes:

> The third is in a doubtful status; perhaps it should be eliminated; on the other hand, we have been inclined to break it into two or three types, to separate intuitions of fact

[68] R. Browning, *Reason and Types of Intuition*, p. 181.

> from intuitions of unarticulated logical connection and from intuition of possible restructuralisations of fact (as the man of practice or the prophet may sense them).[69]

The fourth classification consists of several sub-classes. One of these species is religious insight. It may be objected as to why the fifth — integral experience — is not incorporated in religious insight, instead of being given a separate standing. Radhakrishnan's answer is that continuity between personal religious devotion and mystic experience is at least questionable. But, integral intuition being non-dual gives the complete perceptual intuition.

Browning has worked out in detail the classification of intuition in order to determine the true nature of intuition. His purpose is not to break intuition in severål watertight compartments but to work out what are not intuitions in Radhakrishnan's usage. In brief, the first three divisions have been taken under empirical or lower intuitions. Empirical or lower intuition includes sensory intuition as well as mathematical and logical intuitions. But, it is not successfully operative in the fields of morality and religion. It is pragmatic and effcient in promoting human welfare by way of giving birth to new discoveries in the field of science and technology. The second in valuational intuition which operates in aesthetic, moral and religious spheres. The third one is an integral experience which works at a higher spiritual level. All these various classifications of Radhakrishnan's intuition indicate that his use of this term can be ascertained only in its proper context. Browning designs a name for Radhakrishnan's intuition as "perspectival intuitionism". It seems, we have a sort of relational and perspectival intuitionism. He observes:

---

[69] Loc. cit.

> The perspective may be said to include range or depth. Earlier it was said that some persons have value as their intuitive object; others have God; and others rise to awareness of identity with and in the Absolute.[70]

Keeping in view the classification of Browning, we understand that Radhakrishnan also uses intuition in three different senses — lower, higher and integral. The lower intuition works on sensory level, the higher intuition works on mystical level, and integral intuition connects empirical and mystical levels and gives a comprehensive vision of reality in its totally. It will not be out of place to mention the classification of Radhakrishnan's intuition as made by Arapura. He has also classified Radhakrishnan's intuition under three categories: (i) empirical, (ii) mystical, and (iii) integral experience.

Empirical or lower intuition presupposses two things: (i) the reality with which unity is attained, and (ii) the degree of unity. In empirical or lower intuition, the realities with which the unity is attained, are objects or empirical phenomena. Arapura contends that empirical intuition consists of two types — rational intuition and intuition of feeling. Rational intuition is drawn from the order of conceptualization, while the intuition of feeling from the order of feeling. It may be pointed out that the unities established by empirical intuition are confined to the phenomena.

The second category of intuition is mystical intuition. In mystical intuition, self becomes object of contemplation. It is a kind mystical contemplation of self. Mystical experience is a higher type of intuition which transcends sense experience and reason. In such experience:

> The experience itself is felt to be sufficient and complete. It does not come in a fragmentary or truncated form

[70] R. Browning, *Reason and Types of Intuition*, p. 231.

> demanding completion by something else. It does not look beyond itself for meaning and validity.[71]

It is pointed out that mystical intuition cannot afford to neglect empirical ways of knowing. We realize that empirical intuition. While the former refers to particular matters of fact, the rational and feeling aspects of things, events, relations, structures, etc., while the latter refers to the conditions for knowing them. The self is not a fact among facts, but the truth underlying all facts.

Integral experience is the consummation of empirical or objective and mystical or subjective type of intuition. In other words, subject and object are organically related and integrated. It is fulfilment and completion of all subjective and objective experience in their togetherness and integrity. As such, integral experience is the highest kind of intuitive experience. There are certain differences between mystical intuition and integral experience. In integral experience, we have in place of self the whole person's powers. In place of "Absolute beyond", we have the Absolute conceived as the unity of the beyond and the universe in integral experience. In empirical intuition, we get objectivity or otherness, in mystical intuition, we have got subjectivity or inwardness, but we have got integral and coherent intuitive knowledge which is the central view on intuition in Radhakrishnan's philosophy. Integral experience constitutes the foundation of Radhakrishnan's philosophy and serves as the main principle of its interpretation.

The Application of Reason and Intuition in Science, Art, Ethics and Religion

Reason and intuition operate in each and every sphere of human knowledge. Radhakrishnan tries to show their application in the different fields — science, art, ethics and religion — of

---

[71] S. Radhakrishnan, *An Idealist View of Life*, pp. 72-73.

human activity. He makes a distinction between the inner truth of science, art, ethics and religion, and their outer structures. Reason shapes the outer structures, whereas intuition fathoms the depth of inner truth. Scientific knowledge, artistic experience, ethical consciousness and religious experience are placed under the different grades of human knowledge. There is mutual participation of reason and intuition in the different fields. Science also has a considerable place for flashes of intuition, which illumine new truths and discoveries. Radhakrishnan observes, "Scientific discovery is more like artistic creation in its reaching out after new truth".[72] Art in its perfection merges into ethics. Ethics, at its ultimate point links up with religion. Radhakrishnan points out:

> Strictly speaking, an art independent of morality, which has no roots in our deepest ethical instincts, which does not draw towards the divine in things is not true art.[73]

The art, science, ethics and religion are interconnected since they deal with different aspects of human life and activities. Art and science are not self-contained. Artistic experience and scientific discoveries are valuable not for its formal structure and factual certainty but for its inner meaning. This inner meaning lies in religious insight. Radhakrishnan observes:

> . . . the values of truth, goodness and beauty to a common background, God, the holy, who is both without and within us. The truth we discern, the beauty we feel and the good we strive after is the God we apprehend as believers. While art or beauty or goodness in isolation may not generate religious insight, in their ultimate fusion they lead us to something greater than themselves.[74]

If ethics pretends to stop with itself, it lacks some deeper

[72] S. Radhakrishnan, *An Idealist View of Life*, p. 138.

[73] Ibid., p. 158.

[74] Ibid., p. 159.

content. Ethical consciousness is deeply rooted in religion. There is underlying unity of science, art, ethics and religion. To quote Radhakrishnan:

> The cognitive, the aesthetic and the ethical sides of life are only sides, however vital and significant. The religious includes them all. While science strives to comprehend the law that sustains the universe, while art yearns to reveal the beauty that is worked into the world, while morality struggles to realize the goodness the universe is labouring to achieve, while in their perfection these different aspirations merge into one another, in the process itself, each seems to be complete, though it is true that true art or philosophy or morality cannot be had without all of them in some degree.[75]

Let us consider, in brief, the application of reason and intuition in different fields of human life such as science, art, ethics and religion.

SCIENCE

The application of reason and intuition in the field of science has been much confused due to the misunderstanding that science is solely a matter of observation and reason. It is true that scientific laws are ascertained and determined by reason and higher mathematical knowledge, but their discovery is also often the result of some flashes of intuition. It is the vision of a scientist which prompts scientific discovery. All creative work in science is inspired by intuitive experience and not by dry reasoning. Radhakrishnan states:

> The great scientific discoveries are due to the intuitive genius of the creative thinkers and not the plodding processes of the intellect.[76]

---

[75] S. Radhakrishnan, *An Idealist View of Life*, p. 158.

[76] Ibid., p. 138.

The application of reason and intuition in scientific knowledge presupposes consideration of two aspects:

(i) limitations of scientific knowledge

(ii) intuitive element in scientific knowledge.

In scientific knowledge, the observer is independent of the object. Scientific knowledge gives us only the formal structure of physical existence and not the whole truth. Hence, it is inadequate and limited knowledge. Radhakrishnan states:

> . . . the knowledge obtained by science through the intellectual processes of observation, experiment and inference is inadequate. It gives us only the formal structure of existence, especially physical existence, which can be represented by mathematical equations. Even with reference to physical nature, scientific knowledge does not give us the inner truth. The measurable aspects are not the only ones. We may measure the current of electricity, but we do not know what electricity is. The real being of physical nature does not consist in the abstract structure which science succeeds in representing, but in its inner dynamism.[77]

The inadequacy of scientific knowledge becomes more evident when we proceed to have a look at the conscious processes of living organism. Scientific knowledge gives us quantitative measurements of events in the world. Its process is repetitive and reproductive. Its study is selective and limited.

Intuitive Elements in Scientific Knowledge

The approach of science is objective. In its craze to be absolutely objective, accurate and certain, science ignores the subjective aspect. Reason is used as the tool of objective knowledge. But in spite of its objective approach, science also has its own moments of intuitive illumination. Radhakrishnan observes:

---

[77] S. Radhakrishnan, *Reply to Critics*, pp. 791-92.

> Amid much that is entangled and dark, we have flashes of wondrous insight which appear less the product of reasoning than of revelation. A new law in mathematics is just as much a bit of spontaneous intuition as is a composition in music by Mozart.[78]

Mathematical calculations are sometimes matters of intuitive flash. To relate one number with another and prove the theorem of geometry is a matter of reason. The feeling of mathematical beauty, of the harmony of numbers and forms of geometric elegance, is certainly not possible through reason.

The successful activity of intuition requires a previous study and assimilation of a multitude of facts and laws. We may take it that great intuitions arise out of the depth of thinking and reasoning. Intuition discovers whereas reason proves it. The art of discovery must not be confused with the logic of proof. Radhakrishnan observes, "We forget that we invent by intuition though we prove by logic."[79]

Sometimes, the act of discovery is associated with imagination. As a matter of fact, imagination helps frame hypothesis. Hypothesis is a contemplation of non-existent situations and a review of alternatives. In imagination, there is no assertion but a sort of conjecture. Croce identifies the activity responsible for hypothesis with artistic imagination. But an illuminating hypothesis is not the work of mere uncontrolled imagination. Radhakrishnan says:

> Imagination unvivified by intuition, imagination which is day-dreaming, fancy, reverie or guesswork will not help us to light upon the truth except by accident.[80]

There is a difference between mere guess, which is the work

---

[78] S. Radhakrishnan, *An Idealist View of Life*, p. 138.

[79] Ibid., p. 140.

[80] Ibid., p. 141.

of imagination, and integral knowing. The intuition, which is an activity of the whole being, cannot be gained by mere rational efforts, though it is equally true that it cannot be gained without it. It is wrong to assume that in scientific discoveries, there is complete externality, detachment, indirectness and independence. The intuitive elements are present even in scientific cognition. Radhakrishnan observes:

> The externality of the individual consciousness to the object is transcended in the intuitive apprehension. In it there is a complete fusion of the subject and the object. Even in scientific knowledge, it is not altogether absent. The independence of the observer is only an ideal. Even when the camera takes the place of the human observer, it is the observer who has to fix it in position, who has to interpret the result of the exposure. If, at any stage, "the observer is careless or prejudiced, the whole process becomes a failure".[81]

Science, being a valid form of knowledge, is actually the product of intuitive knowledge. In all intuitive knowledge,

> . . . man ceases to be an impartial spectator. His whole being is at work not merely the powers of observation and inference. It is knowledge by coincidence.[82]

In every form of cognition, the whole self comes into play. Although, in some of the scientific discoveries, the whole self is not realized or expressed. The application of intuition in science is witnessed not in its methodology which is governed by objective approach, but in "the genius" of the man who is engaged in scientific enquiry.

ART

Radhakrishnan observes, "All art is the expression of experience

---

[81] S. Radhakrishnan, *Reply to Critics* (Tudor Publication), p. 792.

[82] Loc. cit.

in some medium."[83] Sculpture has for its medium stone and marble, painting colours, music sounds and poetry words. The intuitive experience is manifested through the work of art. But, reason plays its part in grasping the object and shaping the experience. Radhakrishnan contends that art has got its formal structure as well as inner essence. Reason works on the formal or external structure of art, whereas intuition penetrates into the inner essence. Somebody may say that reason cannot realize artistic experience because it is discursive and analytic in nature. On the contrary, Radhakrishnan holds that reason adds to the value of art. Let us take up music. Every voice is not music. There is a distinction between music and noise. A lay man may harp all the strings of violin but simply harping of strings is not a piece of music. There must be rhythm. Undoubtedly, reason of musician produces music. Similarly, a lump of colour is not painting. A painter portrays pictures in a systematic manner. A sense of mathematical accuracy and ingenuity is required to portray and paint a picture. Every piece of stone is not a piece of artistic sculpture. It is coupled with a keen sense of accuracy and ingenuity. This brings us to the point that reason operates on the external and formal structure of art, whereas intuition reveals its deeper meaning. It may be pointed out that the nature of intuition in science and art is different in certain respects from intuition operating in moral and religious consciousness. Radhakrishnan observes:

> In aesthetic experience we have a type of intuitive knowledge, a personal relationship with the object which is essentially different from what is found in intellectual cognition.[84]

Aesthetic experience implies knowledge of the individual.

---

[83] S. Radhakrishnan, *An Idealist View of Life*, p. 144.

[84] S. Radhakrishnan, *Reply to Critics* (Tudor Publication), p. 793.

Radhakrishnan says, "Works of art express significant individuality".[85] The Work of art bears the deep stamp of individuality. Radhakrishnan holds that any two men could hit on the same law of science, as Darwin and Wallace actually did, but no two men can, ever produce the same work of art. Art is essentially the expression of the whole self, while science in its ordinary usage is the expression of a fragment of the self. Artistic works and aesthetic perceptions are expressions of individuality because the whole self is there at work. A man, whose sensibility is adequately trained, can discriminate between beautiful objects and ugly objects presented to him. The culture of sensibility is dependent on the degree of the development of self. Though Radhakrishnan considers art as an expression of individuality, he does not forget that the self, of which individuality is a mode, has also another mode — universality. Even if art is the self-expression, the self that is expressed is not the narrow one. On closer examinations of Radhakrishnan's writings on art, we find a distinction between "art as vision" and "art as creation". The former is close to self. It is a matter of insight into and experience of reality. Croce is an exponent of "art as vision". He identifies the aesthetic perception, e.g. intuition with its expression. Radhakrishnan views critically Croce's position of the identity of perception of aesthetic value and expression of it. Croce admits that perception cannot be separated from its expression. He does not take into consideration the fact that ". . . inarticulateness stands between experience and expression of the average man".[86] Radhakrishnan differs with Croce for denying that art reveals reality. Art does not merely give us subjective impressions. We can say so if we regard reality as utterly unrelated to knowledge. For Radhakrishnan, art is valuable because it is a way of perceiving and expressing reality. In artistic experience:

---

[85] Loc. cit.

[86] S. Radhakrishnan, *An Idealist View of Life*, p. 148.

> The artist's whole being responds to the object, his feeling is intensified and his imagination stimulated . . . The object enters into the mind of the artist and unfolds its nature in his imagination. The consciousness of the artist enters into the object, sees, feels and vibrates with its truth.[87]

Art gives us a sense of meaningfulness of life. It evokes in us ideas of the larger beauty, justice and charity of the universe. Radhakrishnan suggests that art imparts the knowledge of truth. The element of pleasure is purely incidental. A poet is a revealer of truth. The images not only please our fancies but symbolize the unrevealed. The purest aesthetic consciousness is an aspect of the higher reflection of the spirit on our empirical intuition. Figuratively speaking, art can be called "fusion" or "oneness with" or "absorption into" the spirit. Radhakrishnan in his consideration of aesthetic experience is primarily concerned with integral vision. He does not consider the production of art as an essential part of being an artist. Art also involves the knowledge of the object. In artistic experience, there is a ". . . deliberate suspension of individuality, an utter submission to the real, a complete absorption in the object as it is, so as to breathe its life and enjoy its form".[88]

Art discloses the deeper reality of things. It is the vision of the spirit of things. Art educates and trains sensibility and appreciates the inner reality. It is a mode of self-realization. It enlightens the empirical life with spiritual flavour. Radhakrishnan observes, "It is life come to utterance".[89] The function of art is ". . . to quicken the perception of wonder and surprise, of strangeness and beauty, of the mystery and miraculousness of the world that surrounds us . . .".[90] Art is a

---

[87] S. Radhakrishnan, *Reply to Critics* (Tudor Publication), p. 793.

[88] S. Radhakrishnan, *An Idealist View of Life*, p. 145.

[89] Ibid., p. 146.

[90] S. Radhakrishnan, *The Spirit in Man*, p. 488.

mode of integral insight. The artist ". . . sees the burden of mystery in all things".[91] Radhakrishnan tries to explore the mystery of the universe. This is possible, not by means of his reason, but by intuitive power. Intuition is proved on our pulse and forms the nexus between appearance and reality, matter and spirit. Radhakrishnan lays emphasis on the mysterious nature of the universe which we have to understand not by reason alone but by intuition as well.

ETHICS

Reason and intuition equally work in ethics and yield moral consciousness. When a man is faced with two alternative and conflicting situations in matters of ethics, his reason alone helps him choose the right course.

Radhakrishnan approves the role of reason in shaping ethical consciousness, but he is not interested in routine, mechanical and formalized rational ethics nor in conventional good form, but in "creative good life".[92] As in science, philosophy and art, it is the genius who intuits the truths, so in ethics the discoverer of the moral good is the "moral hero". Radhakrishnan depicts the moral hero as the ideal type, who is marked out by his adventurous path, and who is ". . . akin to the discoverer who brings order into the scattered elements of a science of the artist who composes a piece of music or designs a building".[93] The moral hero aspires to fulfil his spiritual destiny. He follows an inner rhythm in order to realize the self. He plays the game on the chessboard of life with clear vision of the position and with a sure insight. The moral hero has the sense of right and wrong. Integral vision helps resolve the right and wrong of any given situation. Reason

---

[91] S. Radhakrishnan, *The Spirit in Man*, p. 489.

[92] Ibid., p. 490.

[93] S. Radhakrishnan, *An Idealist View of Life*, p. 155.

educates conscience and by intuition one attains automatically the knowledge of his duty. Moral virtue is not simply a matter of reason but arises out of the depth of souls. According to Socrates, "Virtue is knowledge". The knowledge is not mere rational knowledge. It is knowledge which springs from the deeper levels of man's being. It is acquired by the growth of one's consciousness. Radhakrishnan states:

> The deeper a man is rooted in spirit the more he knows directly. To one of ethical sensitiveness, the path of duty is as clear as any knowledge we possess.[94]

In its perception, we come as near to absolute certainty as it is possible for us to do. We have in it a case of intuitive apprehension, though later reflection may discover reasons for its truth. Bradley holds that we know, what is right in a particular case by what we may call an immediate judgement or an intuitive subsumption. Radhakrishnan says:

> He whose life is directed by insight expresses his deeper consciousness not in poems and pictures as the artist does but in a superior type of life. He leaves the world of claims and counter-claims. He is indifferent to the morality which is a matter of checks and balances, for the highest morality which is not the law but love is a necessity of his being. The lives of heros like Buddha and Christ are not merely truthful and austere but beautiful beyond all dream.[95]

RELIGION

Religion, in its deeper aspects, transcends reason. But, it need not decry it. Reason does play an important role in religion also, otherwise it would be difficult to distinguish right faith from superstition. Reason should not be eradicated from the

---

[94] S. Radhakrishnan, *An Idealist View of Life*, p. 156-57.

[95] Ibid., p. 157.

spheres of religion and theology. According to Radhakrishnan, reason has got an important part to play in shaping our religious beliefs and experiences. The role may be secondary but it is significant. There is a level of religious life in which reason has to play a superior role. Religion finds its fulfilment in supra-rational or spiritual or intuitive experience. But, there is also infra-rational life of the instincts impulses, sensations, crude emotions, dogmas — from which all human aspirations have their beginnings. Those infra-rational aspects of life too feel the touch of the religious sense in man. Rituals, ceremonies, offerings and chanting of hymns constitute external phenomena of religion. Man has got higher as well as lower nature. Our lower nature is vitiated by impurities, ignorance, superstition, etc. Here, reason has got to play its legitimate role. It can intervene to enlighten, purify and chasten our nature, which is often dominated by the blind instincts and impulses. The primary function of religion is to awaken the spirit. Radhakrishnan observes:

> If our temples, mosques and churches understand that primary function is to awaken the spirit in us and not impart sacred wisdom, they will convert themselves into houses of God which will have the courage to be comprehensive and welcome believers of varied views and tastes into their spiritual atmosphere.[96]

Creativity in cognitive, aesthetic, ethical or religious activity springs from thought which is intuitive or spiritually quickened. There is no greatness, no sublimity, no perfection whatever be the line, without the touch of this creative energy of life.

Religious consciousness is different from rational or ethical or aesthetic activity. It is also not the sum of these intellectual, ethical and aesthetic activities. It is an autonomous form of

---

[96] S. Radhakrishnan, *An Idealist View of Life*, p. 161.

spiritual life. It includes intellectual, ethical and aesthetic elements, yet it is not confined to them but transcends them. The object of religion is not either the true or the good or the beautiful or a mere unity of them, but God the universal consciousness who includes these values and yet transcends them. Truth, beauty and goodness cease to be the supreme realities and become a part of the being and essence of God. The cognitive, aesthetic and ethical sides are partial aspects of our life, but religious life includes them all. Radhakrishnan states:

> While science strives to comprehend the law that sustains the universe, while art yearns to reveal the beauty that is worked into the world, while morality struggles to realize the goodness the universe is labouring to achieve, while in their perfection these different aspirations emerge into one another, in the process itself, each seems to be incomplete, though it is true that true art or philosophy or morality cannot be had without all of them in some degree.[97]

The essence of religion lies in a comprehensive, synthetic and integral realization of the totality of life. The religious man has the knowledge that everything is significant and there is harmony underlying the conflicts. Man has the capacity to realize the significance and harmony of life. According to Radhakrishnan:

> [religion] is the reaction of the whole man to the whole reality. We seek the religious object by the totality of our faculties and energies. Such functioning of the whole man may be called spiritual life, as distinct from a merely intellectual or moral or aesthetic activity or a combination of them.[98]

He traces the value of truth, goodness and beauty to a common source, while art or beauty or goodness in isolation may not

[97] S. Radhakrishnan, *An Idealist View of Life*, p. 158.

[98] Ibid., p. 69.

generate religious insight; in their intimate fusion, they lead us to something greater than themselves. The religious man lives in a new world which fills his mind with light, his heart with joy and his soul with love. God is seen as light, love and life. Religious experience differs from religious intellectualism which remains confined to superficial religious phenomena and does not enter into the very core of religion. Religious intellectualism believes that interest in religion is prompted by adducing proofs for the existence of God. Religious insight asks us to train our consciousness and educate our sensibility to the level where it can see God. Intuition probes into the nature of God and intuitive seers shrink from precise statement and definitions because definition involves relation and comparison, which are obviously the functions of reason. It is due to this reason that the seers and the mystics all over the world take recourse to symbolic language in order to give expression to the deeper spiritual experiences of their life.

Interpretation of History and Human Destiny

> The forces which determine the process of history are not purely geographical or biological. Climate, topography, soil and race are among the factors which condition historic changes, but they do not determine them. Human society changes according to other principles.[99]

The "other principles" are deeper than those mentioned above. Radhakrishnan contends that history is continuity and advance. This continuity is not mechanical reproduction but creative transformation. Radhakrishnan observes:

> Besides, history is not only seeing but also thinking. Thinking is always constructive if not creative.[100]

---

[99] S. Radhakrishnan, *Religion and Society*, p. 29.

[100] S. Radhakrishnan, *Fragment of Confession*, p. 11.

History is not compilation of facts and dates of accidents. It has got deeper meaning in philosophy. Radhakrishnan remarks:

> History is not recapitulation of facts, but a way of looking at them. It involves interpretation and selection.[101]

The other principles are mental culture, psychological attitude and spiritual training. Radhakrishnan's conception of history conceives it as a realm in which human race marches from bondage of nature to freedom of spirit. He mentions in his *Fragments of Confession* that Collingwood argues that historical thought is the discovery of individuality which is freedom. Thus, history becomes a story of human achievement which is not confined only to geographical, economic, social and other cause, but also extends to the spiritual realm.

Hegel, Marx and Radhakrishnan

Man is not only product of natural and material forces, but he has got deeper aspects of psychological and spiritual longings. Hegel thinks in his *Philosophy of History* about metaphysics of history in terms of monistic idealism. Hegel's thesis is that reality is spirit manifesting itself in nature, in human history, and in the action of man. History, being the development of spirit, expresses itself through successive stages. When spirit reaches the stage of rational freedom, it becomes fully conscious. Hegel points out that world-history does not belong to the realm of matter but to the realm of spirit. The essence of matter is gravity. The essence of spirit is rational freedom.

Hegel's historical process marches forward from one level to another level through the dialectical movement of thesis, anti-thesis and synthesis. All changes, all thinking, all life proceed from affirmation to denial, or from claim to counter-claim, to a new integration which later develops a new

---

[101] S. Radhakrishnan, *Religion and Society*, p. 32.

opposition; and so the movement continues. For Hegel, dialectic is a part of logic. The history becomes the ceaseless march of opposites. The process of thesis, anti-thesis and synthesis goes on until the goal which embodies the whole truth and nothing but the truth is reached.

When we start with the idea of being; the idea of not-being follows naturally and opposition of being and non-being is overcome in the idea of becoming. The process goes on until we reach the "absolute idea". This is the self-development of the idea, according to Hegel. Hegel develops by application of this method, the whole of philosophy of history and natural science as well. For Hegel, history is a continuous self-realization or materialization of minds, and so it must necessarily develop and accomplish itself by the dialectical method. Marx equally applies the dialectical method not to the sphere of ideas and their self-development, but to the material development of society. Both Hegel and Marx believe the historical evolution as dialectical. The difference between Hegelian dialectic and Marxian dialectic is that the former believes that an absolute mind is materializing itself in history and the latter holds that the historical development is conditioned by the material and economic forces. While Hegel gives primacy to ideas, Marx gives primacy to matter. Hegelian dialectic is idealistic. Marxian dialectic is materialistic. Radhakrishnan, instead of affirming a dialectical movement, believes in a sort of spiritual development. To quote Radhakrishnan:

> The development of history is logical for both Marx and Hegel; and it is plausibly accounted for in Hegel, for whom mind is the ultimate reality, and it is more difficult for a materialist to think, that the world develops according to a logical formula.[102]

---

[102] S. Radhakrishnan, *Religion and Society*, p. 31.

Radhakrishnan is critical of the conceptions of history as contemplated by Hegel and Marx. He points out that the historical processes of Hegel and Marx are not free from difficulties. For Hegel, contradiction is the primary principle and opposition is the basis of all advance. Croce raised an objection against Hegelian dialectic in his book *Aesthetic* that Hegel makes a confusion between opposites and distincts. Dialectic is possible, according to Hegel, between opposites which negate each other. For instance, light and darkness negate each other. They are incompatible. The presence of one implies the absence of the other. The opposites cancel each other. But the distincts like truth and beauty, philosophy and art do not exclude each other. Thus, it is a matter of consideration as to how the dialectic of Hegel operates on distinct principles. Further, Marx believes in the inevitability of progress. But history according to Radhakrishnan, is full of examples of decay and retrogression, and cannot be regarded as a continuous development through conflict. There is no guarantee that human progress is inevitable. Moreover, the economic interpretation of history, as contended by Marx, states that economic phenomena, especially economic production, are fundamental and all that we call culture, religion, politics, social and intellectual life are determind by the mode of production and are its immediate consequence. But this contention seems to be partial and one-sided because history does not take into consideration only economic factors, and its mode of production and consumption. Radhakrishnan thinks:

> . . . the emphasis on the importance of economic conditions is correct; the suggestion that they are exclusively determinant of history is incorrect.[103]

According to Radhakrishnan, history is a plan of spiritual

---

[103] S. Radhakrishnan, *Religion and Society*, p. 35.

development. For Kant, history is the gradual moralization of man. For Hegel, it is the progressive unfoldment of the Absolute. For Radhakrishnan, it is a gradual development and spiritualization of man. It is continuity and advance of mankind at large. The continuity is not mechanical reproduction but creative transformation of human race. The difference between Hegel and Radhakrishnan is that the Absolute of Hegel is under the chain of dialectical process or rational process, but the Absolute of Radhakrishnan is free from the chain of dialectical or rational process. Hegel makes out that negation is the power driving the "absolute idea" towards existence and driving existence back towards the "absolute idea" which, in the process, actualizes itself as "absolute mind" or "spirit".

Hegel identifies the Absolute with the cosmic process. It makes little difference whether we say that it is spirit or being which is realizing itself in movement of becoming or that matter, moving in the direction of spirit becomes conscious of itself. But, according to Radhakrishnan, the world of change or non-being is a progressive manifestation of spirit or being. The world process is conceived as a struggle between two antagonistic but indispensable principles of being and non-being. The existence of this world implies the existence of being. Being becomes the foundation of all existence, though it is not itself anything existent but it is spirit.

The Goal of History and the Destiny of Man

Radhakrishnan observes:

> History is neither a chapter of accident, nor a determined drift. It is a pattern of absolute significance.[104]

So, Radhakrishnan specifies that history has got definite purpose and goal. Its goal is to divinize man as well as cosmos

---

[104] S. Radhakrishnan, *Fragments of Confession*, p. 30.

through the process of evolution. Spiritual life is not mere negation of material and animal life but the fulfilment of the human life and its consummation is a historical process. Radhakrishnan states:

> History is not a branch of biology. The drama of human personalities is distinct from life in the animal kingdom. Social sciences which deal with the story of man in society are a separate category from natural sciences.[105]

The human beings work out their evolution, constantly and deliberately. History of mankind reveals that human life is on the path of perfection. The evolution or historical process has not come to an end with the emergence of rational or thinking man. There is all possibility of the emergence of spiritual beings. Human self-consciousness must grow into spiritual-consciousness. Radhakrishnan observes:

> We must pass beyond the dualities and discords of intellect and possess truth as our inherent right. *Ānanda* or joy which is, according to St. Paul, one of the faiths of the spirit, is the stage we have to reach.[106]

The destiny of man lies in the attainment of Divine stage. Radhakrishnan points out:

> The meaning of history is to make all men prophets, to establish a kingdom of free spirits. The infinitely rich and spiritually impregnated future, this drama of the gradual transformation of intellect into spirit, of the son of man into the son of God, is the goal of history. When death is overcome, when time is conquered, the kingdom of the eternal Spirit is established.[107]

This view of history seems to bear a direct impact of the Judaic

105 S. Radhakrishnan, *Fragments of Confession*, p. 29.

106 Loc. cit.

107 S. Radhakrishnan, *Fragments of Confession*, p. 30.

Christian conception of history. The Judaic Christian view as well as Radhakrishnan envisage the complete transformation or divinization of man's existence and the cosmic history. History, according to Radhakrishnan and the Judaic Christian view, is marching towards a definite goal. The goal lies in the complete fulfilment of the historical process. Both Radhakrishnan and the Judaic Christian view believe that the fulfilment of history will be possible only at the end of time. It is not possible in time process. The complete divinization of the world and history, according to Radhakrishnan and Christian view, is possible when the time comes to an end. It is not the end of the cosmic process in time but the end of time. With the end of the time, the Eternity manifests itself fully in the timeless existence.

Radhakrishnan is one with ancient Hindu thought. So far, both believe in man's spiritualization or attainment of liberation. But his view of history and human destiny differs in certain respects from the ancient Hindu view of history. It believed in the cyclic conception of history. History, according to this view, moves in cycles and not in a straight line. There is an emergence of the world and ultimately the dissolution of the world process as there is the birth and death of living beings or as there is the cycle of day and night. According to the Hindu view, nature works for the liberation of spirit and not for its own perfection. This is the meaning of history. It is to endow man with spiritual freedom. In all forms of Indian thought, time is symbolized by birth and death. The world is represented by the wheel of time of births and deaths. Time presupposes change because the world process is a movement of events. The movements occur in time. Thus, change is the essence of existence. The becoming presupposes being. This being is God or spirit. "The aim of the cosmic evolution is to reveal the spirit".[108]

---

[108] S. Radhakrishnan, *Fragments of Confession*, p. 44.

The question of the status of time in cosmic evolution was raised by Kant in his antinomies of Pure Reason. He propounds thesis that the world has a beginning in time and is confined within the limits of space. Then, he advances antithesis that the world has neither beginning in time nor confined in the space but is infinite, as in space so also in time. This antinomy cannot be solved, for according to Kant, reason finds itself in the power of transcendental appearance. Within the limits of the phenomenal world, the contradiction cannot be overcome. We cannot think that time will come to an end in time or that it will go endlessly. How can the end of time occur within time? When the end of cosmic history is reached, we have passed beyond the limits of history. We have transcended time. It is not a question of an end in time but an end of time. So long as there is the struggle, the process of becoming, the overcoming of non-being by being, we have the time process. According to the ancient Hindu thought, as has been stated above, we have the cycle of individual births and deaths as well as the evolution and dissolution of cosmos. There is no completion of the historical process or the end of time. The end of time is realized by man only when he transcends it in his spiritual freedom. According to Radhakrishnan, if it is held as the ancient Hindu thought conceived it, that the final end of history will never be accomplished and there will be perpetual singing and no completion of the song, that is a kind of journeying without any journey's end, then the cosmic process will have no meaning at all. Radhakrishnan observes:

> It cannot be a question of perpetual travelling. We should also arrive. It cannot be interminable singing; there should also be such a thing as completion in a song. There must come a time when all individuals will become sons of God and be relieved into the glory of immortality. When the world is redeemed the end of the plot is reached. Earth and heaven

> would be no more; the timeless and the transcendent alone remains.[109]

The Hindu view seems to be quite meaningful. The journey's end is there for man who has realized his spiritual freedom and transcends the limitations of time process. If the ancient Hindu view held that there was no goal for human spirit then it could be charged with meaninglessness. The goal of history lies in the freedom of spirit. History cannot have any goal for itself excepting the ultimate freedom and perfection of spirit. The consummation of history, according to Radhakrishnan, is the transfiguration and transformation of the cosmos and the destiny of man is spiritualization or divinization of his whole existence. The fulfilment of history lies in revolutionary change in man's consciousness. It is the attainment of wholeness. It overcomes all discords and transcends the element of time in eternity, which we objectify as *brahmaloka*. Radhakrishnan observes, ". . . we have a divine community (*brahmaloka*) where the individual is transformed by contemplation on the being of God into the likeness of that which he beholds."[110] The cosmic purpose of history is fulfilled, when mankind achieves divinity which is its legitimate destiny.

---

109. S. Radhakrishnan, *An Idealist View of Life*, p. 245.
110. Ibid., p. 244.

5

Rabindranath Tagore, Sir Mohammad Iqbal, and J. Krishnamurti

Rabindranath Tagore (1861–1941)

TAGORE'S philosophical thoughts are embodied in his works like *Sādhanā*, *Creative Unity*, *Personality*, *Gitanjali* and *The Religion of Man*. But there is a vast literature in Bengali also. He is mainly a seer, a poet and a thinker but not a dialectician or a systematic philosopher. His writings are full of deep metaphysical insight, poetic suggestions and spiritual illumination. But we do not find a strictly rational exposition and rigorous analysis of metaphysical problems in his writings. Speaking of his *Sādhanā*, Radhakrishnan observes:

> It is a sigh of the soul rather than a reasoned account of metaphysics; an atmosphere rather than a system of philosophy. But we feel that the atmosphere is charged with a particular vision of reality.[1]

What is true of *Sādhanā* is also more or less true of his other writings, which mainly concern themselves with the deeper problems of human life and reality.

Tagore is not a speculative philosopher. His philosophy is based on the spiritual vision, on the intuitive perception of

[1] S. Radhakrishnan, *The Philosophy of Rabindranath Tagore*, p. 4.

the spirit, and of the deepest truths of life and existence. He characterizes this spiritual vision as intuition. Intuition can be defined as a "sudden flash" or "a direct vision" of reality. It is direct consciousness of soul-consciousness. Tagore says:

> The vision of the Supreme one in our soul is a direct and immediate intuition, not based on any ratiocination or demonstration at all.[2]

He believes that experience and enjoyment of God's presence is higher than the rational knowledge of a metaphysician. It is the enjoyment and realization of truth that overflows in his philosophy. His philosophy is not based on reason but on self-experience or intuition. Tagore says that his philosophy springs from "direct vision" or "intuition". He observes:

> This thought of God has not grown in my mind through any process of philosophical reasoning. On the contrary, it has followed the current of my temperament from early days until it suddenly flashed into my consciousness with a direct vision.[3]

Tagore does not arrive at the concept of reality through any process of reasoning or logical deduction. He owes it directly to his early intuitive vision. Tagore realizes in his intuitive vision that beneath the changing phenomena, there dwells the eternal spirit beyond the reach of senses and mind. He speaks of this eternal spirit as god, infinite, supreme person, supreme being, bridegroom or lover, friend, father, man the eternal and so on. The various terminologies employed by him do not make any difference since he believes that reality is one which can be called by different names. He puts it:

> Facts occupy endless time and space; but the truth comprehending them all has no dimension; it is one.

[2] R.N. Tagore, *Sādhanā*, p. 36.

[3] R.N. Tagore, *The Religion of Man*, p. 17.

> Wherever our heart touches one, in the small or the big, it finds the touch of the infinite.[4]

As regards the nature of the ultimate reality, Tagore says that it is *śāntam* (peace or harmony), *śivam* (bliss) and *advaitam* (oneness). It is the concretion of the three values. *Śāntam* is that concord by means of which the entire universe with all the planets and stars is balanced in peace and harmony. It is called *śāntam* because all its ordained laws are in harmony with one another. He feels that there is harmony between the infinite and the finite, between nature and man. The immanence of reality has to be realized in external nature as well as in the depth of human heart. Spirit pervades the entire universe as well as the individual self. In place of chaos, confusion, disorderliness of contradiction, the rythm of harmony reveals the beauty, unity and order in the universe. *Śivam* is that harmony for which man is ever longing. Man attains bliss in harmony with the infinite. *Advaitam* means the realization of that oneness in the soul, which through all disruption and dissension, continues to establish relationship in joy and love. Reality, according to Tagore, is one, infinite, eternal spirit whose nature is essentially *śāntam, śivam* and *advaitam.*

Tagore addresses the supreme as his *jīvan devatā* from whom he always draws inspiration in his life. He maintains that *jīvan devatā* finds joy (*rasa*) in the manifestations of beauty, and creations of art and literature. It is for this reason that He, though one, becomes many. He creates man for playing the game of love with Him. If *jīvan devatā* creates the finite individuals for enacting the love-drama, does it not imply a limitation of His infinity? It is undoubtedly a limitation but it is a self-imposed one. Tagore never likes to confine the *jīvan devatā* with the limits of his own life. God pervades the entire

---

[4] R.N. Tagore, *Creative Unity*, p. 4.

universe and He is called *viśva devatā*, the Lord of the Universe. Spirit is all comprehending and throbs in nature as well as in mankind at large.

Tagore holds that reality is "infinite–finite" being. It is infinite in its essence and finite in its manifestations. He observes:

> And I say of the Supreme Man, that he is infinite in his essence, he is finite in his manifestation is us the individuals.[5]

Reality is the infinite, indeterminate ground and unity of all the finite determinations of it. But, this unifying ground is not to be abstracted from the determinations. Mere knowledge of the finite is as dangerous as an exclusive knowledge of the infinite. One should combine both. In order to make clear the inseparable relationship between the finite and the infinite, Tagore gives the analogy of art-experience. He says:

> The infinite and the finite are one as song and singing are one. The singing is incomplete; by a continual process of death it gives up the song which is complete. The absolute infinite is like a music which is devoid of all definite tunes and therefore meaningless.[6]

Tagore attempts a synthesis of personal and impersonal aspects of God. He assimilates both the theism of Rāmānuja and absolutism of Śaṅkara in his philosophy. Though reality, according to Tagore, is impersonal-personal, he emphasizes more on the personal aspect of reality. To quote him:

> For the Absolute, infinite is emptiness. The finite is something. It may be a mere chequebook with no account in the bank. But the absolute infinite has no cash and not even a chequebook.[7]

[5] R.N. Tagore, *The Religion of Man*, p. 118.

[6] R.N. Tagore, *Personality*, p. 57.

[7] Ibid., pp. 56-57.

Moreover, personal aspect of reality is important from the standpoint of man's religious consciousness which demands that reality must give us "the touch of personal companionship". If personal relations with reality are excluded, the latter would be reduced to an abstraction. He observes:

> There is only one grand tune of all my compositions and it may conveniently be styled as the union of the infinite with the finite in finiteness.[8]

Man is finite if we view him as a psycho-physical personality. He is infinite, if viewed as soul. He combines in himself spirit and nature. "He is earth's child but heaven's heir." The self, says Rabindranath, is ". . . finite in its expression and infinite in its principle".[9] In its finite aspect, the self is conscious of its separateness, and there it distinguishes itself from all others; but in its infinite aspect it "transcends" the limits of the present and the personal and gains ". . . that harmony which leads to its perfection and not its aggrandizement".[10] The finite individual is torn between finiteness and infinity, being attracted by both. He observes, "At one pole of my being I am one with stocks and stones . . . but at the other pole of my being I am separate from all".[11] On the one hand, man belongs to nature and on the other, he is a member of the spiritual world. He is conditioned by natural phenomena and subjected to the law of necessity. He is also free because he is one with the spirit. Man aspires after perfect truth, perfect beauty and perfect goodness. Reason aspires to attain an ideal truth which is complete, harmonious and all-comprehensive, but it is not able to attain this end due to its natural limitations. Reason is unable to grasp the whole. In order to grasp the whole, man

---

[8] R.N. Tagore, *Jīvansmṛti* (first edn.), p. 249.

[9] R.N. Tagore, *Sādhanā*, p. 81.

[10] Ibid., p. 83.

[11] Ibid., p. 69.

must establish kinship with nature and oneness with the Absolute. We can easily notice that the first experience of intuition is found in the consciousness of kinship with nature and later on this consciousness is extended to the supreme reality. Tagore says:

> When I was eighteen, a sudden spring breeze of religious experience for the first time came to my life and passed away leaving in my memory a direct message of spiritual reality. One day while I stood watching at early dawn the Sun sending out its rays from behind the trees, I suddenly felt as if some ancient mist had in a moment lifted from my sight, and the morning light on the face of the world revealed an inner radiance of joy. The invisible screen of the common place was removed from all things and all men, and their ultimate significance was intensified in my mind; and this is the definition of beauty. That which was memorable in this experience was its human message, the sudden expansion of my consciousness in the superpersonal world of man.[12]

Man in his consciousness enjoys oneness with nature. Here, Tagore comes very close to Croce because, at first instance, intuitive experience is viewed as "aesthetic experience". In such experiences, we communicate, participate and appreciate natural beauties because we feel kinship with nature. The fact that we are able to interpret nature, know it, appreciate it, fight and conquer it, shows that it is akin to human consciousness. We could have no communication with nature, if it would have been altogether foreign to us. Tagore believes that there is a close relationship between man and nature. If we separate man from nature, ". . . it is like dividing the bud and the blossom into two separate categories, and putting

[12] R.N. Tagore, *The Religion of Man*, p. 94.

their grace to the credit of two different and antithetical principles".[13] Further, he says:

> The Indian mind never has any hesitation in acknowledging its kinship with nature, its unbroken relation with all.[14]

If we adopt the right attitude to nature, we find the pulse of spirit throbbing through it. Indian mind cultivated consciousness in such a way that everything assumes a spiritual significance. The earth, water, light and fruits are not merely physical phenomena but manifestations of spirit. He observes:

> India intuitively felt that the essential fact of this world has a vital meaning for us; we have to be fully alive to it and establish a conscious relation with it, not merely impelled by scientific curiosity or greed of material advantage, but realizing it in the spirit of sympathy, with a large feeling of joy and peace.[15]

Intuition or "aesthetic experience" can realize the spiritual beauty of the things of nature. Man cannot establish kinship with nature so long as he remains bound in the realm of the finite. The finite reason reduces the universe to the opposites of self and not-self, organism and environment. Intuition or enjoying consciousness can establish union with nature. The universe of mind, ". . . is like a railway station; but the station platform is not our home".[16] There is necessity to rise above the finitude of mind. This is possible when we transcend mind and realize soul-consciousness or attain the vision of reality. God is the highest unity from which all beings proceed and we have to attain union with God. Tagore conceives that spirit throbs into nature. In order to realize spirit, we must establish kinship with nature which is mainfestation of spirit.

[13] R.N. Tagore, *Sādhanā*, p. 7.

[14] Loc. cit.

[15] Loc. cit.

[16] R.N. Tagore, *Sādhanā*, p. 99.

Tagore holds that the individual self is the manifestation of the infinite. He tends to make a distinction between empirical self and soul or spirit. Rabindranath distinguishes the empirical self of man from the spirit. On the surface of his being, man has the ever-changing empirical self. At this level, he does not realize unity with the other selves, with humanity as a whole. But below the surface of his being, this unity is attained by him. Tagore puts it:

> . . . on the surface of our being we have the ever-changing phases of the individual self, but in the depth there dwells the Eternal Spirit of human unity beyond our direct knowledge.[17]

Man's selfish motives and ego-centric attitude obstruct his clear vision of the soul; for these egoistic motives refer only to the limited self in man. When man realizes the existence of soul in him, he transcends the narrow limits of his individuality and becomes conscious of the inner unity which comprehends all. Tagore observes:

> When we are conscious of our soul; we perceive the inner being that transcends our ego and has its deeper affinity with the all.[18]

But when man confuses his soul with the egoistic self, the former loses all its significance. The soul, apprehends the truth by its unity with others. Man remains in anxiety so long as he fails to find the law of uniformity in nature. This law of uniformity is the perception of harmony that lies between human soul and the workings of the world. The realization of this unity between man and the surrounding world gives him immense joy. Self, according to Tagore, has two aspects — finite and infinite. The self in its finite aspect, shows limitations and

---

[17] R.N. Tagore, *The Religion of Man*, p. 17.

[18] R.N. Tagore, *Sādhanā*, p. 27.

separateness. In its infinite aspect, it shows harmony. "In its finite aspect," Tagore remarks, "the self is conscious of its separateness, and there it is ruthless in its attempt to have more distinction than all others. But, in its infinite aspect its wish is to gain that harmony which leads to its perfection and not its mere aggrandizement".[19] In the finite pole, the self maintains its own unique individuality in the universe. Each individual possesses a distinct personality. But self in its infinite pole which is akin to soul must transcend its accumulations or selfishness and share in the fullest measure in the life of the all. When he transcends his egoistic desires and has "deeper affinity with the all", he finds his truth and reaches across the threshold of the infinite. Then, he realizes that he is one with the all. Self in its finite pole indicates individuality and soul in its infinite pole is the embodiment of spirit. Tagore never wants destruction of individuality or annihilation of self. True deliverance of man is the deliverance from *avidyā* (ignorance). There is no need to destroy ignorance or negate reason. He observes:

> It is not destroying anything that is positive and real, for that cannot be possible, but that which is negative, which obstructs our vision of truth. When this obstruction, which is ignorance, is removed then only is the eyelid drawn up which is no loss to the eye.[20]

Tagore thinks that ignorance is a cover which obstructs our vision of the supreme reality. So, there is no need to annihilate self or negate individuality but there is necessity to remove ignorance and attain vision of the true self. There is necessity to know the true self which transcends empirical self. He holds, "To know our soul apart from the self is the first step towards the realization of the supreme diliverance."[21] Man gets

---

[19] R.N. Tagore, *Sādhanā*, p. 83.

[20] Ibid., p. 72.

[21] Ibid, p. 30.

fulfilment in the realization of the supreme self. It is the function of religion not to destroy our nature but to fulfil it. The higher nature in man always seeks for something which transcends itself and yet is its deepest truth. Man has got insistent urge to expand his consciousness, transcend his limitations and attain vision of the universal truth.

Tagore's Religion is the Religion of Man in which the infinite is defined in humanity. The idea of the humanity of our God, or the divinity of man the eternal is the theme of his book, *The Religion of Man*. Tagore accords man the highest place in the universe. Man is the ". . . builder of the heaven, the music maker, the dreamer of dreams".[22] The universe has significance in terms of human values. All values have their origin in human consciousness. Religion concentrates itself on humanity, which illumines our reason, inspires our wisdom, stimulates our love and claims our intelligent service. The core of religion, according to Tagore, consists in worshipping the suffering humanity; because our temple of worship is:

> . . . there where the tiller is tilling the hard ground and where the path maker is breaking stones. He is one with them in Sun and in shower, and his garment is covered with dust.[23]

Tagore's humanism is nurtured on spiritual foundations. He believes that spirit manifests itself in human beings. He says:

> The divine principle of unity has ever been that of an inter-relationship. He misses himself when isolated; he finds his own larger and truer self in his wide human relationship.[24]

---

[22] R.N. Tagore, *The Religion of Man*, p. 123.

[23] R.N. Tagore, *Gitanjali*, no. 11.

[24] R.N. Tagore, *The Religion of Man*, p. 15.

Tagore asserts that religion helps train man in developing the right attitude towards the infinite. In order to realize the divine power in his life, man should discard selfishness and should work for the welfare of the human race as a whole. Then he becomes Viśvakarmā — the world worker — who works for all. Then he realizes the unity of his soul with the soul of the whole humanity. This is the stage of life explained by Buddha as Brahmavihāra or the living in the Supreme. The religion of man consists in the reconciliation of the universal spirit with the individual. He believes in the realization of universal consciousness in the entire human race. It lies in the true realization of the relationship between the infinite and the finite. The religion of man, in reality, is in perceiving one's soul in the union of spirit, that is everywhere.

As has been discussed, reality according to Tagore, is *śāntam* (peace and harmony), *śivam* (bliss) and *advaitam* (oneness). What is the position of evil?

Evil is closely associated with the imperfection of the world. In fact, imperfection is the very essence of evil. As an imperfect being, man suffers from evil. Tagore conceives that evil and imperfection are the natural corollaries of creation.

> The question why there is evil in existence is the same as why there is imperfection, or, in other words, why there is creation at all.[25]

Creation takes place due to the self-limitation of the infinite reality. In other words, God for the purpose of creation involves Himself into imperfect and finite realities. According to Tagore, evil is that which obstructs man from attaining unity with existence. The question, why there is evil or imperfection in the world, is difficult to answer. But it is true that this evil or imperfection is not the final truth. Man has

[25] R.N. Tagore, *Sādhanā*, p. 47.

found that, what is limited is not ". . . imprisoned within its limits".[26] As a matter of fact, imperfection is not the denial of perfection, nor finitude the denial of infinity. Both of them are ". . . completeness manifested in parts".[27] The evil and contradictions are not absolute but relative. Actually, evil and imperfection are due to finitude of human existence. Tagore observes:

> Man has found out the great paradox that what is limited is not imprisoned within its limits; it is ever moving, and therewith shedding its finitude every moment. In fact, imperfection is not a negation of perfectness; finitude is not contradictory to infinity: they are but completeness manifested in parts, infinity revealed within bounds.[28]

Imperfection and evil remain on the rational level. All broken truths are evil. When man realizes universal spirit, evil and pain cease to remain. Rabindranath says:

> Pain, which is the feeling of our finiteness, is not a permanent fixture in our life. It is not an end in itself, as joy is. To meet with it is to know that it has no part in the true permanence of creation.[29]

Evil and error are not permanent, for it cannot accord with the whole. Evil is bound to grow into good, pain into pleasure, finitude into infinite because they are not permanent fixtures of the world. It is possible for man to transcend his finitude, and transmute pain and evil into pleasure and joy. In religious consciousness, man transcends his finitude and realizes oneness with the spirit and, thus, pain and evil cease to exist.

---

[26] R.N. Tagore, *Sādhanā*, p. 48.

[27] Ibid., p. 48.

[28] Ibid., p. 48.

[29] Loc. cit.

The deepest truth can be realized in union and not in separation. The freedom lies in union with Divine. This union is not possible at rational level. Reason cannot create union between finite and infinite. Tagore points out:

> Intellect sets us apart from the things to be known, but love knows its object by fusion.[30]

Love transcends all contradictions of human existence. This shows that Tagore places love or intuition at the highest level of consciousness. Reason moves in duality and involves the distinction between subject and object. Love or intuition aims at union. The distinction between subject and object vanishes in love. Intuition is the perfection of consciousness. Intuition is the light of pure consciousness that emanates from *Brahman*. In order to attain union with the Supreme, we must attain to that summit of consciousness, which is known as love or intuition. Tagore observes:

> It is through the heightening of our consciousness into love, and extending it all over the world, that we can attain *Brahmavihāra*, communion with the infinite joy.[31]

Intuition or soul-consciousness comprehends union between man and God. Love is intuitive by nature and is the only form of experience that comprehends unity. Reason cannot dispense with the distinction between the subject and the object. So long as, this duality exists, the core of the object can never be entered into the subject. Reason is dubious. But, when the subject penetrates into the core of the object, doubt vanishes. Penetration means identity and disappearance of duality. It means love or intuition transcends the level of reason and enters into the depth of human existence, and, thus opens the gate of the world of the infinite. Tagore observes:

---

[30] R.N. Tagore, *Sādhanā*, 159.

[31] Ibid., p. 107.

> The feeling of perfection in love, which is the feeling of the perfect oneness, opens for us the gate of the world of the infinite one, who is revealed in the unity of all personalities.[32]

The true meaning of freedom lies in the realization of union with the Supreme.

The union between the finite and the infinite, man and the Supreme is possible when man transcends reason and gets a glimpse of the intuitive vision. This union is possible in perfect love. The true meaning of human existence is not to be found in its separateness from God and others, but in the realization of its union with them. Love establishes union with the infinite. It does not lead to darkness, but leads to illumination. Tagore says:

> This is the attainment of *bodhi*, or the true awakening; it is the revealing in us of the infinite joy by the light of love.[33]

All our egoistic impulses and selfish desires obscure our true vision of the soul. Reason can give the description of our surface self. The inner being cannot be fathomed by reason. Love can break the barrier of ego and penetrate into the depth of soul. The very essence of love is unity. Love finds its meaning by unifying man with the Supreme. Reason cannot establish the bond of union. Rational understanding is partial and dualistic but the relation of love is complete. Tagore details:

> In love the sense of difference is oblitered and the human soul fulfils its purpose in perfection, transcending the limits of itself and reaching across the threshold of the infinite. Therefore, love is the highest bliss that man can attain to, for through it alone he truely knows that he is more than himself, and that he is at one with the all.[34]

---

[32] R.N. Tagore, *Personality*, pp. 83-84.

[33] R.N. Tagore, *Sādhanā*, p. 84.

[34] Ibid., p. 28.

Man is essentially spirit. There is always quest to realize the true nature of man. He says:

> Man's history is the history of his journey to the unknown in quest of the realization of his immortal self — his soul.[35]

The ultimate aim of man is to find union with the spirit of God. Intuition opens the gate of spiritual life. We can know the Supreme only in love. Tagore observes:

> We cannot attain the supreme soul by successive additions of knowledge acquired bit by bit even through all eternity, because he is one, he is not made up of parts; we can only know him as heart of our hearts and soul of our soul; we can only know him in the love and joy we feel when we give up our self and stand before him face to face.[36]

It is intuition which reveals God and rational knowledge. Intuition is just like light which illumines other objects as well as itself. Intuition is self-revealing. It is the vision of the Supreme Reality. At this stage:

> Man becomes perfect man, he attains his fullest expression, when his soul realizes itself in the infinite being . . ..[37]

Soul-consciousness overcomes all limitations of mind. When soul-consciousness or intuitive vision arises, man finds his affinity with the Supreme.

In *Sādhanā,* Tagore upholds the case of soul-consciousness or intuitive vision. He specifies:

> Intellectual knowledge is partial because our intellect is an instrument, it is only a part of us, it can give us information about things which can be divided and

[35] R.N. Tagore, *Sādhanā*, p. 33.

[36] Ibid., p. 37.

[37] Ibid., p. 40.

> analysed and whose properties can be classified, part by part.[38]

Intellect sets us apart from the things to be known. Love knows its object by fusion. The intuition or soul-consciousness realizes its unity in the Supreme one. He says, ". . . but our apprehension of truth in our soul is immediate and through direct intuition."[39] It is seen that the term "love" expresses the meaning of intuition at its best. Love is the consciousness of the soul. It is knowing by one's entire being. In epistemology, the faculty of knowledge, which establishes union, is known as intuition. In human experience, the power which creates union between man and the divine is known as love. P.T. Raju observes:

> The comprehension of unity is called intuition from the standpoint of knowledge, and love from that of human experience. As Tagore's philosophy aims at the understanding of the suprahuman in terms of the human, he calls it love.[40]

Realization of our soul is love. It is love or intuition which makes realization possible. Religious experience is the consciousness of soul. It is an intimate realization through intuitive vision. Reason declares truth as inexplicable and unknowable. To quote Tagore:

> Then we have our mind; and mind seeks its own food. Mind has its necessity also. It must find out reason in things. It is faced with a multiplicity of facts; and is bewildered when it cannot find one unifying principle which simplifies the heterogeneity of things. Man's constitution is such that he

---

[38] R.N. Tagore, *Sādhanā*, p. 159.

[39] Ibid., p. 36.

[40] P.T. Raju, *Idealistic Thought of India*, p. 329.

> must not only find facts, but also some laws which will lighten the burden of mere number and quantity.[41]

In order to attain synthetic vision, we have to transcend reason by means of intuition. Tagore asserts that *Brahman* cannot be known by reason. Truth is deeper than rational demonstration. Intuition alone can fathom the depth of divine mystery and release man from the bondage of ignorance.

Man possesses an urge to achieve freedom from bondage. This is evident from the lowest level of freedom to the highest summit of salvation. Man asserted in his bodily structure his first proclamation of freedom against the established rule of nature. The capacity of man to stand erect has given our body its freedom of posture, making it easy for us to turn on all sides and realize ourselves at the centre of things. Further, man adopts freedom of view. This freedom of view is the mental freedom. But man is conditioned by death, disease and decay. He does not enjoy true meaning of freedom at the psycho-somatic level. He is not fully free because his freedom of view is constantly influenced by desire, interest, prejudice and passion. According to Tagore, the true freedom lies in self-realization. When man attains self-realization, he exceeds himself and there lies the true meaning of freedom. He becomes fully aware that he is not imperfect but incomplete at the rational level for "... the human mind it has its circular shell of limitations".[42] The deeper truth — infinite dwells in finite and man can attain the ideal of unity — is revealed in intuition. Intuition is the deeper realization of one's own inner spirit. To be true is to become one with truth. The salvation of the finite lies in the deeper realization of spirit.

Man's ultimate goal is the realization of the Supreme or the infinite seated in the lotus of our heart. To realize our

[41] R.N. Tagore, *Personality*, p. 3.

[42] R.N. Tagore, *The Religion of Man*, p. 65.

oneness with the Supreme Being is the highest aim of our life. Tagore observes:

> But whatever may be the name and nature of his religious creed, man's ideal of human perfection has been based upon a bond of unity running through individuals culminating in a Supreme Being who represents the eternal in human personality.[43]

The salvation of man lies in him freeing his personality from the narrow limitations of selfhood, from the narrow bigoted perspective of his selfishness; his fulfilment consists in breaking the bonds of his isolated, narrow and private self. The destiny of man lies in bringing himself into contact with the All. Man can realize freedom which is the legitimate destiny of mankind in universal consciousness and finally it leads to oneness with the infinite. Tagore observes, "It was an inspiration for freedom, the freedom which enables us to realize *dharma*, the truth of Eternal Man".[44]

Sir Mohammad Iqbal (1876–1936)

Iqbal was greatly impressed by Henry Bergson, Nietzsche, Jalaluddin Rumi and some other Islamic thinkers. The metaphysics of Iqbal seems to have been considerably influenced by the great mystic poet Rumi. His book, *Masnavi,* is the source of many basic conceptions of Iqbal. Both Rumi and Iqbal agree that reason cannot give us the experience of God. Reason fails to comprehend the ways of the working of the Divine. Rumi was essentially a mystic and, for him, experience was more than reason. Reason is always conditioned by the finitude of human existence. According to Iqbal, intuitive experience is a better guide to religious life than reason.

---

[43] R.N. Tagore, *The Religion of Man*, p. 147.

[44] Ibid., p. 155.

The Ultimate Reality, according to Bergson and Iqbal, is not a pure being or static and passive existence, as the immobile and immutable reality cannot give rise to the world of change or becoming. Things can be derived from force and dynamic principles, but, we cannot derive force from static and motionless existence. Therefore, the ultimate principle is a dynamic living energy and not a static one. Iqbal observes, "We can derive 'things' from movement; we cannot derive movement from immobile things".[45] But, it is required to be mentioned that Iqbal does not follow Bergson's conception of the *elan vital*. Reality is not a blind force for Iqbal. The Ultimate Reality is not merely a flow of events, nor a directionless, aimless and random movement. It has consciousness and will. For Bergson, the *elan vital* is not consciousness nor is will, a quality of the former. Moreover, there is a distinction between will and consciousness. For Bergson, consciousness is the evolved product of the creative will. Iqbal rejects the view that reality is a blind force. It is not tenable to conceive that all creation, movement and change are without direction, aim and purpose. According to Iqbal, reality is God. It is a conscious personality. It directs, guides and creates the cosmos. God has self-determination and will. Iqbal is also against the monistic conception of reality which is devoid of individuality, self-will or self-determination. Iqbal postulates God, who is a conscious personality, in place of the *elan vital* of Bergson as the ultimate, dynamic and supreme self.

God is the Ultimate Ego. He has ego and like a human self, He has an organizing capacity. He controls the finite egos of individuals and organizes the universe. He creates realities and new worlds according to His will. Iqbal conceives that in evolution, there is the gradual ascent and creation of new realities, which are higher and superior to what existed before.

---

[45] S.M. Iqbal, *The Reconstruction of Religious Thought in Islam*, p. 48.

The Ultimate Ego holds the finite selves as a garland holds the pearl-beads without obliterating the individuality of the finite selves. God holds them in His own being. The finite selves are related to one another; God as an organic reality holds them in His existence. The Ultimate Ego is called the Absolute because the cosmos and the finite selves exist in His all-inclusive being. Iqbal observes:

> Thus a comprehensive philosophical criticism of all the facts of experience on its effcient as well as appreciative side brings us to the conclusion that the Ultimate Reality is a rationally directed creative life. To interpret this life as an ego is not to fashion God after the image of man. It is only to accept the simple fact of experience that life is not a formless fluid, but an organizing principle of unity, a synthetic activity which holds together and focalizes the dispersing dispositions of the living organism for a constructive purpose.[46]

The operation of thought or finite reason, which is essentially symbolic and discursive in character, veils the true nature of life. It can only picture it as a kind of universal current flowing through all things. Iqbal realizes the importance of intuition which alone can reveal reality. He observes:

> "Intuition reveals life as a centralizing ego. This knowledge, however, imperfect as giving us only a point of departure is a direct revelation of the ultimate nature of reality. Thus the facts of experience justify the inference that the ultimate nature of reality is spiritual, and must be conceived as an ego.[47]

It is clear from the above exposition that God has personality. But, it does not mean that He has finite existence. Individuality

---

[46] S.M. Iqbal, *The Reconstruction of Religious Thought in Islam*, pp. 57-58.

[47] Ibid., p. 58.

does not, in case of the ultimate ego, imply finitude. If God is an ego and as such an individual, how can we conceive Him as infinite? Iqbal observes:

> The answer to the question is that God cannot be conceived as infinite in the sense of spatial infinity. In matters of spiritual valuation mere immensity counts for nothing.[48]

Space and time are possibilities of the ego. They are partially realized in the shape of our mathematical space and time. Beyond Him and apart from His creative activity, there is no time and space to close Him off in reference to other egos. The Ultimate Ego is, therefore, neither infinite in the sense of spatial infinity nor finite in the sense of the space-bound human ego, whose body closes him off in reference to other egos. The infinity of the Utimate Ego consists in the infinite inner possibilities of His creative activity of which the universe, As known to us, is only a partial expression. Iqbal says:

> In one word God's infinity is intensive, not extensive. It involves an infinite series, but is not that series.[49]

Time, according to Iqbal, is an essential element in the ultimate reality. He makes an attempt to distinguish between real time and serial time. In serial time, there is division between past, present and future. Real time transcends them. Iqbal observes:

> But the real time is not serial time in which the division of past, present and future is essential; it is pure duration, i.e. change without succession . . ..[50]

Real time is pure duration in which distinction between "now" and "then" does not exist. In serial time, the distinction

---

[48] S.M. Iqbal, *The Reconstruction of Religious Thought in Islam*, p. 61.

[49] Ibid., p. 61.

[50] Ibid., p. 79.

between past, present and future can be made. McTaggart assumes the serial nature of time in which distinctions between past, present and future exist. He considers the serial nature of time as final. Iqbal observes:

> If we regard past, present and future as essential to time, then we picture time as a straight line, part of which we have travelled and left behind, and part lies yet untravelled before us. This is taking time, not as a living creative movement, but as a static absolute, holding the ordered multiplicity of fully shaped cosmic events, revealed serially, like the pictures of a film to the outside observer.[51]

Bergson conceived that reason as a spatializing activity cannot reveal the true nature of reality. Iqbal maintains that though reason spatializes and makes use of only mechanical categories, it has also a deeper movement in which it synthesizes the elements of our experience. Man's finite reason remains confined to serial time and does not touch real time or pure duration. While distinguishing his conception of reason from that of Bergson, Iqbal says:

> The nature of thought according to Bergson is serial; it cannot deal with movement except by viewing it as a series of stationary points. It is, therefore, the operation of thought, working with static concepts, that gives the appearance of a series of immobilities to what is essentially dynamic in its nature. The co-existence and succession of these immobilities is the source of what we call space and time.[52]

According to Iqbal, Bergson takes the partial view of intelligence and creates the dualism of will and thought. In the Ultimate Ego, there is no duality of will and consciousness. Bergson was not correct in conceiving reality to be merely a

[51] S.M. Iqbal, *The Reconstruction of Religious Thought in Islam*, pp. 54-55.

[52] Ibid., p. 49.

creative will or vital energy. He has, thus, subordinated thought to will and created a dualism of will and thought. This dualism may be found in the finite selves, where the discursive thought or lower reason operates. But thought in God has identity with His creative energy. It is not the same as finite reason or discursive thought. In God, there is no duality between thought and being. Iqbal observes:

> This is really due to the partial view of intelligence that he takes. Intelligence, according to him, is a spatializing activity; it is shaped on matter alone, and has only mechanical categories at its disposal.[53]

But thought or reason, according to Iqbal, has a deeper meaning. Further he states:

> While it appears to break up reality into static fragments, its real function is to synthesize the elements of experience by employing categories suitable to the various levels which experience presents. It is as much organic as life.[54]

Iqbal criticizes both Ghazali and Kant for failing to see that thought, in every act of knowledge, passes beyond its own finitude. Iqbal holds that Kant, in German thought, and Ghazali, in Islamic thought, exposed the pretensions of reason. Kant's *Critique of Pure Reason* revealed the limitations of human reason and reduced the whole work of the rationalists to a heap of ruins. Philosophical scepticism of Ghazali did the same work in the world of Islam in breaking the back of that ". . . proud but shallow rationalism which moved in the same direction as pre-Kantian rationalism in Germany".[55] Iqbal further points out that there is one important difference between Ghazali and Kant. Kant, consistently with his

---

[53] S.M. Iqbal, *The Reconstruction of Religious Thought in Islam*, p. 49.

[54] Loc. cit.

[55] S.M. Iqbal, *The Reconstruction of Religious Thought in Islam*, p. 5.

principles, could not affirm the possibility of a knowledge of God. Ghazali, having realized the limitations of "analytic thought", moved to mystic experience. In mystic experience, he found an independent content for religion. But, Iqbal, distinguishing his position from Ghazali, observes:

> But the revelation of the total infinite in mystic experience convinced him of the finitude and inconclusiveness of thought, and drove him to draw a line of cleavage between thought and intuition. He failed to see that thought and intuition are organically related and that thought must necessarily simulate finitude and inconclusiveness because of its alliance with serial time.[56]

Iqbal points out that Kant and Ghazali could not realize the deeper meaning of reason. Ghazali erected a barrier between thought and intuition due to the fact that he could not recognize the higher and deeper meaning of thought than its logical or intellectual understanding. Iqbal says:

> The idea, that thought is essentially finite and for this reason unable to capture the infinite, is based on a mistaken notion of the movement of thought in knowledge. It is the inadequacy of the logical understanding which finds a multiplicity of mutually repellent individualities with no prospect of their ultimate reduction to a unity that makes us sceptical about the conclusiveness of thought. In fact, the logical understanding is incapable of seeing this multiplicity as a coherent universe.[57]

Intellectual understanding of Iqbal is very similar to the finite reason of Sri Aurobindo and technical reason of Paul Tillich. In fact, the logical understanding is taken in the sense of reasoning or logical understanding of religious problems. It is incapable to see the multiplicity of the universe as a coherent

[56] Loc. cit.

[57] Loc. cit.

whole. Its only method is generalization based on resemblances, but its generalizations are only fictitious unities which do not affect the reality of concrete things. Iqbal observes:

> In its deeper movement, however, thought is capable of reaching an immanent infinite in whose self-unfolding moment the various finite concepts are merely moments. In its essential nature, then, thought is not static; it is dynamic and unfolds its internal infinitude in time like the seed which, from the very beginning, carries within itself the organic unity of the tree as a present fact. Thought is, therefore, the whole in its dynamic self-expression, appearing to the temporal vision as a series of definite specifications which cannot be understood except by a reciprocal reference.[58]

According to Iqbal, both Kant and Ghazali could not apprehend the higher nature of thought or reason. Reason in its higher nature passes beyond its own finitude. He says:

> Both Kant and Ghazali failed to see that thought, in the very act of knowledge, passes beyond its own finitude. The finitudes of Nature are reciprocally exclusive. Not so the finitudes of thought which are, in their essential nature, incapable of limitation and cannot remain imprisoned in the narrow circuit of their own individuality.[59]

Reason, in its deeper aspect, enjoys freedom and serves as a pointer to the infinite. Iqbal holds, ". . . thought demolishes the walls of its finitude and enjoys its potential infinitude".[60] It is a gross mistake that thought is altogether limited and narrow. Its higher movement and deeper meaning become

---

[58] S.M. Iqbal, *The Reconstruction of Religious Thought in Islam*, p. 6.

[59] Loc. cit.

[60] Loc. cit.

possible only because of the implicit presence in its finite individuality of the infinite, which keeps alive within it the flame of aspiration and sustains it in its endless pursuit.

> It is a mistake to regard thought as inconclusive, for it too, in its own way, is a greeting of the finite with the infinite.[61]

Iqbal seems to be anxious to prove that man should not abandon reason in order to realize the ultimate truth. If, as it is generally maintained that thought is related to the world, and if the world has to be renounced for the ultimate reality, it implies that thought has to be left behind. It is held that intuition alone, and not thought can reveal to us the ultimate truth. Iqbal maintains that neither the world nor thought should be left behind. It was a mistake of Ghazali, Kant and Bergson that they have not noticed a deeper aspect of thought. In its deeper moment, reason does not remain merely analytic and discursive. It leads us to the conclusion that Iqbal understands reason in its two aspects — analytic and synthetic. Analytic reason is static, whereas synthetic reason is dynamic. Analytic reason is lower, whereas synthetic reason is a higher one. P.T. Raju observes:

> Iqbal is not unaware of the fact that thought, which is used in our ordinary practical life, is mechanistic and that as such it cannot reveal to us reality in its purity. That is why he says at another place that lying close to our normal consciousness, there are potential types of consciousness which can "open up the possibilities of life-giving and knowledge-yielding experience". But this deeper consciousness is not opposed to thought; it is thought in its synthetic activity, by virtue of which the manifold fuses into one and serial time becomes pure duration and an eternal now.[62]

---

[61] Loc. cit.

[62] P.T. Raju, *Idealistic Thought of India*, pp. 384-85.

As regards relation between reason and intuition, Iqbal holds that it is a mistaken notion to hold reason and intuition as opposed to each other. There is no opposition between thought and intuition. Iqbal, very correctly, observes:

> Nor is there any reason to suppose that thought and intuition are essentially opposed to each other. The one grasps reality piecemeal, the other grasps it in its wholeness. The one fixes its gaze on the eternal, the other on the temporal aspect of reality. The one is present enjoyment of the whole of reality; the other aims at traversing the whole by slowly specifying and closing up the various regions of the whole for exclusive observation. Both are in need of each other for mutual rejuvenation. Both seek visions of the same reality which reveals itself to them in accordance with their function in life.[63]

Reason sharpens our insight. It prepares us for deeper understanding of religious problems. In its higher sense, reason takes a unitary view of the whole of reality. In order to secure a complete vision of reality, Iqbal says that sense-perception, reason and intuition must be harmonized. To quote Iqbal:

> In the interest of securing a complete vision of reality, therefore, sense-perception must be supplemented by the perception of what the Quran describes as "Fuad" or "Qalb", i.e. heart . . ..[64]

The "heart" is of kind a inner intuition. It brings us into contact with aspects of reality other than those open to sense-perception. Iqbal contends, "It is, according to *Quran*, something which 'sees' and its reports, if properly interpreted, are never false".[65] However, it is not a mystical faculty. It is rather a mode of dealing with reality in which sensation, in

---

[63] S.M. Iqbal, *The Reconstruction of Religious Thought in Islam*, p. 2.

[64] Ibid., p. 15.

[65] Loc. cit.

the philosophical sense of the word, does not play any part: yet the intuitive experience, thus opened to us, is as real and concrete as, any other experience. To describe it as psychic, mystical or supernatural does not minimize its value as experience. Here, reason plays a dominant role. It prepares the ground for higher vision. The experience is as true as any other experience. Iqbal says:

> There seems to be no reason, then, to accept the normal level of human experience as fact and reject its other levels as mystical and emotional. The facts of religious experience are facts among other facts of human experience and in the capacity of yielding knowledge by interpretation, one fact is as good as another.[66]

The organic unity of knowledge is possible only at the level of intuitive experience. Intuition gives us direct knowledge of the truth. It is an extraordinary experience. It aims at comprehending the whole of reality. The unique experience is revealed only to a few persons. But, everyone can have intuitions of his own self in moments of crucial decisions, when he goes deep to the bottom of his self.

Characteristics of Intuition

Iqbal believes that mystic experience is not cut-off from other sources of knowledge. In this way, we find that his mystic experience is intuitive in nature. He gives general observation on the main characteristics of mystic intuition.

Intuition is an immediate experience. It is a supra-sensuous and supra-rational experience of reality. Intuition comprehends reality as a whole. In this respect, it does not totally differ from other levels of human experience. Iqbal observes:

> As regions of normal experience are subject to interpretation of sense-data for our knowledge of the external world, so

[66] S.M. Iqbal, *The Reconstruction of Religious Thought in Islam*, p. 15

> the region of mystic experience is subject to interpretation for our knowledge of God.[67]

The immediacy of intuitive experience means that we know God directly just as we know other objects.

Intuition of mystic experience gives an unanalysable totality of experience. In such experience, the subject identifies itself with the object. The distinctions between the self and not the self, and the subject and the object disappear in intuition. Reason divides the knower from the known, and the subject from the object. In intuition, we cannot have any division of this kind. In intuition or mystic experience, there is no isolation of one knowledge from the other. Intuition gives reality with its past, present and future possibilities. That is why, we receive in it an unanalysable experience. Let us illustrate it with an example given by Iqbal himself. When one experiences the table before him, innumerable data of experience merge into the single experience of the table. We select out of the manifold data that fall into a certain order of space and time, and round them off in a reference to the table. In the intuitive or mystic state, however vivid and rich it may be, thought is reduced to a minimum and such an analysis is not possible. But this difference of the intuitive state from the ordinary rational consciousness does not mean discontinuance with the normal consciousness. In either case, it is the same reality which is operating on us. Iqbal states:

> The ordinary rational consciousness, in view of our practical need of adaptation to our environment, takes that reality piecemeal, selecting successively isolated sets of stimuli for response. The mystic state brings us into contact with the total passage of reality in which all the diverse stimuli merge into one another and form a single unanalysable unity in

---

[67] S.M. Iqbal, *The Reconstruction of Religious Thought in Islam*, p. 17.

which the ordinary distinction of subject and object does not exist.[68]

Intuition or mystic experience reveals to us a super-personal self. It is an active communion between self and God. There is an experience of the "Beyond", of the greater self outside us in all our intuitive experience. It is not a passive or reflective consciousness. It emerges due to the direct, active and personal encounter of self with God. Iqbal's conception of "other self" resembles Otto's numinous experience of "the wholly other". Iqbal observes:

> . . . to the mystic, the mystic state is a moment of intimate association with a unique otherself, transcending, encompassing and momentarily suppressing the private personality of the subject of experience.[69]

One may raise the question: how does Iqbal say that mystic experience involves a direct contact with the supreme self? Iqbal answers that just as we do not perceive the self of another man and yet immediately infer that he has a self, in the same way, in communion with God, we perceive Him and infer that He has a personality. Iqbal says:

> Yet we feel that our experience of other minds is immediate and never entertain any doubt as to the reality of our social experience.[70] Likewise, in mystic experience or intuitive experience, we encounter the supreme self.

Intuitive experience is incommunicable. It is more like a feeling than a thought. The interpretations, which the mystic puts on the content of his religious consciousness, can be conveyed to others in the form of propositions. But, the content of mystic

---

[68] S.M. Iqbal, *The Reconstruction of Religious Thought in Islam*, pp. 17-18.

[69] Ibid., p. 18.

[70] Ibid., p. 19.

experience cannot be transmitted because it baffles language and all symbolic expressions. Iqbal finds:

> The incommunicability of mystic experience is due to the fact that it is essentially a matter of inarticulate feeling, untouched by discursive intellect. It must, however, be noted that mystic feeling, like all feelings, has a cognitive element also; and it is, because of this cognitive element that it lends itself to the form of idea.[71]

Intuition seeks its expression in thought. Iqbal holds that religious feeling is objective and not a subjective fancy. He states:

> Considering its content, the mystic state is highly objective and cannot be regarded as mere retirement into the mists of pure subjectivity.[72]

Religious feeling has got certain direction and it is not a haphazard feeling without any direction. A direction implies some objective. It always refers to something beyond the present self. Here, we find that there is a close resemblance between Iqbal's religious feeling and Otto's "numinous experience". Both believe that religious feeling is not subjective but objective. Both Iqbal and Otto conceive that we feel about some object when we encounter God who is "other self". In spite of the fact that religious experience is incommunicable, it can be subjected to intellectual and pragmatic tests. Iqbal says:

> Happily we are in possession of tests which do not differ from those applicable to other forms of knowledge. These I call the intellectual test and the pragmatic test. By intellectual test I mean critical interpretation, without any presupposition of human experience, generally with a view to discover

---

[71] S.M. Iqbal, *The Reconstruction of Religious Thought in Islam,* p. 20.

[72] Ibid., p. 18.

> whether our interpretation leads us ultimately to a reality of the same character as is revealed by religious experience.[73]

In conclusion, we can say that according to Iqbal, religion holds out the prospect of nothing less than a direct vision or intuitive experience of reality. In this respect, it presents a contrast with philosophy. The spirit of philosophy is one of free and rational inquiry. It suspects all authority. Its function is to examine the uncritical assumptions of thought. In this pursuit, it may finally end in the denial or a frank admission of the incapacity of pure reason to reach the Ultimate Reality. The essence of religion is faith based on intuitive experience. It ultimately transcends reason. But though religious consciousness ultimately transcends sense-experience and reason, it does not negate or discard them. It is concerned with the whole man. As Iqbal observes:

> Religion is not a departmental affair; it is neither mere thought, nor mere feeling, nor mere action, it is an expression of the whole man.[74]

J. Krishnamurti (1895–1986)

If philosophy is love of wisdom, then J. Krishnamurti can rightly be called a philosopher. Unlike academic philosophers, he is not interested in constructing structures of reality. He also does not indulge in the dialectical criticism of the other philosophical systems. He does not propound any view of his own concerning reality. He is a philosopher who teaches a way of life. It is a way which leads to the unconditioning of mind, its utter freedom from the conditions of existence. It is the unconditioned mind alone which, according to him, can have a direct awareness of reality.

Reality, according to Krishnamurti, cannot be understood

---

[73] S.M. Iqbal, *The Reconstruction of Religious Thought in Islam*, p. 25.

[74] Ibid., p. 2.

by mental activities or reasoning. Reality is beyond time and space. Thought-process is always conditioned by time and space. Thought, which is in time, cannot apprehend reality which is timeless. Truth is not static but dynamic. It is living and moving. Thought-process or reasoning gives birth to idea which is based on image and memory. Truth is not an idea. It is not the image of something. Krishnamurti observes:

> Truth is not something static; it has no fixed abode, it is not an end, a goal. On the contrary, it is living, dynamic, alert, alive.[75]

If truth is a fixed point or static, it is not truth. Truth is unknown. A mind, which always moves in the realm of image and memory, cannot grasp reality which is dynamic. Mind will never find reality because it is made up of the known, it is the result of the past, the outcome of time. Mind is the instrument of the known, hence it cannot find the unknown. It can only move from the known to the known. When a mind is seeking truth, it is seeking its own self-projection and not truth.

> But a mind that is seeking reality, seeking God, is seeking the known. When you think of God, your God is the projection of your own thought, the result of social influences. You can think only the known, you cannot think of the unknown. You cannot concentrate on truth. The moment you think of the unknown, it is merely the self-projected known. God or truth cannot be thought about. If you think about it, it is not truth.[76]

Truth cannot be sought by reason or mental activity.

> Truth is in every leaf, in every tree; it is to be known from moment to moment. No one can lead you to truth; and if anyone leads you, it can be to the known.[77]

---

[75] J. Krishnamurti, *The First and the Last Freedom*, p. 152.

[76] Ibid., pp. 152-53.

[77] Ibid., p. 153.

Krishnamurti analyses the concept of mind and shows its finitude. He categorically says that reality or truth cannot be realized in terms of concepts but through direrct experiencing which carries to one beyond name and form. Truth cannot be given. Truth is a matter of realization. There must be "a state of mind in which there is direct perception".[78] There is no perception when there is resistance. "Understanding comes through being aware of what is."[79] We miss truth when our mind begins to translate, interpret truth according to its own conditioning. To know exactly "what is" the real, the actual without interference of dualistic reason or mental categories is only possible when mind is still. Mind is fragmentary and partial in nature. It is very elusive. This little mind, which is always conditioned with pre-conceived notions, prejudices, ideas, memory and images, cannot grasp the truth or reality. In order to understand the truth, we have to free our mind from all conditioning and come in direct contact or immediate awareness with truth.

Krishnamurti makes a distinction between understanding and intellectual understanding. He observes:

> I do not mean by the word "understand" mere intellectual understanding. One can never understand anything intellectually; do what it will, the cunning intellect can never grasp the quality of love, for example. The intellect can talk about it, write volumes about it, but the intellect cannot possibly feel it, or sense the quality, the perfume, the nature of love. And the intellect is all we have. We have so cunningly, so clearly developed the intellect, that when we use the words, "I understand", we mean that we understand intellectually — which is sheer nonsense. Nobody can understand anything merely intellectually. Either one understands or does not understand. You can understand only when you

[78] J. Krishnamurti, *The First and the Last Freedom*, p. 20.

[79] Ibid.

> give your whole being — body, mind, heart, everything that you have — to understand, including the intellect.[80]

So, this is clear that understanding of reality involves the totality of the being. In such an understanding of reality, emotion, will and reason are completely harmonized. Mind, according to Krishnamurti, is dualistic and always moves in the realm of duality of the knower and the known, but understanding which is direct experiencing transcends this duality. Reason is taken in the sense of "thought-process" or "reasoning". Krishnamurti observes, "Reason, however subtle and logical, is a process of thinking."[81] The process of thinking or reasoning starts with previous knowledge. So, thought is always linked with the past knowledge. It is not altogether free from the past knowledge. Thought is the response of memory and image. Krishnamurti says, ". . . thought is the response of the past, of experience as memory."[82] Reason can give an idea of reality. Idea is the outcome of thought-process. There can be no idea without thought-process. Krishnamurti observes:

> So the thought-process is the response of memory, is it not? You would have no thoughts if you had no memory; and the response of memory to a certain experience brings the thought-process into action.[83]

The response of memory, which is the thought-process, creates an idea. Therefore, the idea is always conditioned. He further says:

> That is to say the idea is the result of the thought-process, the thought-process is the response of memory, and memory is always conditioned. Memory is always in the past, and that memory is given in the present by a challenge. Memory

[80] Talks by Krishnamurti in Europe (1965), p. 19.

[81] J. Krishnamurti, *Commentaries on Living*, vol. III, p. 204.

[82] Ibid., p. 88.

[83] J. Krishnamurti, *The First and the Last Freedom*, p. 53.

> has no life in itself; it comes to life in the present when confronted by a challenge. And all memory, whether dormant or active, is conditioned.[84]

Reason or thought is capable of every form of abstraction. Reason can give concepts which are ideas created by mental projections. Carlo Suares states:

> Thought is capable of every form of abstraction. It creates concepts, it calls Being, Absolute, Eternity, and so on, and the thinker then imagines that these inverted projections, thrown up by his ignorance, are Reality. The truth of the matter is that the thinker prefers to stay in ignorance and uncertainty rather than explore the secret desires and unconfessed motives which make him believe in his system. His belief, his certainty, his faith, are not knowledge. The latter being the self-revelation of the total process of our consciousness, contains neither concepts nor dogmas, nor any formulation of the world.[85]

So, reason can remain confined to ignorance. The understanding of the reality involves man's total existence. We can understand the total structure of existence when our whole being is involved. Reason can give knowledge but not understanding of truth. Krishnamurti makes a further distinction between learning and knowledge. He uses the term learning in a special sense different from knowledge. He states:

> Learning is something entirely different from knowledge. It is very easy to accumulate knowledge, to gather information, store it up through experience, through reading, through reaction, and so on — store them up and from that knowledge act, which is what most of us do. But to learn is something entirely different because the moment you have learnt, which is the past, it has become knowledge. Learning

---

[84] J. Krishnamurti, *The First and the Last Freedom*, p. 54.

[85] Suares Karlo, *Krishnamurti and the Unity of Man*, pp. 23-24.

> is a constant process, a movement in which there is no accumulation at all. Most of us look at any problem through what we already know, through our accumulations, through our knowledge, through our rememberances, through our experience, through our conditionings, and so we prevent ourselves from learning about the problem.[86]

Learning is different from knowledge because knowledge gives us static concepts but learning is an act — an act of the active present.

> It is the verb to learn, it is a movement. But that which has been learnt has already become a static thing. So learning is dynamic and immediate.[87]

It is in direct contact with the fact. To understand anything, one must come immediately and directly into contact with the fact. But, we do not come into contact with the fact, because we either try to analyse it or avoid it or find the cause of it.

We have come to know the nature of thought-process or reasoning. Thought, according to Krishnamurti, is repetitive and not creative. Krishnamurti holds that creativity is possible when one hears "the voice of intuition". He recognizes that voice of intuition helps to create. He also holds that one should not follow or imitate anybody but arouse the voice of intuition. Reason is repetitive, mechanical and imitative. But, the voice of intuition is an inner urge. The term intuition can be best defined, "That insistent urge of the spirit, who gives the lower nature no peace until he is obeyed".[88] Further, he observes:

> The noblest guide each of us has is this voice, this tyrant, this intuition; and it is in cultivating, in ennobling, and in

---

[86] Talks by Krishnamurti in Europe, p. 4.

[87] Loc. cit.

[88] J. Krishnamurti, *The Kingdom of Happiness* (see footnote), p. 11.

> perfecting this, that we arrive at the goal — our own goal.[89]

We want to attain the Ultimate Truth. The Ultimate Truth is the goal. But our reason or thought which moves in the realm of ideas cannot realize the truth. Reason confirms to a certain type and makes ourselves fit into moulds not of our own making. This is fatal to the developement of perfect intuition. Intuition is creative and not repetitive like thought. It springs from the inner depth of the being. Krishnamurti says:

> And so long as you obey that voice, the intuition, you cannot err; it is in trying to follow the orders, the ideas, the visions of others that you go wrong.[90]

When we move in the realms of ideas, memories and images, there is likelihood to miss the reality and distort the fact. But, when we follow the inner voice, we cannot err in discovering reality. In intuition, there is a perfect harmony of emotions and of mind. It is the voice of the true self. Krishnamurti opines, "Intuition is the whisper of the spirit, intuition is the guiding word in our life."[91] Intuition is understanding by our total being. The emotion and the reason are perfectly harmonized. It is not a mental activity which is fragmentary but "voice from within". Krishnamurti holds that feelings and emotions are not required to be curbed or curtailed but sublimated and perfected in intuition. He observes:

> The idea that we should have no feelings and emotions is absured and unspiritual. The more you are bubbling over with feelings, the better; but you will find you have to control them; and if you do not, you suffer.[92]

---

[89] J. Krishnamurti, *The Kingdom of Happiness*, p. 12.

[90] Ibid., p. 14.

[91] Ibid., pp. 14-15.

[92] Ibid., p. 15.

According to Krishnamurti, the only authority is the voice of intuition. He holds that spiritual person should not follow the voice of others but he should recognize that voice of intuition which is from within. He observes:

> You must hear for yourselves that call, that voice which only comes through experience, through thought, through feelings.[93]

Intuitive knowledge — immediate awareness of total being — is true knowledge, for in this, the knower and the known are not two different things. Mind or reason creates division between the knower and the known. Krishnamurti frequently uses the word "awareness" which is akin to intuition. When one understands fact in direct contact, one is aware of the fact. He holds that fact may be an objective fact, a psychological fact and a spiritual fact. So, the fact in Krishnamurti's usage is not restricted to the objective fact. To be aware means to come in direct contact with facts. When man comes in direct contact, he becomes free from the background of past image and memory. Reason or analytic process cannot free us. It is not possible to analyse the whole content of our consciousness and, thereby, be free through the process of analysis. According to Krishnamurti, the analyser is not altogether different from that which he is analysing. He may separate himself from that which he analyses, but the analyser is part of that which he analyses. For example, if a man is angry, the man who analyses anger is still part of the anger. Therefore, the man is the analyser as well as the analysed. They are a joint phenomenon. Actually, they are not two separate forces. The difficulty in analysing ourselves, unfolding, looking at ourselves step by step, watching every reaction, every response is incalculably difficult and long. There must be a much simpler, a more direct way. The analysis cannot lead us to freedom. The thinker and

---

[93] J. Krishnamurti, *The Kingdom of Happiness*, p. 48.

the thought is a joint phenomenon. The thinker is trying to analyse that which he thinks. It will not free him from the background. Actually, the thinker analyses thought with the help of previous image and memory. So here the thinker is conditioned by memory and image. If the mind is free from the duality of the thinker and thought, then what is its state? Mind is blank. When mind is free from analytic process with all its implications, it becomes free and is capable of looking directly. So, thought is the result of time. Thought is the result of environment, of social and religious influences, all part of time. Now, can thought be free from time? That is, thought which is the result of time, can it stop and be free from the process of time? The problem is: how can a mind, which is the result of thought, be free from the background? Awareness is the direct experiencing, where the thinker is the thought and thought is the thinker. Awareness transcends the duality between the thinker and the thought. There is pure awareness as such. Krishnamurti thinks that when man is aware, then only he can be free from mental influence. The division between the thinker and the thought creates contradiction. Krishnamurti observes:

> . . . the root of contradiction is this division between the thinker and the thought; and the two cannot be integrated. But if you observe the structure of the thinker, you will see that the thinker is not when thought is not. It is the thought that breeds the thinker. . ..[94]

There is necessity to understand this whole structure, not as an intellectual process, but to be totally aware of fact. This awareness is like seeing something, it is like looking at a flower. We never actually look at a flower, because we look with our minds, with our thoughts, with our ideas, opinions, with our botanical knowledge of that flower. So it is thought

[94] J. Krishnamurti, *The First and the Last Freedom*, p. 33.

that looks. Our thoughts, ideas, opinions, judgements, botanical knowledge interfere with our looking. It is only when we can look at something completely then we are in direct contact with that thing. Awareness is looking at or "what it is". It is without the interference of the past as knowledge, as ideas, as a conclusion, as an experience, then surely one is directly in contact with the fact. If one looks so attentively, one will find that there is no experiencer and the thing experienced, no thinker and the thought, no observer and the thing observed. There is no centre from which one looks. He observes:

> Are you looking at fear as an observer, fear being the observed? Are you the thinker, observing the thing which is called fear? or are you looking at fear, but not as an observer, and therefore there is no censor, no centre from which you are looking, so that fear is the only fact.[95]

In a state of awareness there is no duality between the thinker and the thought, the observer and the thing observed. This state of awareness is akin to intuition. This is not knowing by reasoning but by directly experiencing. In a state of awareness mind becomes silent. Moreover, the mind cannot ride the tide of inward awareness without first being aware of outward behaviour, outward gestures, costumes, shapes, the size and colour of a tree, the appearance of a person, of a house. It is the same tide that goes out and comes in, and unless we know the outward tide, we will never know what is the inward tide.

Krishnamurti also distinguishes awareness from mystical apprehension. It is not mysterious something to be practised. It is the simple awareness of outward as well as inward things. The method which Krishnamurti suggests is very simple. He says that one shall be passively aware without choice. Krishnamurti wants to look at life in its wholeness and in actuality without any distraction of mind. He holds that mind,

---

95. J. Krishnamurti, *The First and the Last Freedom*, p. 15.

which is dull, cannot understand the nature of life. The mind must be extraordinarily alert and active. It should be "extensively aware" of all dimensions of life. Mind can be extensively aware through positive as well as negative approaches. The positive approach is the process of analysis, examination, asking, tearing to pieces, following and destroying. When the process of analysis in complete, one should discard the positive activity.

Now, the mind is in a state of negation. Negation in the sense that it is not expecting an answer, not looking for a way out. Having inquired, analysed, having wandered around, tried all the positive ways, followed the various paths, and not having found any answer; mind is completely in a state of negation. Now, when the mind is in a state of complete negation, man can approach anew all his problems, and then he will find that they can be resolved totally and completely because it is the mind itself that has been creating the problem. The mind that is in a state of complete negation because it has understood the whole process of following, denial, acceptance, the process of positive inquiry, positive assertions it is only such a mind whose action is freedom, and therefore it has no problem. The mind that is alertly aware of itself, that is fully conscious of its own activities, for such a mind, there is self-knowing. Self-knowing is the beginning of wisdom. Self-knowing brings freedom; and when there is freedom from the known, which is the very image of pleasure, then the mind enters into quite a different state, into quite a different dimension: The mind is completely quiet, totally still, but not through determination, not through wish, not through the desire for pleasure, not through the avoidance of pain. It is a total stillness in which thought is absent. Thought is of time and, therefore, this stillness is not of time.

If the mind is alert and extensively aware, it will be engaged in choiceless awareness. If the mind is dull, it is crowded with image, memory and pre-conceived notions, and becomes a victim of the efforts of memory. Thus, in the negative approach, memory becomes a very big obstacle in understanding the reality, for its one concern is to translate the unknown in terms of the known. Memory clothes the unknown with the images with which it is familiar. So, reason, which is a mental activity, cannot apprehend reality. The mind comes face to face with the unknown when it is passively aware of it. If the mind continues its state of alertness, it will be able to frustrate all efforts of memory at transfiguring the unknown into the known. The moment memory has imposed upon the unknown an old image or a modified image of old experience, the alert mind will put it aside declaring it, not this-not this. Thus, it is only an alert mind that can understand reality. The dull mind is sure to get itself caught in the vortex of images, where memory super-imposes upon the unknown.

The dull mind functions under the conditions of existence and filled with memory, image and pre-conceived notions. Intuitive knowledge is possible when the person is free from all sense of the past and the future, that is, when he is free from "psychological memory". It is only when the mind is emptied of psychological memory, that the intuitive perception of life can come. It is this intuitive perception that gives man freedom. As long as the mind is dull and is filled with psychological memory, there is no hope of the light of intuition. Krishnamurti says, "It is only the empty cup that can be filled." The mind, that is emptied of all the content of memory, can receive the illumination of intuition. So, reason can prepare the ground for intuitive realization which is immediate knowledge. It springs from the depth of the being. When the mind is emptied of memory and image, it becomes ready to receive that which comes from the deeper depth of existence. If a man is free from the influence of mind which works with image and memory, the light of intuition can be perceived by him, and it is in the light of intuition that there lies man's liberation.

The process by which Krishnamurti leads us to intuitive realization is through choiceless awareness. The passive but alert awareness is awareness with our entire being. It is our psychological memory that leads us away and conditions life all the time. Krishnamurti says that "that which is conditioned" cannot perceive the unconditioned. Truth is unconditioned. It can be realized only by an unconditioned mind. But, memory all the time imposes conditions upon us, thus preventing us from looking at life in an unconditioned manner. The greatest obstacle to man's liberation, therefore, is the mind which is based on images and memory, and which is conditioned by time. To be free from the conditioning factors of mind or reason is the main problem before man. If he becomes free from the influence of reason or mind, he will then be able to look at life free from all distractions. So, Krishnamurti visualizes that the mind should become free from all movement in time. The mind that is free from all movement in time is a still mind. A mind or thought is in time, but when the stillness of mind comes, it transcends time. Krishnamurti observes:

> The enclosure of the mind in an idea or the avoidance of people who make life complicated does not bring about stillness of mind. Stillness of mind comes only when there is no process of isolation through accumulation but complete understanding of the whole process of relationship. Accumulation makes the mind old; only when the mind is new, when the mind is fresh, without the process of accumulation — only then is there a possibility of having tranquillity of mind. Such a mind is not dead, it is most active. The still mind is the most active mind but if you will experiment with it, go into it deeply, you will see that in stillness there is no projection of thought. Thought, at all levels, is obviously the reaction of memory and thought can

> never be in a state of creation. It may express creativeness but thought in itself can never be creative. When there is silence, that tranquillity of mind which is not a result, then we shall see that in that quietness there is extraordinary activity, an extraordinary action which a mind agitated by thought can never know. In that stillness, there is no formulation, there is no idea, there is no memory; that stillness is a state of creation that can be experienced only when there is complete understanding of the whole process of the "me". Otherwise, stillness has no meaning. Only in that stillness, which is not a result, is the eternal discovered, which is beyond time.[96]

The mind, which is chained to idea, cannot apprehead reality. The mind that has become still is unconditioned, free from all distractions. It is such a mind that can receive the light of truth or god or reality. In the stillness of the mind, there is complete freedom from memory. In such a state, man is able to look at life with the awareness of his whole being. Such awareness brings man to the realization of truth.

The choiceless awareness, negative approach and the stillness of the mind are interrelated. They go together to form an integrated life of the individual. Perfect action for man is possible only in the stillness of mind. With choiceless awareness and negative approach, the mind becomes empty of its contents. In the state of tranquillity of mind, there arises love. Krishnamurti observes:

> In the state of tranquillity of mind that is really still, there is love. And it is love alone that can solve all our human problem.[97]

The problem is how to bring an end to this separative process of reason. Reason cannot put an end to itself. Krishnamurti holds:

---

[96] J. Krishnamurti, *The First and the Last Freedom*, p. 279.

[97] Ibid., p. 114.

> We see the ways of the intellect but we do not see the way of Love. The way of Love is not to be found through intellect. The intellect with all its ramifications, with all its desires, ambitions, pursuits must come to an end for love to come into existence.[98]

Rightly, he observes, "So love can come into being only when the mind is not there".[99] Intuition or love can bring man to freedom and perfection. He says, "Awareness is freedom, it brings freedom, it yields freedom . . .".[100] When reason is silent, there is a union between subject and object in love. Krishnamurti stands for the blending of head and heart, wisdom and love, reason and intuition. This experience is a sort of total awareness in which will, emotion and mind are integrated. We see the ways of reason but we do not see the way of love. The way of love is not to be found through reason. "So love can come into being only when the mind is not there."[101] When love arises, the duality between the subject and the object lapses. Only then, it is possible to find out what God is, what truth is. So long as we remain confined to reason or thought-process, there is duality between the thinker and the thought, and we cannot grasp reality. Reason is always conditioned by its ideas which are based on memory and image. Krishnamurti observes:

> Now, we are trying to find truth through intellect, through imitation — which is idolatry, only when you discard completely, through understanding, the whole structure of the self, can that which is external, timeless, immeasurable, come into being. You cannot go to it; it comes to you.[102]

---

[98] J. Krishnamurti, *The First and the Last Freedom*, p. 119.

[99] Loc. cit.

[100] J. Krishnamurti, *The First and the Last Freedom*, p. 174.

[101] Ibid., p. 119.

[102] Loc. cit.

6

Conclusion

THE foregoing discussions on the concepts of reason and intuition lead us to the conclusion that reality or the Absolute cannot be apprehended through reason or mental categories. Intuition alone can fathom the depth of reality. Reason can serve only as a pointer to the Absolute, but it cannot reach it. Intuition alone can attain unity with it. This truth has been amply illustrated in the philosophies of the great thinkers whom we have studied in the course of the present book, specially in that of Sri Aurobindo, K.C. Bhattacharyya and S. Radhakrishnan.

According to Sri Aurobindo, our formal or finite reason is involved in interminable conflicts. The contradictions between indeterminate and determinate, one and many, infinite and finite, etc. are irreconcilable at the level of the finite or formal reason. But they can be resolved by the higher reason or the Logic of the Infinite. According to Misra, ". . . the conception of the Logic of the Infinite is Sri Aurobindo's main contribution to philosophy".[1] It has great significance for modern thought and specially for Absolutism, both Indian and Western. Sri Aurobindo has been able to establish his Integral Advaitism on the basis of his conception of the higher reason or the Logic of the Infinite. This may be regarded as a unique contribution of Sri Aurobindo in the field of metaphysics.

---

[1] R.S. Misra, *Integral Advaitism of Sri Aurobindo* (Preface), p. vii.

Another significant contribution that Sri Aurobindo makes is with regard to his theory of integral or supramental knowledge. He makes a clear-cut distinction between the intuitive knowledge and the supramental knowledge. Intuition, according to him, is affected by the subjectivity of human existence. It cannot grasp the integral reality. Man can have a direct and all-embracing vision of reality only when he attains supramental consciousness in the course of evolution. Thus, unlike Śaṅkara, Rāmānuja and other great philosophers of the past, Sri Aurobindo does not regard intuition as the highest source of knowledge. This, in our opinion, is a most revolutionary idea of Sri Aurobindo and it constrains us to look at the age-old problem of knowledge from a different perspective. The supramental knowledge may or may not be attained by man. It is difficult, rather impossible, to say anything for or against the possibility of man's attaining the supramental knowledge on strictly logical grounds. But the contention of Sri Aurobindo that man in the present state of his development cannot enjoy a direct and all-embracing vision of reality even through intuition seems to have sufficient force and logic in it and it cannot be easily set aside.

Sri Aurobindo also marks a radical departure from tradition in his ideas of salvation and the goal of human life, and of history. Though he admits the liberation of the individual soul from the cycle of birth and death, he does not regard it as the goal of man's life. The real goal of man's life is not individual salvation but collective salvation. It is not only the salvation of human spirit but of nature as well. Not only the human spirit has to attain fulfilment ultimately but the whole historical process is heading towards that fulfilment, according to Sri Aurobindo. Thus, we find that Sri Aurobindo has given a deeper meaning to the concepts of reason and intuition, and tries to approach the problem of knowledge from an entirely fresh perspective. He also shows distinct originality and freshness in developing the ideas of cosmic evolution which is entirely spiritual in nature, of the emergence of supermen or gnostic beings, of the collective salvation and the fulfilment of nature and history.

K.C. Bhattacharyya is an analytic and critical thinker. His philosophical method is analytic. As has been discussed before, Bhattacharyya believes in "cognitive inwardization". The state of cognitive inwardization can be attained only by analysis. His most important contribution is that he shows the supreme freedom of the subject. This freedom of the subject is established not by dialectical reasoning but by critical analysis of the subjective experience as well as of the objective world. He shows great understanding and insight in defining the nature of metaphysics, the nature of theoretic consciousness or reason, of the different objects of reason, etc. He does not essentially give new truths but he certainly provides new insight into the truths of logic, epistemology and metaphysics. The central concept of his philosophy — the subject as freedom — is essentially derived from the Advaita Vedānta. But, his exposition of the freedom of the subject seems to be distinctly original. His originality lies in his analytic and critical method, and in his providing deep insight into the different metaphysical, epistemological and logical problems. Even when he does not give new truths, one certainly after reading him does not fail to feel the impact of a great mind. One starts thinking in a fresh way and with a deeper understanding over the problems which were known to him before. The formulation of the analytic and critical method and its application in the field of metaphysics and in unravelling the nature of the ultimate reality or the unconditioned seems to be the most significant contribution of Bhattacharyya. Though he takes recourse to the analytic and critical method of reflection, he also shows the limitations of reflective consciousness. Reason in his philosophy not only distinguishes the subject from the object, the real from the appearance, etc. but it also becomes aware of its own limitations. While it subjects the facts of experience to critical examination and valuation, it also turns the searchlight of criticism on itself. Reason becomes critical of itself and thus becomes acutely conscious of its limitations. This consciousness itself paves the way for the realization of the higher or spiritual consciousness, which ultimately aims at the realization of subject as freedom itself.

Radhakrishnan gives a comprehensive and deeper meaning to the concepts of reason and intuition. The most significant contribution of Radhakrishnan lies in his application of reason and intuition in the different fields of human experience. He does not take reason and intuition as constituting any kind of polarity. They are, according to him, not opposed to each other. Intuition, according to him, fulfils reason but does not negate it. Radhakrishnan takes intuition in the sense of integral experience. It is something which is all-inclusive and which gives a real and comprehensive knowledge of the universe as well as of the transcendent reality. Radhakrishnan's interpretation of reason and intuition in a deeper and comprehensive way helps him in having a correct appreciation of the reality as a whole which includes the individual, universal and transcendent orders of existence. Another significant contribution of his thought is that he finds the operation of reason and intuition in the different fields of life such as science, art, ethics and religion. Intuition, according to him, is something which not only makes one aware of the transcendent reality but also enables one have a deeper understanding and appreciation of the truths of science, art, ethics, religion and of the other fields of human creativity. Though, metaphysically, he is a Vedāntin belonging to the Advaita school, he introduces certain new ideas concerning salvation and the goal of history. Salvation of the individual does not seem to interest him so much as the salvation of the society as a whole. History, according to him, is also moving forward and is heading towards some sort of fulfilment. In this respect, he comes very close to Sri Aurobindo, though he does not envisage the possibility of collective salvation and the fulfilment of history in as clear a way as Sri Aurobindo.

One most significant feature that one finds in Sri Aurobindo and Radhakrishnan and some modern Indian thinkers is that they show great interest in man's life in the world and they seem to be deeply interested in the spiritualization of his secular life. The real aim of man's life, according to them, is not only the attainment of individual liberation, but it is the enrichment and all-round development and fulfilment of his collective life. These thinkers do not believe in any polarity between the spiritual life and secular life. The different spheres of man's secular life are to be illuminated and transformed by the light of spirit. His life as a whole is to be spiritualized. Human society as a whole has to attain, according to these thinkers, a higher reflective and spiritual level. Human society has to attain a level of existence where it will be free from all discords, strifes, disparity, selfishness, etc. and where life will be guided in a natural way by the light and truth of spirit.

Rabindranath Tagore also, like Sri Aurobindo and Radhakrishnan, is a great champion of spiritualization of life. The spirit, according to him, is to be realized in its deepest aspects not only within man but also in the world outside. The awakened spirit of man, according to him, manifests itself in the different fields of human creativity — science, art, literature, philosophy, music, ethics, etc. Thus, Tagore gives a deeper and richer content to man's understanding of religion and spiritual experience. He does not believe in any gap between spiritual life and secular life. This gap is felt only so long as man is not conscious of the eternal spirit and its working in the world order. Man has to realize unity not only in himself but in the whole of human society. Spiritual realization, according to him, really becomes meaningful only when man engages himself in the great creative activities in the different fields of life. Thus, the attitude of Tagore towards man's life in the world is more or less the same as that of Sri Aurobindo and Radhakrishnan. All these three great thinkers aim at the all-round progress, enrichment and fulfilment of man's life individually as well as collectively. They seem to be possessed of the most optimistic and dynamic attitude towards life, both secular as well as spiritual. This attitude has had a powerful impact on the development of their world views and their envisaging the goal of human life and of history.

Sir Mohammad Iqbal was a great Muslim thinker of undivided India. He tried to reconstruct the Islamic thought in the modern light. Like Sri Aurobindo and Radhakrishnan, he conceives and interprets reason in a deeper sense. His main contribution to the "philosophy of religion" is that he envisages the deeper meaning and moment of thought which do not come in conflict with intuition. The abstract or lower thought is in opposition to intuition but the higher or deeper thought paves the way for an organic and intuitive vision of reality. He also makes a significant contribution by distinguishing real time and serial time. He equates real time with pure duration of Bergson in which there is no division between past and present. The serial time is taken as a straight line in which the distinction between "now" and "then" exists. He conceives that reason in its lower aspect remains confined to serial time and does not apprehend real time, which is pure duration. He takes reality as dynamic and ever flowing. Thought cannot grasp the ever-flowing reality because it is abstract and tries to grasp reality through its static concepts. The another contribution by Iqbal is regarding the position of man and the world. Iqbal conceives that man is not different from God, but he is also not identical with Him. He does not want negation of the individual egos. He says that the individual egos are related to the Supreme Ego as pearl beads are woven in a garland. In this way, Iqbal makes significant and substantial contribution to our understanding of the nature of reason and spiritual experience and of time, ultimate reality or God and man's relation with Him.

J. Krishnamurti is a great champion of the philosophy of the "unconditioned". He impresses on man one central truth with great persuasion and force and it is the necessity on the part of man to free himself from all kinds of conditioning. He asks man to free himself altogether from the impact of his tradition and all other influences that have conditioned his life so far. He has to free himself from all authority — human or Divine. Man cannot have a correct understanding and appreciation of truth so long as he looks at life and reality in the light of tradition, authority or other influences. So, the best way for him is to unconditon his mind from everything. This will alone enable him attain stillness and peace of mind. It is only in this way that his spirit will manifest in him in its pristine purity. The attainment of the unconditioned state of existence is, according to Krishnamurti, the real truth of man's life. His insistence on freeing oneself from the authority of tradition, scriptures, etc. and the attainment of the unconditioned state of mind may be said to be the chief contribution of J. Krishnamurti. He is a thinker who does not give any new truths or new values of life. What he actually does is that he teaches man to develop a correct attitude towards life or, more correctly, he teaches man to free himself from all views and conditioning, and enjoy the undisturbed silence or peace of mind. There lies, according to him, man's freedom and his fulfilment.

Thus, we find that the great Indian thinkers of modern time have made significant and substaintial contributions to the various fields in phiosophy. They have certainly enriched our understanding of the nature of reason and intuition or spiritual experience and their importance and role in man's life. They start enquiry into the deeper truths of metaphysics and religion with utmost seriousness and devotion. Philosophy, according to them, is something which vitally concerns man's life, individually as well as collectively. It is something living and concrete and not a mere abstract discipline of idle speculation, remote from life and existence. Philosophy, in their views, is not simply a way of thought but it is also a way of life. In this respect, these philosophers are in perfect agreement with their illustrious predecessors of the past. Philosophy, in this ancient land, has never been divorced from life. It had given meaning and direction to man's life in the past. It is performing the same noble and spiritual function today.

Bibliography

Aurobindo, Sri., *The Life Divine*, Pondicherry: Sri Aurobindo Ashram, first edn., 1955.

———, *Isha Upaniṣad*, Calcutta: Arya Publishing House, third edn., 1941.

———, *Kena Upaniṣad*, Pondicherry: Sri Aurobindo Ashram, first edn., January 1952.

———, *Ideal and Progress*, Pondicherry: Sri Aurobindo Ashram, fourth edn., January 1951.

———, *Letters of Sri Aurobindo*, Bombay: Sri Aurobindo Circle, fourth series, first edn., 1951.

———, *Bankim-Tilak-Dayananda*, Calcutta: Arya Publishing House, first edn., November 1940.

———, *The Renaissance in India*, Chandernagore: Publishing House, September 1920.

———, *The Ideal of the Karmayogin*, Pondicherry: Sri Aurobindo Ashram, seventh edn., 1950.

———, *The Problem of Rebirth*, Pondicherry: Sri Aurobindo Ashram, first edn., January 1952.

———, *Savitri*, Pondicherry: Sri Aurobindo International University, first edn., January 1954.

———, *The Ideal of Human Unity*, New York: Sri Aurobindo Library, first edn., 1950.

———, *Essays on the Gita*, Calcutta: Arya Publishing House, second edn., 1944.

———, *Essays on the Gita*, Calcutta: Arya Publishing House, first edn., 1944.

———, *The Riddle of This World*, Calcutta: Arya Publishing House, 1933.

———, *The Human Cycle*, Pondicherry: Sri Aurobindo Ashram, first edn., 1949.

———, *The Synthesis of Yoga*, Pondicherry: Sri Aurobindo Ashram, first University edn., 1955.

Arapura, J.G., *Radhakrishnan and Integral Experience*, Calcutta: Asia Publishing House, 1966.

Bahm, A.J., *Types of Intuition*, University of New Maxico Press, 1960.

———, *Philosophy, An Introduction*, America: John Wiley and Sons, Inc., 1953.

Barrett William and Henry D. Aiken (ed.), *Philosophy in the Twentieth Century, An Anthology*, vol. I, New York: Random House 1962.

Banerjee, S., *A Short Treatise on 'The Life Divine'*, vol. II, part I, Pondicherry: Sri Aurobindo Ashram, 1957.

Bergson, H., *The Creative Mind* (tr. by Andison L. Middle, New York: Philosophical Library, 1946.

———, *An Introduction to Metaphysics* (tr. by Hulme), New York: The Liberal Art Press, second edn., August, 1955.

———, *The Two Sources of Morality and Religion*, New York: Doubleday Anchor Books, (paperback), 1935.

———, *The Creative Evolution* (tr. Arthus Mitchell), New York: The Modern Library, 1944.

Berdyaev, Nicolas, *Freedom and the Spirit*, Geoffrey Bles, London: The Centenary Press, third edn., May, 1944.

———, *Spirit and Reality*, Geoffrey Bles, London: The Centenary Press, third edn., May, 1946.

Bhattacharyya, H. (ed.), *The Cultural Heritage of India*, Calcutta: The Ramakrishna Mission, Institute of Culture (vol. IV, second edn., revised and enlarged), 1956.

Bhattacharyya, K.C., *Studies in Vedantism*, Calcutta University Studies no. 3, 1909.

———, *The Subject as Freedom*, Amalner: Indian Institute of Philosophy, 1930.

———, *Studies in Philosophy*, vol. I (ed. Gopinath Bhattacharyya), Calcutta: Progressive Publishers, August 1956.

——— *Studies in Philosophy*, vol. II (ed. Gopinath Bhattacharyya), Calcutta: Progressive Publishers, May 1958.

Bradley, F.H., *Appearance and Reality*, London: Oxford University Press, second edn., ninth impression, 1962.

———, *The Principles of Logic*, vols. I and II, London: Oxford University Press, 1950.

Brightman, E.S., *Introduction to Philosophy*, New York: Henry Holt and Co., 1925.

Broad, C.D. *The Mind and Its Place in Nature*, London: Routledge and Kegan Paul Ltd., 6th impression, 1951.

Bouquet, A.C., *Hinduism*, London: Hutchinson's University Library, 1948.

———, *Comparative Religion*, England: Penguin Books Ltd., seventh edn., 1967.

Burgh, W.G., *The Life of Reason*, London: Macdonald & Evans, 1949.

Burtt, E.A., *Types of Religious Philosophy*, New York: Harper & Row Publishers, 1951.

Butler, D.C., *Western Mysticism*, Grey Arrow edn., 1960.

Caird, John, *An Introduction to the Philosophy of Religion*, Glasgow: Jackson Sons & Ltd., 1936.

Cark, W.E., *Indian Conceptions of Immortality*, Cambridge: Harvard University Press, 1934.

Carrel, A, *Man the Unknown*, London: Hamish Hamilton, 17th impression, April, 1961.

Carr, E.H., *What Is History*, Penguin Books, 1961.

Chardin, Pierre Teilhard De, *The Phenomenon of Man*, Fotana Books, 1958.

Chand, T., *Influences of Islam on Indian Culture*, Allahabad: The Indian Press (Publications) Pvt. Ltd., second edn., 1963.

Chowdhury, H., *Sri Aurobindo: The Prophet of Life Divine*, Calcutta: Sri Aurobindo Pathmandir, first published in 1951.

Chowdhary Haridas and Spiegelberg Frederie (ed.), *The Integral Philosophy of Sri Aurobindo*, London: George Allen & Unwin Ltd., first published, 1960.

Cohen, M.R., *Reason and Nature*, Glencoe, IIlinois: The Free Press Publishers, 1959.

Collingwod, R.G., *The Idea of History*, Oxford University Press, (paperback edn.), 1961.

Croce, Bendetto, *Aesthetic* (tr. by Douglas Ainslie), London: Macmillian and Co., 1929.

Das, Bhagavan, *The Essential Unity of All Religions*, Banaras: The Kasi Vidya Pitha, 1939.

Das, A.C., *Sri Aurobindo and the Future of Mankind*, University of Calcutta, 1934.

———, *Sri Aurobindo and Some Modern Problems*, Calcutta: General Printers and Publishers Private Ltd., first edn., 1958.

Dasgupta, K.C., *Monism, A Critical Survey*, Calcutta: K.C., Gupta, October 1954.

Dasgupta, S., *Tagore's Asian Outlook*, Calcutta: S. Dasgupta, 8 May, 1961.

———, *A History of Indian Philosophy*, vol. II, Cambridge University Press, reprint, 1952.

Dasgupta, S.N., *Hindu Mysticism*, London: The Open Court Publishing Co., 1927.

———, *A History of Indian Philosophy*, Cambridge University Press (vol. I, first edn., 1922, Reprint, 1932).

Datta, D.M., *The Six Ways of Knowing*, University of Calcutta, 1960.

———, *The Chief Currents of Contemporary Philosophy*, published by S. Kanjilal, Calcutta University Press, second edn., 1961.

Devi, Maitreye, *Tagore by Fireside*, Calcutta: Rupa & Company, first published in January 1961.

Datta, K. Guru, *Existentialism and Indian Thought*, The Indian Institute of World Culture, Bangalore, third edn., 1960.

Durant, Will, *The Story of Philosophy*, London: Ernest Benn, 1929.

Estoborn, Sigfrid, *The Religion of Tagore*, Mysore: The Christian Literature Society for India, first printed, 1949.

Ewing, A.C., Reason and Intuition, London: Oxford University Press, 1942.

Farquhar, J.N., *The Crown of Hinduism*, London: Humphray Milford, Oxford University Press, 1919.

———, *Modern Religious Movements in India*, New York: The Macmillian & Co. Ltd., 1918.

Ferm, V. (ed.)., *Religion in the Twentieth Century*, New York: The Philosophical Library, 1948.

Frazer, R.W., *Indian Thought Past and Present*, London: T. Fisher Unwin Ltd., 1915.

Galloway, George, *The Philosophy of Religion*, Edinburgh: T. & T. Clark, 1956.

Gandhi, Kishore H., *Sri Aurobindo and the World Crisis*, Bombay: Sri Aurobindo Circle, 1949.

Ghosh, Sisir Kumar, *The Later Poems of Tagore*, Bombay: Asia Publishing House, 1961.

Gibb, H.A.R., *Modern Trends in Islam*, Illinois: The University of Chicago Press, third impression, 1954.

Giri, Swami Mahadevananda, *Vedic Culture*, Calcutta: University of Calcutta, and Hardwar: Sannyas Ashram, 1947.

Gokhale, B.G., *Indian Thought Through the Ages*, Bombay: Asia Publishing House, 1961.

Green, T.M., *Moral Aesthetic and Religious Insight*, New Jersey: Rutgers University Press, 1957.

Gupta, Nalini Kanta, *The Yoga of Sri Aurobindo*, Part Two Pondicherry: Sri Aurobindo Ashram, 1943.

———, *The Approach to Mysticism*, Part Two, Madras: Sri Aurobindo Library, first edn., 1943.

Happold, F.C., *Mysticism — A Study and an Anthology*, London: Penguin Books, 1963.

Harper, Ralph, *Existentialism: a Theory of Man*, Cambridge: Harvard University Press, second Printing, 1949.

Hegel, G.W., The Philosophy of History, New York: Dover Publication Inc., 1956.

Hiriyanna, M., *Outlines of Indian Philosophy*, London: George Allen and Unwin, 1951.

Hocking, W.E., *The Meaning of God in Human Experience*, New Haven: Yale University Press, 13th printing, March 1955.

———, *Types of Philosophy*, New York, Chicago, Atlanta: Charles Scribner's Sons 1939.

Hoffding, H., *The Philosophy of Religion*, London: Macmillian & Co. Ltd., 1914.

Inge, W.R. et al. (eds.)., *Radhakrishnan Comparative Studies in Philosophy*, Presented in Honour of his Sixtieth Birthday, London: George Allen and Unwin Ltd., first published in 1951.

Inge, W.R. *Mysticism in Religion*, London: Hutchinson's University Library.

Isherwood, Christopher (ed.), *Vedanta for Modern Man*, New York: Harper and Bros, first edn., 1957.

Iyengar, K.R. Srinivasa, *Sri Aurobindo*, Calcutta: Arya Publishing House, 1945.

Iqbal, S.M., *The Reconstruction of Religious Thought in Islam,* London: Oxford University Press, 1934.

———, *The Secret of the Self* (tr. by Reynold A. Nicholson), London: Macmillian & Co. Ltd., 1920.

———, *The Development of Metaphysics,* London: Luzac & Co., 1908.

Jack, Homer, A., *Wit and Wisdom of Rabindranath Tagore,* New Delhi: New Book Society of India, first edn., 1961.

James, W., *The Varieties of Religious Experience,* New York: Collier Books 1961.

Joad, C.E.M., *The Counter Attack from the East,* London: George Allen and Unwin, 1933.

———, *Guide to Philosophy,* London: Victor Gollancz Ltd., 1948.

———, *Guide to Modern Thought,* London: Faber and Faber Ltd., 1948.

Jones, Rufus M., *Studies in Mystical Religion,* London: Macmillian and Co. Ltd., 1923.

Kabir, Humayun, *Immanuel Kant on Philosophy in General,* Calcutta: University Press, 1935.

———, *The Indian Heritage,* Calcutta: Asia Publishing House, third edn., revised and enlarged, November 1955.

Kapali Sastri, T.V., *Sri Aurobindo: Lights on the Teachings,* Calcutta: Sri Aurobindo Pathmandir.

Kaul, R.N., *Immediacy, Reason and Existence,* Allahabad: Udayana Publications, 1965.

Kingsland, W., *Rational Mysticism,* London: George Allen and Unwin, first edn., 1924.

Krishnamurti, J., *The Kingdom of Happiness,* London: George Allen & Unwin Ltd., for Star Publishing Trust, Eerde, Omnsen, Holland, first published in 1927.

———, *The Master of Culture* (ed. by Rajagopal), London: Victor Gollancz Ltd., 1965.

———, *Commentaries on Living* (ed. by Rajagopal), London: Victor Gollancz Ltd., fifth impression, 1967.

———, *Education and the Significance of Life,* London: Victor Gollancz Ltd., sixth impression, 1968.

———, *Freedom from the Known* (ed. by Mary Lutyens), London: Victor Gollancz Ltd., 1969.

Langley, G.H., *Sri Aurobindo, Indian Poet, Philosopher and Mystic,* David Mariowe Ltd., Royal India and Pakistan Society, 1949.

Leuba, J.H., *The Psychology of Religious Symbolism,* London, 1929.

Lewis, H.D., *Contemporary British Philosophy,* London: George Allen and Unwin, third series, second edn., 1961.

Lovejoy, A.O., *The Reason, The Understanding and Time,* Baltimore: The Johns Hopkins Press, 1961.

Malkani, G.R., *Vedantic Epistemology,* Amalner: Indian Institute of Philosophy, 1953.

———, *Metaphysics of Advaita Vedanta,* Amalner: Indian Institute of Philosophy, 1961.

Maitra, S.K., *Studies in Sri Aurobindo's Philosophy,* Banaras: Benaras Hindu University, 1945.

———, *The Vision of India,* Calcutta: Culture Publishers, May 1947.

———, *The Spirit of Indian Philosophy,* Benaras Hindu University, first edn. July, 1947.

———, *Sri Aurobindo: A Homage,* third revised and enlarged edn., April, 1950.

———, *The Meeting of the East and the West in Sri Aurobindo's Philosophy,* Pondicherry: Sri Aurobindo Ashram, first edn., January 1956.

———, *An Introduction to the Philosophy of Sri Aurobindo,* Pondicherry: Sri Aurobindo Ashram, 1965.

Mehta, R., *Intuitive Philosophy,* Madras: The Theosophical Publishing House, 1950.

Milburn, R.G., *The Religious Mysticism of the Upanisads,* Calcutta: R. Cambray & Co., 1919.

Misra, R.S., *Integral Advaitism of Sri Aurobindo,* Banaras: Banaras Hindu University, first edn., 1957.

Morgan, W.K. (ed.), *The Basic Beliefs of Hinduism,* Calcutta: The Y.M.C.A. Publishing House, Indian edn., 1955.

Motwani, K. (complied), *Sri Aurobindo on Social Sciences and Humanities for the New Age, An Anthology,* Calcutta: Orient Longmans, first published, 1962.

Moore, Charles A. (ed.), *Essays in East-West Philosophy,* Honolulu: University of Hawaii Press, 1951.

Mukerjee, Radhakamal, *The Theory and Art of Mysticism,* Bombay: Asia Publishing House, first Indian edn., 1960.

Mukerji, A.C., *The Nature of Self,* Allahabad: The Indian Press Ltd., second edn., 1943.

———, *Self,Thought and Reality,* Allahabad: The Indian Press Ltd., Enlarged second edn., 1957.

Müller, M., *The Six Systems of Indian Philosophy,* Varanasi: Chowkhamba, Sanskrit Series Office, New Impression, 1919.

Mure, G.R.G., *An Introduction to Hegel,* Oxford: Olarendon Press, 1940.

Murti, T.R.V., *The Central Philosophy of Buddhism,* London: George Allen and Unwin, 1955.

Murty, K.S., *Revelation and Reason in Advaita Vedanta,* London: Asia Publishing House, 1961.

Naravane, V.S., *Modern Indian Thought,* Bombay: Asia Publishing House, 1964.

Nicholson, R.A., *The Mystics of Islam,* London: G. Bell & Sons Ltd., 1914.

Niebuhr, R., *The Nature and Destiny of Man,* vol. I.

Nikhilananda, Swami, *Hinduism,* London: George Allen and Unwin Ltd., first published in Great Britain, 1959.

Northrop, F.S.C., *The Meeting of East and West, An inquiry concerning World Understanding,* New York, Macmillian Co., 1946.

———, *The Logic of the Sciences and the Humanities,* New York: Macmillian Co., 1953.

Nouy, Lecomte Du, *Human Destiny,* the New American Library, May, 1956.

Otto, Rudolf, *Mysticism East and West,* New York: Meridian Books third printing, August, 1959.

———, *The Idea of the Holy,* Penguine Books, 1959.

Prakash, D.R. (ed.), *Tagore Centenary Souvenir,* New Delhi: Tagore Memorial Publications, 1961.

Parameswaran, C., *Dayananda and the Indian Problem,* Lahore: Swami Vedananda Tirtha, July, 1944.

Paton, H.J., *Kant's Metaphysics of Experience,* vol. I, London: George Allen and Unwin Ltd., second impression, 1951.

———, *The Modern Predicament,* New York: Copllier Book, 1962.

Pearson, N., *Sri Aurobindo and the Soul Quest of Man,* vol. I, London: George Allen and Unwin Ltd., 1st published in 1952.

Peterfreund, S.P. and T.C. Denise: *Contemporary Philosophy and Its Origins,* Affiliated East-West Press, 1968.

Prabhavananda, Swami, *Vedic Religion and Philosophy*, Madras: Sri Ramkrishna Math.

Plato, *The Republic*, London: Macmillian and Co. Ltd., 1916.

Pringle, P., *The Idea of God in the Light of Recent Philosophy*. Oxford, 1916.

Purani, A.B., *Sri Aurobindo: Some Aspects of His Vision*, Bharatiya Vidya Bhavan, first edn., July, 1966.

Radhakrishnan, S., *The Reign of Religion in Contemporary Philosophy*, London: Macmillian and Co. Ltd., 1920.

———, *The Religion We Need*, London: Ernest Benn Ltd, 1928.

———, *Kalkior, The Future of Civilization*, London: Kegan Paul, Trench: Tribner and Co. Ltd., 1929.

———, *Eastern Religions and Western Thought*, Oxford University Press, 1939.

———, *Eastern Religions and Western Thought*, Oxford University Press, second edn., 1940.

———, *Freedom and Culture*, Madras: G.A. Natesan and Co., second edn., 1942.

———, *Religion and Society*, London: George Allen and Unwin Ltd., 1947.

———, *Great Indians*, first published in 1949.

———, *Indian Philosophy*, vol. II, London: George Allen and Unwin Ltd., reprinted, 1951.

———, *The Principal Upaniṣads*, London: George Allen and Unwin Ltd., 1953.

———, *History of Philosophy*, London: Eastern and Western, vol. II, George Allen and Unwin Ltd., first published, 1953.

———, *East and West — Some Reflections*, London: George Allen and Unwin Ltd., Mc Gill University, 1954.

———, *Recovery of Faith*, George Allen and Unwin Ltd., first published in 1956.

———, and C.A. Moore (eds.), *A Source Book in Indian Philosophy*, Princeton University Press, 1957.

——— and Muirhed (eds.), *Contemporary Indian Philosophy*, London: George Allen and Unwin Ltd., third edn., 1958.

———, *The Dhammapada*, New York: Oxford University Press, 1958.

———, *The Bhagavadgita*, London: George Allen and Unwin Ltd., fifth impression, 1958.

———, *East and West in Religion,* London: George Allen and Unwin Ltd., fourth impression, 1958.

——— and P.T. Raju (eds.), *The Concept of Man,* London: George Allen and Unwin Ltd., first published, 1960.

———, *The Brahma Sutra: The Philosophy of Spiritual Life,* London: George Allen and Unwin Ltd., first published in 1960.

———, *The Philosophy of Rabindranath Tagore,* Baroda: Good Companions Publishers, first published in India, 1961.

———, *An Idealist View of Life,* London: George Allen and Unwin Ltd., 1961.

———, *Thought and Reality,* London: George Allen and Unwin Ltd., 1937.

Raju, P.T., *Idealistic Thought of India,* London: George Allen and Unwin Ltd., 1953.

Ranade, R.D., *A Constructive Survey of Upanishadic Philosophy,* Poona: Oriental Book Agency, 1926.

Ray, Benoy Gopal, *Contemporary Indian Philosophers,* Allahabad: Kitabistan, 1947.

Rhine, J.B., *New Frontiers of the Mind,* London: Faber and Faber Ltd., 1937.

Rhys, Ernest, *Rabindranath Tagore — A Biographical Study,* London: Macmillan and Co. Ltd., 1917.

Rolland, R., *The Life of Ramakrishna,* Almora: Advaita Ashram, Mayavati, third edn., 1944.

Roy, Anilbaran, *Sri Aurobindo and the New Age,* John M. Watkins, first published in 1940.

Runes, D.D. (ed.), *Treasury of Philosophy,* New York: The Philosophical Library, 1955.

Russell, B., *History of Western Philosophy,* London: George Allen and Unwin Ltd.,Third Impression, 1948.

———, *Mysticism and Logic,* London: George Allen and Unwin Ltd., 11th Impression, 1959.

Saksena, S.K., *Nature of Consciousness in Hindu Philosophy,* Banaras: Nand Kishore and Bros., 1944.

Santayana, S.K. *The Life of Reason,* London: Archibald Constable and Co. Ltd., 1905.

Schilpp, A. (ed.), *The Philosphy of Sarvepalli Radhakrishnan,* New York:

The Library of Living Philosophers, Tudor Publishing Company, first edn., 1952.

Schweitzer, A., *Indian Thought and its Development,* Wilco Publishing House, 1960.

Sharma, D.S., *Hinduism Through the Ages,* Bombay: Bhartiya Vidya Bhawan, 1956.

Sharma, R.N., *The Philosophy of Sri Aurobindo,* Meerut: Kedarnath Ramnath, second edn., 1963.

Sharma, C.D., *A Critical Survey of Indian Philosophy,* Motilal Banarasidass, 1964.

Smith, N.K. (tr.), *Immanuel Kant Critique of Pure Reason,* New York: The Modern Library, 1958.

Spencer, Sidney, *Mysticism in World Religion,* Penguin Books, 1963.

Stace, W.T., *Time and Eternity,* Princeton University, 1952.

———, *Religion and the Modern Mind,* London: Macmillian and Co. Ltd, 1953.

———, *The Philosophy of Hegel,* Dover Publications Inc., 1955.

———, *Mysticism and Philosophty,* London: Macmillian & Co. Ltd., 1961.

Stock, J.L. *Reason and Intuition,* London: Oxford University Press, 1939.

Tagore, Rabindranath, *Creative Unity,* London: Macmillian and Co. Ltd., reprinted, 1962.

———, *Gitanjali,* London: Macmillian and Co. Ltd., reprinted, 1962.

———, *Personality,* London: Macmillian and Co. Ltd., Indian edn., reprinted 1959.

———, *Religion of Man,* London: Unwin Books Ltd., first published in 1961.

———, *Reminiscences,* London: Macmillian and Co. Ltd., reprinted, 1962.

———, *Sādhanā,* Macmillian and Co. Ltd., reprinted, 1962.

———, *Towards Universal Man,* New York: Asia Publishing House, 1961.

Tagore Centenary Volume, published by the Singapore Tagore Centenary Celebration Committee, 1961.

Thilly, F. and Ledger Wood, *A History of Philosophy,* Allahabad: Central Book Depot.

Thompson, Edward, *Rabindranath Tagore: Poet and Dramatist*, Oxford University Press, second revised and reset, 1948.

Tillich, Paul, *Systematic Theology*, vol. I, Chicago: The University Chicago Press, 1951.

———, *Biblical Religion and the Search for Ultimate Reality*, Chicago: The University Chicago Press, 1952.

Titus, H.H., *Living issue in Philosophy*, New York: American Book Company, fourth edn., 1964.

Underhill, E., *The Essentials of Mysticism*, London: J.M. Dent and Sons Ltd., 1920.

———, *Mysticism Meridian Books*, New York, ninth Printing, July, 1960.

Verma, V.P., *Modern Indian Political Thought*, Agra: Lakshmi Narain Agrawal, 1961.

Vogel, A.A., *Reality, Reason and Religion*, London: Longmans, Green and Co., 1959.

Wild, K.W., *Intuition*, Cambridge: Cambridge University Press, 1938.

William, M., *Religious Thought and Life in India*, London: John Murry, 1883.

Whitehead, A.N., *Religion in the Making*, Cambridge: Cambridge University Press 1930.

Whitehead, A.N., *The Function of Reason*, Beacon: Beacon Press, 1958.

Younghusband, Sir Francis, *Dawn in India*, London: John Murrary, 1931.

Zacharias, H.C.E., *Renascent India*, London: George Allen and Unwin Ltd., 1933.

———, *Renascent India*, London: George Allen and Unwin Ltd., 1933.

Zaehner, R.C., *Hindu and Muslim Mysticism*, London: University of London, 1960.

———, *Mysticism, Sacred and Profane*, Oxford University Press, 1961.

———, *Hinduism*, Oxford University Press, 1962.

Journals

Bagchi, Kalayan Kumar, "Notion of Epistemology in Prof. K.C. Bhattacharyya," *Philosophical Quarterly*, July, 1963, pp. 93-101.

Bhattacharyya, Kalidas, "A Brief Account of the Writings of K.C.

Bhattacharyya", Appendix II in *Krishnachandra Bhattacharyya Memorial Volume,* Amalner, 1938.

Burch, George, "Contemporary Vedanta Philosophy" in Three Series, *Review of Metaphysics,* March, 1956 (pp. 485-504), June 1956 (662-80) and September, 1958 (pp.122-57). K.C. Bhattacharyya in Series I March 1956, pp. 485-96.

Burch, George, "The Definite and the Indefinite,"*Krishnachandra Bhattacharyya Memorial Volume,* Amalner, 1938. Something about Krishnachandras' Alternative Forms of Absolute.

Chowdhary, Prabhas Jivan, "Meaning of Existence," *Krishnachandra Bhattacharyya Memorial Volume,* Amalner, 1958.

Das, Ras Bihari, "Krishna Chandra Bhattacharyya", *The Modern Review,* April, 1934, pp. 435-39.

———, "Logic Metaphysics and Religion," *Krishnachandra Bhattacharyya Memorial Volume,* Amalner, 1958.

Gupta, N.K., "Human Progress" (an Article Contributed on 72th Birthday on 15th May, 1944) *Sri Aurobindo Mandira Third Annual),* Calcutta: Sri Aurobindo Pathmandir.

Lal, Basant Kumar, "Existentialism and the Philosophy of K.C. Bhattacharyya", *Philosophical Quarterly,* April, 1959, pp. 31-42.

Malkani, G.R., *Existence Philosophical Quarterly,* October, 1937 (pp. 163-78) and January, 1938 (pp. 231-55).

———, "Some Points of K.C. Bhattacharyya's Concept of Philosophy", *The Philosophical Quarterly,* vol. XXIII, no. 2, July, 1950.

Maitra, S.K., "The Integral Vision of History" (An Article Contributed to 73rd Birthday of Sri Aurobindo), *Sri Aurobindo Mandir Annual,* Calcutta: Sri Aurobindo Pathmandirs 1945.

Misra, R.S., "The Concept of Reason in the Systematic Theology of Paul Tillich", *Religion and Society,* vol. XIII, no. 2, Bangalore, 1966.

Talks by Krishnamurti in Europe, 1965, Madras: Krishnamurti Writings Inc.,

Talks by Krishnamurti in USA, 1966, Madras: Krishnamurti Writings Inc. 1967.

Talks by Krishnamurti in India, 1967, Madras: Krishnamurti Writings Inc., 1968.

Talks by Krishnamurti in India, Madras: 1966, Published by Krishnamurti Writings Inc. 1967.

Varadachari, K.C., "What Is Intuition According to Tagore, Radhakrishnan and Aurobindo", Bombay: *The Aryan Path,* August, 1935.

The Encyclopaedia Britannica (Relevant volumes).

The Encyclopaedia of Philosophy (Relevant volumes).

The Encyclopaedia of Religion and Ethics (Relevant volumes).

The Encyclopaedia of Religion and Religion by Royston Pike, Allen and Unwin, 1951.

Index